Freedom, Eudaemonia, and Risk

Capitalist Thought: Studies in Philosophy, Politics, and Economics

Series Editor: Edward W. Younkins, Wheeling Jesuit University

Mission Statement

This book series is devoted to studying the foundations of capitalism from a number of academic disciplines including, but not limited to, philosophy, political science, economics, law, literature, and history. Recognizing the expansion of the boundaries of economics, this series particularly welcomes proposals for monographs and edited collections that focus on topics from transdisciplinary, interdisciplinary, and multidisciplinary perspectives. Lexington Books will consider a wide range of conceptual, empirical, and methodological submissions. Works in this series will tend to synthesize and integrate knowledge and to build bridges within and between disciplines. They will be of vital concern to academicians, business people, and others in the debate about the proper role of capitalism, business, and business people in economic society.

Books in Series

On the Private and Public Virtues of an Honorable Entrepreneur by Felix R. Livingston
The Ontology and Function of Money: The Philosophical Fundamentals of Monetary Institutions by Leonidas Zelmanovitz
Andrew Carnegie: An Economic Biography by Samuel Bostaph
Water Capitalism: Privatize Oceans, Rivers, Lakes, and Aquifers Too by Walter E. Block and Peter Lothian Nelson
Capitalism and Commerce in Imaginative Literature: Perspectives on Business from Novels and Plays edited by Edward W. Younkins
Pride and Profit: The Intersection of Jane Austen and Adam Smith by Cecil E. Bohanon and Michelle Albert Vachris
The Seen, the Unseen, and the Unrealized: How Regulations Affect Our Everyday Lives by Per L. Bylund
Global Economics: A Holistic Approach by Clifford F. Thies
On the Private and Public Virtues of an Honorable Entrepreneur: Preventing a Separation of the Honorable and the Useful by Felix R. Livingston
Perspectives on Ayn Rand's Contributions to Economic and Business Thought by Edward W. Younkins.
The Dialectics of Liberty: Exploring the Context of Human Freedom by Roger E. Bissell, Chris Matthew Sciabarra and Edward W. Younkins
Markets against Modernity: Ecological Irrationality, Public and Private by Ryan H. Murphy
The Moral Case for Profit Maximization by Robert White
Perspectives on Ayn Rand's Contributions to Economic and Business Thought edited by Edward W. Younkins
On the Private and Public Virtues of an Honorable Entrepreneur: Preventing a Separation of the Honorable and the Useful by Felix R. Livingston
Global Economics: A Holistic Approach by Clifford F. Thies
Freedom, Eudaemonia, and Risk: An Inquiry into the Ethics of Risk-Taking by Kathleen Touchstone

Freedom, Eudaemonia, and Risk

An Inquiry into the Ethics of Risk-Taking

Kathleen Touchstone

LEXINGTON BOOKS
Lanham • Boulder • New York • London

Published by Lexington Books
An imprint of The Rowman & Littlefield Publishing Group, Inc.
4501 Forbes Boulevard, Suite 200, Lanham, Maryland 20706
www.rowman.com

6 Tinworth Street, London SE11 5AL, United Kingdom

British Library Cataloguing in Publication Information Available

Library of Congress Cataloging-in-Publication Data

Names: Touchstone, Kathleen, author.
Title: Freedom, eudaemonia, and risk : an inquiry into the ethics of risk-taking / Kathleen Touchstone.
Description: Lanham : Lexington Books, [2020] | Series: Capitalist thought: studies in philosophy, politics, and economics | Includes bibliographical references and index. | Summary: "This book uses the philosophies of Objectivism, rule-utilitarianism, and neo-Aristotelianism to argue that ethical risk-taking is vital for economic flourishing —Provided by publisher.
Identifiers: LCCN 2020033331 (print) | LCCN 2020033332 (ebook) | ISBN 9781498596992 (cloth) |ISBN 9781498597005 (epub) Subjects:
LCSH: Risk—Moral and ethical aspects. | Risk—Social Aspects—Philosophy. | Decision making—Philosophy.
Classification: LCC HM1101 .T68 2020 (print) | LCC HM1101 (ebook) | DDC 302/.12—dc23
LC record available at https://lccn.loc.gov/2020033331
LC ebook record available at https://lccn.loc.gov/2020033332

Dedicated to D. S. Lliteras

Contents

List of Tables

Acknowledgments

Very special thanks to Ed Younkins, editor of the Lexington Books series *Capitalist Thought: Studies in Philosophy, Politics, and Economics*, for suggesting that I submit a book proposal. I'm grateful to Bryndee Ryan for her instruction in the proposal process. I am also grateful to Joseph Parry for his thoughtful suggestions on the book, and I thank him, Joseph Gautham, and Alison Keefner for their editorial guidance. Thanks also to Chris Matthew Sciabarra for reading draft versions of two chapters and for his encouraging remarks. And, of course, thanks to my husband, D. S. Lliteras, for his continued devotion to me and to my work. These acknowledgments do not imply an endorsement of any of the ideas contained herein.

One of themes of this book is the necessity of making errors in order to learn, to discover, and to create. Geoff Colvin estimated that an Olympic figure skater may have to fall 20,000 times in the course of a career to achieve excellence. Faulty reasoning might suggest that thousands of errors are synonymous with excellence. Of course, reduction of errors is the objective. Yet, there are experts in risk management who maintain that elimination of all error is impossible because of the "human factor." Although some philosophers claim that we can never be certain of anything—that there is only probable truth—of this I am certain, errors remain in this book. For these, I take sole credit (and blame).

Introduction

Capitalism depends on risk-taking entrepreneurs. According to economic theory, it is rational to undertake a risky endeavor if the expected compensation exceeds the expected loss. Yet people take risks—they risk failure, even to the point of risking their lives—when there is no apparent sufficient compensation. One of the purposes here is to address the question, why would a person rationally choose to risk his life if life is the ultimate value? A keyword in this question is "rationally." That is, the question assumes that humans have the capacity to reason. There are some people who are foolhardy ("irrational")—some who play Russian roulette, for instance—and they may have "reasons" for risking their lives (e.g., for "kicks"), but I am not addressing those kinds of decisions. "Risk" is a second keyword. The fundamental risk is that associated with one's survival; however, there are other risks that are related to the quality of one's life, such as the risk of one's wealth or to one's health. There are also failures of other kinds. Another keyword is "choose," which presumes that a person has the freedom to choose as well as the inherent capacity to do so. The fourth concept is "life." The basic risk at issue is one that is binary, of life or death—one for which the risk of death is high. However, "life" is a more encompassing term than "survival." Finally, when discussing risk, the concept of "probability" is relevant.

Broadly considered here are freedom, "life," and the risk of failure. Chapters 1 through 6 consider the first two of these: freedom and life. The purpose of those chapters is to lay a foundation for the discussion of risk in chapters 7 through 9. Given limited space, I cannot address all possible views related to these concepts. Primarily, I present my contributions as they relate to them. Of course, my ideas did not spring forth fully formed like Athena from the head of Zeus. For their foundation, I draw from schools of thought associated with libertarians and classical liberals—which include contributions on these subjects by Objectivists and neo-Objectivists, neo-Aristotelians, and rule utilitarians. I do not delve significantly into divergent points of view within each of these philosophies. In some cases, I point out points of apparent agreement and divergence within these schools of thought, but the treatment is not comprehensive.

One principle upon which I rely is the Benevolent Universe Premise (BUP), which essentially states that if a person acts ethically (rationally), he can expect success in the long term. It is a principle that is associated with Objectivism (although it may have been first articulated by Isabel Paterson); however, it is implicit in writings associated with other schools of thought. It can be found in the writing of Aristotle and is implicit in the writings of some rule utilitarians. Although the BUP is not exclusively associated with a particular school of thought, it has been articulated explicitly by Objectivists. I should add the qualification that it is my interpretation of the BUP that I employ in various contexts.

The BUP states that if one acts rationally he can expect long-range success. A person may fail, but failure is incidental or accidental. This does not mean that if failure occurs it is not a tragedy; it means that failure is the "not to be expected." A basic measure of success is survival. That is, fundamentally, the BUP deals with life, death, and risk. In this basic context, risk implies that the probabilities of success (life) and failure (death) are relevant. The full measure of success is given by the term "flourishing." The BUP presumes the freedom to act on one's decisions. It is "optimistic" in outlook in that the probability of failure is small. In other words, the BUP regards man as efficacious. If he is ethical and lives in a society consistent with his nature (freedom), he can expect his chosen course of action to result in a positive outcome—that is, survival (and in a broader sense, flourishing)—in the long term. Short-term setbacks may happen and failure is possible, but failure is the not to be expected. There is no certainty; probabilities are involved because "accidents" may occur. From a macro perspective, this is generally true in relatively free societies. That is, generally speaking, the inhabitants tend to live longer lives and experience higher standards of living than those in non-free countries. It has been argued that this is because freedom is more consistent with man's nature. It permits humans to act voluntarily on their own judgments. Individuals in free countries are at liberty to voluntarily pursue risky ventures. Some pursue new businesses, for instance—which, according to economic theory, may be undertaken if the expected returns exceed the expected costs.

Decision rules exist that are not consistent with the "optimism" associated with the BUP; for instance, the maximin and the minimax criteria. These two criteria may be used when probabilities are unavailable (Salvatore 1996, 568–70). Rawl's theory of justice employed the maximin principle, which basically ranks the worst possible outcomes and selects the best of the worst outcomes (Oyeshile 2008, 66). This criterion is pessimistic in that it assumes for each alternative, the worst possible outcome will prevail. When the decision maker's opponent is "nature," the criterion can be viewed as being premised on a "malevolent" universe. When one's opponent is another person, the maximin approach is regarded as "cowardly" (Baumol 1977, 460).

In a different context, "cowardice," or more broadly "risk aversion," has been associated with diminishing marginal utility for alternatives expressed in units of money. For instance, a risk-averse person would not accept a fair bet. For example, that person would not accept a bet on a coin tossed with a balanced coin (where the probabilities for the outcomes are 50/50). A risk-neutral person (constant marginal utility) would be indifferent about a fair bet, and a risk taker (increasing marginal utility) would accept a fair bet. Of course, in free societies there are risk takers. That is, there are some individuals who take risks for which the odds are against them, or for which the expected costs appear to exceed the expected benefits. For instance, some individuals (say, firefighters and police officers) pursue careers in which the probability of death or injury is high (and the compensation is relatively modest), and society is generally better off for it. These choices do not appear to fit neatly within the BUP.

Chapters 1 through 6 lay a foundation for the discussion of risk in the latter chapters. Although I discuss material associated with the schools of thought mentioned above, many of the arguments I present are mine. Insofar as schools of thought are concerned, I'm less interested in analyzing or rearranging bones discovered by other archeologists than I am in finding new bones. And if what I discover appear to be bones missing from an existing skeleton that's partially constructed, I try to fit them in. If they are bones that belong to a different creature, then I try to assemble them as best I can.

Although I attempt to include most of the essential steps to my arguments, they are nevertheless abbreviated. They are given a fuller treatment in the references that are given. I do not regard my argument for charity or children or government, etc. to be "the" argument. I tend to think, typically, that if something is worthwhile, there is more than one way to arrive at why it has merit. That is, more than one reason or chain of reasoning can be given for it. In some cases, an argument can be made for something and yet arguments can also be made against it. I think this is true of the government, for instance. I have not found (nor developed) an argument for government that is flawless because by its nature government is flawed in that it is coercive. However, anarchy suffers from conceptual flaws as well.

Chapter 1 deals with freedom, which entails a discussion of rights. In chapter 1, I present an example that supports negative rights, specifically, the noninterference principle. Although negative rights are said by some to be based on man's capacity to reason, my illustration does not require sophisticated reasoning on the part of the individuals involved, but relies upon probabilities under the assumption of no prior information. The example is not associated with any particular philosophical school. In chapter 1, I also present my case that positive rights (to care for children from their parents) are fundamental rights. This position is not consistent with the views in either Objectivism or libertarianism. Also, in chapter 1, I offer my case for limited government (based on children's right to care if abandoned by caregivers, and justice on their behalf if killed or abused by caregivers). This position is not in keeping with that of anarcho-libertarians and is different from arguments for government given by Objectivists and other libertarians and classical liberals.

In chapter 2, I discuss "life"; specifically the Aristotelian concept of eudaemonia. Some neo-Aristotelians (such as David Norton) as well as Objectivists regard the individual as having a single over-arching purpose in life. Unlike that position, I argue "reproductivity" (childcare) is ethically on a par with productivity. That is, parenting is an essential part of flourishing. Life is more complex when there is more than one demand on a person's time and resources. This is relevant to the discussion on virtuosity given in chapter 8. Colvin (2008) maintains that excellence in a single discipline requires a devotion to the pursuit of focused practice for many years, which continues throughout the career. He also notes that this level and intensity of practice is more of a challenge for a person who has more than this one demand on his time and energy. Nevertheless, Colvin points out that anyone, even those who are not virtuosos, can become better at their occupations.

In chapter 3, I discuss "life" as being the ultimate value within a system of ethics. Although the emphasis of my argument is different, it is essentially in agreement with that of Objectivists. It is a position that is associated with some neo-Aristotelians as well as some "rule utilitarians." In chapter 3, my discussion of "life" focuses on the significance of life's finality (limitedness), not simply life's contingency (represented by a positive probability of death at any given time). Of relevance to this discussion is PV/T (expected life divided by potential life), a ratio I put forth to discuss ethics within two contexts—one related to ethical behavior and the other related to the improvement of skills. My contribution to decision-making, given in chapter 3, employs my interpretation of the BUP to address decisions involving ethical and unethical alternatives.

In chapters 4 through 6, I continue the discussion of ethical decision-making, primarily as it pertains to charity and to children, as well as address preference scales. My cases for children (chapter 4) and for charity (chapter 5) differ from Objectivists and neo-Objectivists. I have developed a criterion for giving, which is based on the BUP. Because I regard the BUP as being either explicit or implicit in several schools of thought (Objectivism,

Aristotelianism, and to some extent, rule utilitarianism), I do not think the principle is limited to any particular school. In chapter 5, I argue that decisions involving expenditures (of income, time, and other resources) on children and on charity can be arrayed on ordinal scales separate from the preference scale for oneself. This position is unlike that found in traditional economic theory, as well as unlike that of Objectivists, and some utilitarians (specifically, Ludwig von Mises)—all of whom view preferences as being arrayed on a single preference scale. Chapter 6 considers arguments for taking risks for which the probability of death could be high.

Chapters 1 through 6 summarize arguments of mine that have been presented elsewhere. I have presented new material in those chapters as well. In chapters 7 through 9, I present arguments that have not been presented elsewhere in any form. In chapter 7, I present a new definition of the concept of probability. As Weatherford (1982) points out, there is no one accepted theory of probability. The prevailing definitions of probability all suffer from limitations partly because of what is referred to as the analytic-synthetic dichotomy—that is, an analytic proposition may be capable of being verified but is unrelated to reality; whereas synthetic propositions are reality based but are incapable of being verified. Objectivist epistemology provides an avenue for resolving this dichotomy. It also helps resolve the problem of infinity that plagues the relative frequency theory of probability. Although Objectivist epistemology is useful, the definition of the concept of probability that I propose is mine. This definition of the concept of probability is not normative but descriptive. It encompasses the prevailing definitions of probability (with qualifications). To discuss its application to some of the prevailing definitions of probability, I introduce three epistemological categories (which do not appear in the literature on Objectivist epistemology). These categories are not presented as being either definitive or conclusive. They are of relevance within the context of this discussion. Chapter 8 deals with decision-making when the risk of death (or failure) is high. This kind of decision does not appear to be consistent with the BUP. For a theoretical background, I draw from theories in risk management. For my part, I address the issue by returning to the ratio PV/*T*. Chapter 9 gives some "Final Thoughts."

CHAPTER OVERVIEWS

Freedom allows people to take risks, even those that may be life threatening to the risk takers. They have a right to do so—so long as they do not infringe on the rights of others, but is this ethical? Economists cannot answer this question, because economics is ethically neutral. Some rule utilitarians (Hazlitt 1998, 21, 25–26, 33–34; Yeager 2001, 62, 85) regard the Aristotelian notion of eudaemonia, or satisfaction with one's whole life, as the aim toward which an ethical person's actions should be directed. Mises essentially agreed with this view ([1949] 1996, 154). There are authors (Younkins, "Menger, Mises, Rand, and Beyond," 2005, 367; Den Uyl and Rasmussen, "Life, Teleology, and Eudaimonia," 1986, 75), who have observed that the Objectivist view of "life qua man" as man's ultimate value is essentially the same as eudaemonia. If life is the objective toward which actions should be aimed—why would a rational person risk it? More to the point, is it ethical to risk one's life when there is no apparent adequate compensation?

From my essay "On Life and Value within Objectivist Ethics":

> Risk for the sake of risk, playing Russian roulette, for instance, is unethical. However, in cases for which it is possible, the perfection of a skill is designed to reduce risk. This is ethical (or can be). Athletes and firefighters do not take risks simply for the sake of it. They perfect skills in order to achieve excellence, thereby reducing risks. The same is true for risks that do not result in death, but can result in failures of other kinds. Dancers and musicians reduce risk of failure by improving their skills. A life well lived is not simply one in which the risk of death or failure is minimized, but may be one in which a person perfects his skills so as to minimize those risks. (Touchstone 2018, 64)

Free market capitalism, or simply capitalism, is regarded as free—that is, voluntary—association. This is a broader perspective than that which focuses narrowly on economic exchange or markets. This view covers all voluntary interactions. It is the freedom to engage voluntarily with others or not to engage. It is the freedom to live and to flourish—or to fail, as long as one's actions do not infringe on the rights of others. Chapter 1 gives an overview of rights. Negative rights apply to adults, according to those writing in the Aristotelian tradition, such as Rasmussen and Den Uyl (1991, 44) as well as libertarian Rothbard (1998, 97) and neo-Objectivist Machan (*Classical Individualism*, 1998, 122). Rasmussen and Den Uyl (1991, 104) have argued that individuals require a sphere of moral territory in order to flourish. In the first part of chapter 1, using the "desert island scenario," I present an example (from Touchstone [2015, 196–98]) that supports the noninterference principle in a state of nature in which there are two castaways. I then discuss positive rights, which are considered by Rasmussen and Den Uyl (1991, 82, 107) to be derivative. However, I present my case that the positive rights to care for a child from his parents is not derived from the actions of his parents (although they are responsible for satisfying those rights). It is also true that a child's negative rights are not derived from his parents' actions. The source of all rights that a child has is based on his nature as a human being. That positive rights are fundamental for all human beings are illustrated by a "state of nature" setting for the Primary Social Unit, PSU (mother and child) (Touchstone 2006, 89–104, "Rand, Rothbard, and Rights Reconsidered," 2010, 23–25). The PSU argument for positive rights does not extend to adults—doing so would infantilize adults (which would contradict the basis for positive rights to parental care, which is to provide adequate nurturance in order for a child to mature). Also discussed is my case for limited government. Finally, I briefly discuss the rights of children and the unborn as they relate to organ donation and fetal tissue use—tangentially discussing this in relation to their use in creating human parts and hybrids with human faculties.

Chapter 2 considers the Aristotelian concept of eudaemonia, or what Den Uyl and Rasmussen have referred to as flourishing, which they have described as striving toward one's potentiality or excellence. Ayn Rand, the founder of Objectivism, saw a person's maintenance of his life and happiness as in a sense inseparable (Touchstone 2015, 180n6). Den Uyl and Rasmussen stated that Rand's view is best envisioned as a eudaemonistic theory (1986, 75). They believed that David Norton's insights in this regard are more developed than Rand's. Rand regarded man's life as his ultimate value, and productive work as his central purpose. To Norton (1976, 311–13), it is by specialization that people benefit from what others create by way of fulfilling their inherent destinies; however, the "market" for one's talents is largely ignored in his discussion. Like Norton, Rand regarded a man's destiny as singular, but unlike Norton she tied it more directly to the market. She also linked it more directly to his survival (Touchstone 2006, 224–25, 2018, 79–80n15).

Rand and Norton envisioned a person as having a single destiny around which other decisions are made. In contrast, I regard many people as having more than one purpose: a productive purpose for pay that provides the means of fulfilling a destiny as well as providing for one's survival, and reproductivity (caring for one's child or children), which is non-remunerative and is not directly tied to one's survival. I regard reproductivity to be a productive activity; however, it is sufficiently different from productivity to be categorically separable. I also see it on a par with productivity within the hierarchy of a person's values system. Because a person's purpose is not singular, this complicates decision-making since more than one purpose continually vies for top place.

Finally, in chapter 2, I discuss Rand's BUP, which basically states that if one acts rationally (ethically), one can achieve long-range success—success being life qua man. Virtues are those actions that promote or preserve one's life (if pursued consistently). What is difficult to explain in this context is why a person would (rationally) willingly risk his life if life is his ultimate value. Perhaps more difficult to explain is why a person would willingly pursue a profession in which he risks his life on a continual basis. In chapter 2, I briefly address this question, which I consider more fully in chapter 8.

Chapter 3 considers what is meant by "life" in a person's value system, particularly as it relates to life being the ultimate value. Life can be regarded as being lived "moment to moment" or lived "as a whole." In ethical decision-making, it is life as a whole that is the relevant context. In chapter 3, the distinction between the two is considered from different perspectives. First I present an illustration (from Touchstone [2015] and [2018]) that isolates longevity and examines the effect of living a more virtuous life on the "expected life" (PV) relative to the "potential life" (*T*) for two beings—one who is mortal and another who is potentially immortal. Specifically, it addresses the effect of a more ethical life (which, other things equal, tends to lower the mortality rate) on the expected life span, PV. The changes in the PV values relative to *T* are examined for each being. It is shown that a finite life (or at least a "limited" one) provides a relative context for ethical decision-making; whereas a potentially infinite life cannot provide a relative context.

Secondly, I present a simple illustration (see Touchstone [2018, 64–66]) that considers the question: does one live to eat or eat to live—that is, is a person's purpose short-term satisfaction or one's life long term? I conclude that if the emphasis is one's life as a whole, a person can achieve both. If the focus is on short-term consumption, then longevity will be sacrificed. Finally, I consider the argument that life is the ultimate value stressing action. It is essentially the same case as Rand's except for emphasis. The significance of "life as a whole" becomes apparent when comparing the choice between an ethical course of action and an unethical alternative. Based on my interpretation of the BUP, the expected loss of an ethical action can be ignored (because it is the not-to-be-expected if a person acts ethically); however, this is not the case for the unethical alternative. The expected loss (the probability of loss multiplied by the value of the loss) cannot be dismissed because it is endemic to the action, and it not insignificant. This is not only because the probability of failure (death) is larger for the unethical action, but also because the loss encompasses the value of the entirety of one's life (Touchstone, "Economic Decision-making and Ethical Choice," 2008, 178–80). What comprises the "entirety of one's life" is also briefly addressed.

Chapter 4 considers two broad categories by which virtues may be discovered. One is an empirical approach advanced by evolutionary ethicists that derives ethics by examining social norms that have stood the test of time. The other is an abstract approach that isolates a few variables and "observes" their interaction in order to arrive at a conclusion or conclusions that may be generalized to a broader and more realistic setting—in particular, the so-called Crusoe approach. The latter approach, which examines interaction in a "state of nature," has been used to illustrate the "mutual gains from trade" that can result from voluntary interaction of two parties. In chapter 4, this "trader principle" is discussed within the context of three models of increasing complexity. In a brief discussion, I also apply the evolutionary approach to recent developments related to language.

Both the Crusoe approach and the evolutionary approach to the discovery of virtues have their limitations. One limitation of the Crusoe approach is that the conclusions that are drawn from the analysis are confined to the nature of the parties that are observed. As a result of the utilization of this approach by Rand ("The Objectivist Ethics," 1964, 25–26, 32; "The Nature of Government," 1964, 107) and libertarian Rothbard (1998, 35–36) as well as others, I do not think sufficient importance has been placed on "reproductivity" (i.e., childcare by parents) in the systems of values that Rand and others have developed. In the final section to chapter 4, I present my argument—which is based on the trader principle broadly interpreted—that reproductivity is a primary virtue (Touchstone, "Reproductivity, Capital Theory, and Objectivist Ethics," 2010, 229–31).

Chapter 5 examines decisions under "certainty." Of course, the future is never certain. By certainty in this context, I mean that the probability of failure (in this case death) is so low that it can be dismissed from consideration. The decisions considered in this chapter are those for which the direct beneficiary is someone other than the decision maker. According to Objectivist Ethics (OE), virtues are life affirming for the person in question. Giving to others would seem to be unethical or at least ethically neutral since the primary beneficiary is not oneself. Reproductivity would seem to be primarily other oriented; and, in fact, it is unilateral from the perspective of the child. In OE, parenting is considered one of many productive activities and is regarded as being morally optional. However, the case I make in chapter 4 is that reproductivity is globally or intergenerationally reciprocal. It is also separate from and on a par with productivity. In chapter 5, my case for charity is similar to the case for reproductivity in that it is based on a broad interpretation of reciprocity. The Objectivist position on charity is that it is not a primary virtue. It is secondary at best. Even a minor sacrifice could be seen as unethical in OE. However, my position is that even if a person regards a charitable contribution as a sacrifice in a narrow sense (in the sense that the cost exceeds his psychological or monetary return), charity may not be a sacrifice in the broader context of one's whole life. This is, in part, because many if not most people are born with an inheritance of knowledge and/or of freedom for which they cannot repay. Basic knowledge is a "public good" in part because its producers discovered it without receiving adequate compensation, if any. This is similarly true for freedom. A person who receives these bequests cannot repay his benefactors directly, but he can give to others (whom he regards as deserving). In this sense, such gifts are not "sacrifices" in the broad sense. By giving to others, a person is re-paying or maintaining this inheritance.

The ethical problem with unilateral transfers is that, given that they are not primarily self-preserving, there is no established dividing line between oneself and others. In chapter 5, I provide rough rules of thumb for both charitable giving and for (basic) expenditures for one's child. A rule of thumb for expenditures on charity follows from the BUP (Touchstone, "Ethical Principles, Charity, and a Criterion for Giving," 2008, 47–48). As a rough guideline, expenditures for one's child could be equal to an annual sinking fund amount based on the investment in one's human capital (derived from one's parents' expenditures) (Touchstone 2016, 47). In my view, potential expenditures on one's child and on charity can be (in part) separable from each other as well as from expenditures for oneself.

Austrian economists, such as Ludwig von Mises ([1949] 1996, 233), see decisions on spending as ranked on a single scale of preferences. This view is consistent with the prevailing economic thought on preferences (Alchian and Allen 1977, 25–26; Becker 1995, 7). Similarly, Rand (1990, 31) viewed decisions related to values as all being arrayed on a single ordinal scale. Based on the guidelines for charity and for one's child that I propose, I argue that potential charitable expenditures and potential expenditures for one's child may each be ranked ordinally on separate scales from the scale for oneself. Because these expenditures are ranked on separate scales, they do not compete directly with expenditures for oneself (Touchstone 2016, 48–51).

Chapter 6 continues with the discussion of ethical decision-making. The basis for the discussion is my application of the BUP to ethical decision-making under uncertainty. The primary focus in this chapter is on decisions in which the loss of one's own life cannot be ignored. It begins by discussing ethical decisions in general. That is, virtues are actions that result in long-term success when consistently followed and therefore may be regarded as conforming to a "strict causal chain." This follows from the BUP, which states that failure is the "not-to-be-expected"; thus, the probability of failure can be ignored. Consequently, an unwavering adherence to virtues is the "best way to bet." This is illustrated specifically by considering a decision between an ethical action and an unethical alternative. As briefly mentioned in chapter 3, when choosing between an ethical action and an unethical alternative, the expected loss for the former can be ignored, but it cannot be ignored for the latter. Because of the enormity of the loss for the unethical action, in making a decision between an ethical and an unethical action, calculation (of expected gains and losses for each alternative) is not necessary. That is, the better course of action (in terms of successful results long term) is to consistently choose the ethical action.

For those people who strive to be ethical, most decisions are not between ethical and unethical alternatives, but involve choosing between or among ethical courses of action. This chapter considers these kinds of decisions; that is, decisions involving only ethical alternatives. Because these decisions only involve ethical actions, the expected loss (related to death) may be ignored for the alternatives for a given decision in many cases. However, in some cases the loss may be large for a particular alternative and would have to be taken into account (e.g., if one of the alternatives would result in placing the person's livelihood in considerable jeopardy). The more difficult decisions to explain within a value system (in which life is the ultimate value) are those for which the risk of death is significant (Touchstone, "Economic Decision-Making and Ethical Choice," 181–85). That is, why would a person rationally risk his life for another person or for an abstract principle? Some rationales for these decisions are also addressed in chapter 6.

A discussion of risk inherently involves referring to probabilities. One problem concerning the concept of probability is that there is no single accepted definition for probability (Duffey and Saull 2008, 11). In chapter 7, I offer a definition of the concept of probability that can be viewed as overarching in the sense that it is sufficiently broad to encompass a variety of definitions of probability (with qualifications). As background, chapter 7 briefly discusses three theories of probability: classical, relative frequency, and subjective. Their limitations are also addressed. Because I am proposing a definition of a concept of probability, I present the Objectivist definition of a "concept" as well as the Objectivist notion of "concepts of consciousness." Because the concept of infinity is integral to some of the definitions of probability, the concept of infinity as a "concept of method" is given. Presented also is a brief overview of the Objectivist position on the analytic-synthetic dichotomy. In order to discuss the prevailing definitions of probability within the context of the proposed definition of the concept, I present three epistemological categories—theory, prediction, and reality (which I do not regard as exhaustive or definitive, but are presented in order to address the proposed definition within the context of the prevailing theories of probability). Infinity can be used in the first two categories, but is not a concept that applies to reality.

Based on the proposed definition, there is no "estimation" of probabilities. There may be better or worse probability values in that they may be closer or farther from the actual proportions that they predict, but they are nevertheless probabilities. The definition that is proposed is descriptive not normative. It encompasses (with qualifications) other existing definitions of probability. With the proposed concept, the idea of a "true probability" that is equal to a long-run proportion based on an infinite number of trials is a theoretical possibility, but it is not one that exists in reality. A "long-run" proportion (whether based on a finite or on a theoretically infinite number of trials) is a probability if it is used to predict, but the actual proportion that is predicted in the real world is not a probability. It is a proportion, which if, in turn, is used to predict, will then become a probability. A range of proportions (whether they are discrete values or are on a continuous scale) used in prediction is comprised of probabilities. That is, all of them are probabilities, not estimates of probabilities. They are used to estimate or predict a proportion or proportions. The proportions that are predicted become probabilities if, in turn, they are used in prediction.

I discuss the proposed definition of the concept of probability within the context of "orthodox" theory and Bayesian theory. I also discuss it within the context of computer learning systems, specifically principal component analysis and adaptive resonance theory. Although I regard chapter 7 as important in that it offers a new definition of the concept of probability, it can be omitted without loss of continuity for those who are not interested in this subject.

Chapter 8 examines risk taking, particularly in the case of physically dangerous occupations. A free society not only depends on the risk taking of entrepreneurs, it also relies upon the risk taking of combat soldiers, firefighters, and police officers as well as those in other high-risk occupations. People in these occupations typically have a higher tolerance for and preference for risk than others. Inherent differences in preferences and in talents can to some extent affect occupational choice. Dangerous occupations are more often employed by men. Over 90% of work-related deaths are men. (Of course, 100% of pregnancy-related deaths are women. I realize that the contexts are different for these two percentages.)

Although inherent abilities matter, Colvin (2008) made clear in a book by the same name "talent is overrated"—or it can be. As Colvin illustrated again and again, skills improve with deliberate practice. This is well known in the field of risk management. Individuals learn by doing and this lowers the accident rate associated with certain activities. Risk management explores the relationship between learning and risk. As Duffey and Saull (2008, 3; italics in original) stated: "[*T*]*he Learning Hypothesis is based on the well-known proposition that humans learn from their mistakes.*" Writing on engineering, this is more forcefully stated by Henry Petroski: "we *must* have such errors and mistakes in order to improve" (2008, 9; italics in original).

In examining this relationship in risk management, Duffey and Saull (2008, 25, 28, 192–93) found that the same equation that they estimated at the organization/industry level was applicable at the individual training level. The relationship between risk and learning at the individual level is illustrated in the Universal Law of Practice equation: $E^* = e^{-3t^*}$, where E^* is a non-dimensional error rate and t^* is a non-dimensional practice time equal to t/t_T, where t_T is maximum practice (2008, 508). At the organizational/industrial level, the learning rate constant, 3, was estimated based on world data on errors and on experience from several technological systems that included 800 data points covering a period of 200 years (see Duffey and Saull 2008,

52–53, 506). That is, experience at the macro level was found to be equivalent to training at the individual level.

Duffey and Saull (2008, 215; italics in original) stated: "*[L]ack of experience represents the greatest risk!*" Risk of failure is greatest at the outset of an experience (2008, 161). Duffey and Saull (2008, 60, 404) set the probability of a beginner making an error at about 63% (i.e., [1 – 1/e]). This figure is particularly unsettling when the risk a person faces is death. Firefighters and others in dangerous occupations risk their lives daily. Because the risk of failure is the greatest for those with no experience, firefighters first train for this occupation in controlled environments, which involves simulating life-threatening situations and learning to respond successfully. In risky occupations, it is not possible to train for every contingency. Firefighters continue to learn on the job. This is the case for most professions that involve risking death. It is also true for vocations and avocations that can result in failures of other stripes. Individuals take on risky endeavors not to fail, but to attain excellence. This is achieved through learning skills that reduce the risk of failure.

In chapter 8, in order to examine the effect of training, I re-introduce a simple equation that was first introduced in chapter 3 in the discussion of the expected life of a person for a given early death rate (which is inversely related to virtue). In chapter 3, the objective of the person was longevity, which was achieved by living a more virtuous life (thus reducing the early death rate or "force of mortality," r). To gauge improvement, the expected age (PV) was compared with the potential life span (T). Instead of a person's life, the focus in chapter 8 is on a defined task which has an end. The task could be a training module for a risky occupation, such as firefighting. It could likewise apply to any task with a fixed pattern or routine, such as a monologue or a piece of music. Because of the availability of literature on the subject, in chapter 8, I examine a piece of music. From my article "Rand and the Austrians: The Ultimate Value and the Non-interference Principle":

> By way of analogy, one could think of a piece of music as having a potential life to a musician. One objective of the musician is to make it to the end of the piece—which I will call time T. Time T is the time at which the piece, in effect, "dies." T is its potential life. If the musician has a "fatal error" before the end of the piece, this would be analogous to an "early death." The musician would prefer to play the piece as well as he can (ideally, with no errors) and to make it to the end. In playing, the musician is interested in how well he is doing throughout, with the objective of playing it to the end. The end, "death," is not an objective or a goal. The objective is to "keep the piece alive" until T. Making it to the end is one measure of success, but not the only measure. Doing so with as few errors as possible is another. Playing the piece completely and beautifully is the ultimate goal. (Touchstone 2015, 186)

The fatal error rate, r, would be an average rate for a given piece of music played at a given tempo for a particular musical instrument and rehearsal level and for a given proficiency of the musician. The expected "life" of the piece of music, say PV, could be measured relative to T. The objective would be to achieve excellence through practice thereby reducing r so as to increase PV/T, ideally to equal one. The musician would prefer to reduce the number of errors—particularly "fatal errors." This is achieved through practice. The musician must risk failure in order to achieve excellence. It is through practice that the risk of failure is reduced.

At the outset, the decision to learn a difficult piece of music, or more generally to pursue a risky discipline, may appear to be "irrational," in the sense that the risk of failure is high. There may be "less risky" endeavors that a person could pursue. A relatively high risk of failure would tend to be true of any period of practice or rehearsal evaluated in isolation early on. However, as proficiency is achieved, the risk is reduced. A challenging endeavor should be considered in its entirety, not based solely on isolated periods as skills are learned.

Chapter 9 is titled "Final Thoughts." Its focus is primarily on PV/T by revisiting some points made in previous chapters concerning its usage in different contexts. In chapter 3, the equation was used to show the relationship between the expected age at death, PV_1, and the force of mortality, r, within the context of the pursuit of virtue. In chapter 8, the equation was used to show the relationship between the expected life span of a task (specifically, a musical piece) and the failure (mortality) rate as a person gains excellence in performance. Aristotle would refer the former improvements as virtues related to morality and the latter as intellectual virtues related to the professions or the arts. Both categories of virtue (moral and intellectual) require striving for a kind of excellence that is achieved through practice to reduce errors. My final "final thought" is: "Virtues may be actions that serve to preserve or maintain our lives, but they are not methods designed to avoid risks. They are tools we can utilize to handle them."

Chapter 1

Freedom to Flourish

INTRODUCTION

The primary focus of this chapter is on rights. First, negative rights as natural rights will be discussed, followed by an illustration that supports the noninterference principle using the two-person desert island device. Second, it is noted that a prevailing consensus is that negative rights apply to adults, not children. Following that is a discussion of the source of positive rights, particularly the right to care of children by parents. Next is a discussion of rights under a two-person scenario I call the Primary Social Unit (PSU) that is comprised of a mother and child. Then an argument is presented that children's rights to care from parents are natural rights. This is followed by a section on government, which includes an overview of two cases for limited government, a brief discussion on the inalienability of rights, and a consideration of some of the coercive aspects of government. Finally, the rights of the unborn and some related rights issues are addressed.

NEGATIVE RIGHTS AND THE NONINTERFERENCE PRINCIPLE

Classical liberals, libertarians, and Objectivists maintain that basic rights are negative. Negative rights delimit the actions of others *vis-à-vis* the rights holder. Specifically, the obligation negative rights impose on others is one of nonaction—that they not interfere with or infringe upon the person or property of another. This means that one person cannot force another to perform a positive action (Rothbard 1998, 100). Negative rights confer upon the rights holder a positive right to action—to act on one's autonomous, voluntary judgment (Rand, "Man's Rights," 1964, 94).

Objectivists, as well as many libertarians, such as Rothbard (1998, 155), view (natural) rights as following from man's nature. Specifically, according to the founder of Objectivism, Ayn Rand (Rand, "What is Capitalism," 1967, 16–18), they stem from that aspect of his nature on which his survival depends—his rational faculty. Rights set the conditions for man's survival. Reason, which is man's means of survival, is neither automatic nor infallible. It takes effort and humans may make mistakes. (In fact, as will be addressed in chapter 8, in many instances they must make errors in order to learn.) They must be free to act on their own judgments, even if they make errors, so long as their actions do not infringe on the rights of others.

Even though rights relate to action, they are not actions per se. They are boundary setting. They provide a sphere of moral territory (Rasmussen and Den Uyl 1991, 104; Machan, *Classical Individualism*, 1998, 122). Natural rights are said to precede and exist separate from custom or convention of any particular community or society. Nevertheless, there is a connection between natural law and positive law. According to Rasmussen and Den Uyl, natural rights provide the normative basis for a legal system. They likewise provide guidance for the construction of a constitution (1991, 112).

In *The Ethics of Liberty*, Rothbard (1998, 31) examined the establishment of rights in a state of nature employing the familiar "Crusoe" abstraction. That is, first it is assumed that a man alone, Crusoe, is stranded on an island; then a second man, Friday, arrives on the scene. Rothbard then discussed the gains from trade as a basis for cooperation. Gains from trade are typically illustrated as being realized when traders engage in an exchange of those products for which each person has a comparative advantage. Specialization on the basis of comparative advantage can result in more output (1998, 35–36). However, more value (in a "utility" sense) can result from trade, even when there is not "more" in a physical sense, as long as each trading partner is more satisfied after the exchange has taken place.

The gains from interaction are not limited to the exchange of goods and services, but also apply to knowledge, friendship, and reproduction. "Reproductivity" is often ignored in the literature. One and one can yield more than two, but this cannot be known before any interaction has ever taken place. The positive sum nature of exchange remained undiscovered for a long time. Trade is still seen by many as zero sum or worse. It took some time before humans grasped the concept of paternity in reproduction. (There is debate about whether relatively recent "primitive" societies had an understanding of the concept; e.g., see Pulman [2004].) The mutual benefits that can emerge from interaction are not self-evident.

If the mutual benefits to interaction were obvious before the fact, there would be a strong incentive for cooperation between two strangers, such as Crusoe and Friday. Because they are not, and because it is assumed that both castaways suffer from amnesia (and therefore are unaware of any experiences or principles they may have known before being stranded on the island [Rothbard 1998, 29]), they may engage in interactions that are less than cooperative. Ethical evolutionists look to current standards of morality as providing a basis for ethical principles, having stood the test of time, so to speak (Hayek 1973, 43–48). A desert island scenario in which there has been no prior interaction provides a blank slate insofar as social standards are concerned (see Touchstone [2015, 196–98]).

When Crusoe is confronted with the arrival of a second man, he may turn to his own feelings for guidance. If he feels threatened by the presence of another, he may gather that since he values his own life, Friday (who, like himself is a human being, and, therefore, may reason similarly), also values his life. Thus, Crusoe may surmise that they both will draw the same conclusion—which is that both can protect their own lives by respecting each others' lives. Crusoe would be pursuing a principle that would apply equally to himself as well as others. This generalization from one's own feeling to others does not always lead to the establishment of a respect for "rights." If Crusoe was attracted to Friday and, using his feeling as a basis for abstraction, concluded that the attraction was mutual and he unilaterally acted on the basis of that reasoning, he could be in violation Friday's right to noninterference. Feelings are a weak basis for the establishment of principles. Nevertheless, when there are no other humans to observe, one's self may provide the sole basis for generalization to another or others.

Crusoe could take his cue from the animal kingdom, and conclude (as some have—rightly or wrongly) that the "law of the jungle" is "kill or be killed." If so, from Crusoe's perspective, looking at the alternative decisions with which he is confronted and the probability of dying under each decision, he may reason as follows. He faces two alternative decisions: he can either decide to kill Friday or not to kill Friday. With no other knowledge, he assumes that he and Friday are evenly matched. If he decides to kill Friday, he therefore would have a 50% chance of dying. The second alternative is to choose not to kill Friday. If he chooses not to kill Friday, then Crusoe faces two alternative choices from Friday's perspective. Friday will either choose to kill Crusoe or he will not. The probability associated with each of these alternatives is 50%. If Friday chooses not to kill Crusoe, then given that Crusoe has already decided not to kill Friday, Crusoe faces a 0% chance of dying. If Friday chooses to kill Crusoe, then Crusoe's (joint) probability of dying is 25%; that is, the probability that Friday will choose to kill Crusoe (50%) multiplied by

Crusoe's chance of dying (50%, again because of the assumption that they are equally matched). Of the two alternatives, the better choice for Crusoe is to not initiate violence (to kill) Friday because it presents a better chance that he will not die. If he also thinks that Friday will reason as he does, this improves Crusoe's probability of survival even more.

The asymmetry in the probabilities that each castaway faces occurs because each person knows more about himself than he does the other person (for instance, see Salvatore [1996, 564]). The assumption of equiprobability for two alternatives is typical when no other information is available. The assumption may be flawed, but that is not particularly relevant here since people often do not have perfect information when they make decisions and may have to rely on less than perfect assumptions. It depicts a possible probability structure that Crusoe could envisage, and one I think is tenable. Although this illustration doesn't establish the noninterference principle per se, it does make a case that supports noninterference (2015, 196–98).

NEGATIVE RIGHTS ARE FOR ADULTS

According to Rand, the single obligation that rights require is that each person must respect the rights of others (Rand, "The Wreckage of the Consensus," 1967, 227). Rasmussen and Den Uyl stated that rights are universal and must be applied uniformly (1991, 84). To Rand, the source of rights stems from man's rationality, by which she meant its mature state of being. Similarly, Rasmussen and Den Uyl limited their investigations to understanding the adult manifestation of the human organism (1991, 44). To Machan (*Classical Individualism*, 1998, 122), rights provide adults with a sphere of moral territory. Likewise, it was Rothbard's position that negative rights apply to adults (1998, 97).

In contrast to the previous authors, Herbert Spencer envisioned every person as possessing equal rights—including children. Individual rights are derived from human faculties. The extent to which children's faculties are less developed than an adult's is irrelevant. Rights are equal, regardless of whether faculties are equal or not. Children have the right to exercise whatever faculties they have ([1892] 1954, 156–57). According to Spencer, the problem with assigning less than 100% self-ownership is discerning at what point a child becomes an adult. As with adults, each child has a sphere of noninterference. Any coercion whatsoever infringes upon the child's rights, whether that involves punishment or forced education ([1892] 1954, 158, 168).

Rothbard (1998, 45–46) seemingly agreed with Spencer, asking the question: if there is less than 100% self-ownership, how is partial ownership to be determined? He saw no viable alternative. Yet his comments on children contradict that statement and are themselves contradictory. He stated that children have "potential" ownership of themselves. He also stated that the mother is the "natural" owner by virtue of homesteading (1998, 98–99). (However, as mentioned below, the homesteading argument would seem to apply to the child *vis-à-vis* the mother rather than vice versa. The child is the homesteader and would, by that argument, "own" the space inside the mother until birth.) According to Rothbard, parents can sell their child without the latter's consent. The child has the right to leave home regardless of his age or circumstance, at which time the child attains full self-ownership. The child is obligated to follow the rules set down by the parents so long as he lives in the latter's home. Rothbard set no age (minimum or maximum) at which a parent can forcibly evict a child from the house (1998, 103–104).

Although Rothbard claimed that a child has the negative rights of not being killed or tortured by his parents (1998, 100), this in effect is not the case. Rothbard advocated anarchy (anarcho-capitalism) in which each person is responsible for retribution in the event of rights violation. Children would have to rely on their parents to protect their rights. Hoppe (1998, xli) stated that Rothbard's position was that "any state interference in the autonomy of families should be anathema." Thus, if the parent or parents violate a child's rights (i.e., they abuse, torture, or murder the child), and it is left to the very same parent(s) to protect those rights, in essence the child has no rights.

POSITIVE RIGHTS

It was Rothbard's contention that the sole right of the individual was the right to noninterference. Thus, a parent cannot be compelled to care for his child because this would necessitate a positive obligation for the parent to act. Therefore, the parent is under no legal requirement to feed or otherwise care for his child; that is, a parent has the right to neglect his child even if it results in the child's death (1998, 100). Positive rights impose obligations to act with respect to others. Positive rights, unlike negative rights, are not universal. They are special rights that are particular and contingent (Rasmussen and Den Uyl 1991, 107, 113, 84). No one person has the positive right to compel another person to act without his consent, unless the latter has violated the former's negative rights. Rasmussen and Den Uyl noted that there are special relationships that one person may have with others (e.g., parent to child) that "may imply certain obligations that are not easily reducible to consent alone" (1991, 107). The child's right to care is derived from the parents' actions in deciding to have the child. Thus, positive rights are derivative (1991, 82, 107).

Of the authors considered thus far, Rothbard was the most restrictive in his interpretation of "consent." Rothbard's view was shared by Williamson Evers. To Rothbard (1998, 134) and Evers (1978, 7–8), positive rights can only be based on contract and only for that which is alienable. Only physical products are alienable. A person's will is not alienable; therefore, contracts for labor services would be unenforceable. Rothbard provided a way around this problem and that is by the person who hires the services of another securing a penal or performance bond, which is an agreement on the part of the worker to pay an amount of money if he fails to deliver services that have been promised. Money is alienable (1998, 138–39).

Although Rothbard did not mention this explicitly, a way around the proscription against alienating one's will is implicit in his theory of rights. If the worker reneges on both the promise to work and the performance bond payment, he can be placed in a position of involuntary servitude ("just slavery") to the claimant until the debt is met. Involuntary servitude is permitted—in fact, it may be required—in the event a person defaults on a penal or performance bond contract (or otherwise violates the rights of another), according to Rothbard (1998, 86). In Rothbard's philosophy, this circuitous route to the provision of care from the parents would be unavailable to a child since the child cannot enter contractual agreements such as these with his parents (1998, 98).

Roger Bissell's argument for the right to childcare from the parent is a liability argument. To Bissell: "The right to child support … springs from the same basic source as the right to compensation for disablement when caused by someone else" (1981, 30). A person who is rendered disabled by a drunk driver is entitled to compensation. The driver may not have intended the outcome, but the intent is not an issue here, nor is prior consent needed between the driver and the injured party, because the positive rights of the latter are the result of an infringement of his negative rights. Similarly, with regard to reproduction, intent is irrelevant and a contract is unnecessary. The liability argument is valid; however, it has the drawback (based on my interpretation) of putting birth in the category of an infringement of the rights of the child (Touchstone 2006, 117–18). By this argument, the positive right to childcare is derivative.

In contrast with the Bissells's case (as I interpret it), I do not view the positive right to childcare as derivative. That is, this positive right is not reciprocity based, as is trade or the violation of a negative right. I view it as a basic right, the source of which is based on human nature—a human's rational faculty; specifically, its development. Also, unlike Rasmussen and Den Uyl, I do not view the positive right to childcare as a special right. It is universal because it is required for every human being who is born.

THE PRIMARY SOCIAL UNIT

In his derivation of negative rights, Rothbard (1998, 29) used the desert island device, first starting with a man alone, Crusoe, and then adding a second man, Friday. Rights become relevant with the presence of another man. Rand limited her discussion of ethics and rights to two possibilities, man alone on an island and man living among others under an appropriate government. Rand regarded living among others as optional (Rand, "The Nature of Government," 1964, 107). Living alone on a desert island may be optional for a man; however, no one is born alone. As Peikoff (1991, 231) acknowledged: "every organism owes its existence" to reproduction. By the nature of what a human being is, there is one relationship that is not an option and that is the relationship between a mother and child. I have referred to this as the PSU (Touchstone 2006, 89–104; Touchstone, "Rand, Rothbard, and Rights Reconsidered," 2010, 23–25).

Negative rights are universal, according to Evers, "because they are generalizations based on the nature of man and reality" (1978, 3). Likewise, I would argue that a child's positive right to care from parents (or from the mother when the analysis is limited to the PSU) is universal because it is applicable to every human being and stems from a human's nature and reality. An adult's negative rights follow from his nature; that is, his rational faculty. Rand's case is tied to man's survival. Man has no automatic means of survival. To survive, he relies on his rational faculty, which is not automatic; it takes effort. It is also fallible—which means he may make (and, I would add, may need to make) errors. His reason informs his actions—which he must perform in order to survive. Others should not infringe upon or interfere with a person's (an adult's) exercise of his rational faculty or the decisions he makes (the actions he takes) that follow therefrom, so long as they do not infringe on another person's rights. Similarly, I argue, by his nature, a human being is born with no automatic means of survival. His rational capacity, on which his survival depends, is not automatic—it takes time and effort to develop. In fact, it requires *years* to develop, and it cannot be developed by a human in isolation. The positive right to care is required for the development of the rational faculty that is necessary for the survival of every person who is born (Touchstone, "Rand, Rothbard, and Rights Reconsidered," 2010, 21–22).

Rothbard referred to the man on the desert island as the "most elementary human situation and problem" (Hoppe 1998, xxii). It is not a social unit, however. For that, more than one person is required. The decision for two adults (such as Crusoe and Friday) to form a social unit is optional because of the nature of what maturity entails—adults are independent. The smallest unit that is required by nature is that of mother and child. It is a social unit, not only because it consists of more than one person, but also because it is long term in nature—which is a defining feature of a society. A one-time encounter is not a social unit. That is why the interaction between adults that results in reproduction is not by necessity a social unit. Whether or not any further association becomes of long-term duration is optional. The PSU is a two-person scenario consisting of a child and an adult. It is primary because it is the first social unit encountered by every human being. It is universal because it is required for every person. It is also necessary because it is tied to the survival of one of the person's in the unit. (It is also the case that the PSU is vulnerable.)

If society is limited to adults, then it may be generally true, as Rand ("The Fountainhead," 1961, 81–82) has suggested, that one man's survival does not depend *fundamentally* upon another person. The nature of the PSU is one of dependency. It is not dependency per se that renders the PSU a required social unit. Rights are involved. The rights that would be relevant in this social unit would be the positive right to care of the child. The negative right of the child not to be killed is unnecessary within the confines of the PSU. By the nature of what childcare is—that is, sustaining the life of the child—the negative right to not be killed would add a superfluous layer of rights. When the child is young, the negative rights of the mother would not be relevant in the sense that the child would not be culpable if he harmed the mother. (By that I mean that when a child is very young, if he were to harm the mother in some way, the typical avenues for seeking recourse for rights violations would not apply.) The only right that is relevant for the PSU (when the child is young) is the positive right to care for the child. Thus, the primary right (in the sense of the first right a human has) would be the positive right to care as a child. In Objectivism, rights are tied to survival. The PSU is tied to the survival of the child—which means the survival of every human who is born (Touchstone 2006, 89–104; Touchstone, "Rand, Rothbard, and Rights Reconsidered," 2010, 23–25).

Of course, as a human matures his negative rights become relevant (as would the mother's within the PSU), and his positive right to care diminishes. The fact that a human does not have positive rights throughout his entire life is irrelevant insofar as universality is concerned. Within the context of the PSU, a person does not have negative rights throughout his entire life either. What makes rights universal is that they apply to every person, not that they apply throughout every person's life.

As an aside, the PSU is an abstraction to understand the rights of human beings at the very early stage of development. It is not a basis for understanding a society of adults, as others have suggested (Held [1990]; Hewitson [2001, 240–41]). An implication of using the PSU as the basis for establishing relationships among adults is that adults continue to be regarded as if they possess the positive rights of children. That is, it tends to infantilize adults. There has been a recent cultural trend in this direction in the United States. Ironically—or perhaps not, this has been coupled with a shift away from an observance of the right to life of infants.

CHILDREN'S RIGHTS TO PARENTAL CARE ARE NATURAL RIGHTS

Natural rights are negative, according to Rasmussen and Den Uyl (1991). They exist merely because a person is a human being. They apply to every person. They are basic—which means they are not derived from other rights. Positive rights are particular rights that apply to specific persons due to circumstances that apply to them alone (1991, 80–82). This applies to voluntary trade between consenting adults. Consent is required for trade to take place. Trade is bilateral in nature. As Rand ("The Objectivist Ethics," 1964, 31) expressed it, value is exchanged for value. Consent is also an issue for interaction that involves the sphere of physical space around a person. Exchange can be economic, but it also can involve the exchange of information, friendship, and other types of social interaction. Infringement of negative rights results from default on trade, arson, theft, vandalism, trespassing, assault, rape, murder, and so on.

Infringement of rights also occurs when negligence results in the injury or the death of a person or the destruction of property. With an infringement of rights there is what I have referred to as a "truncated exchange" (Touchstone 2006, 43). That is, one person uses another person's person or property without the consent of and/or compensation to the victim. The "interaction" is unilateral in that sense. However, it is bilateral from a "rights" perspective (i.e., from the perspective of justice). The person whose rights have been infringed upon is thus "owed" retribution, redress, and/or restoration for that which has been violated.

A child's right to care from his parents is not a result of consent, since children cannot give consent to be conceived or born. Nor is the relationship between parents and children based on reciprocal exchange. The transfer is unilateral from parents to the child. The child is under no obligation to give anything in return. Even if child-rearing is viewed as an "investment" (in human capital), it is one for which the return accrues (primarily) to the child, not the parent. According to Rasmussen and Den Uyl (1991, 82), a child's right to care from the parents is derived from the parents' actions—their decision to have the child. The liability argument (as discussed above) for the right of care for a child from his parents is that the parents' actions resulted in a condition of helplessness of a person; therefore, the parents must be responsible for that person's care. In effect, the basis for the right to care is an infringement of negative rights. By this argument, birth is an infringement of the child's rights. One important difference between reproduction and liability for personal injury is that, even though both result in conditions of helplessness of a person, the former results in the *creation* of a person; the latter does not.

The outcome of the action of a child's parents is that a child is produced. It can thus be seen as a productive activity. That is reproduction is production (for the Objectivist position, see Peikoff [1991, 302] and Rand, Alvin Toffler's *Playboy* Interview with Ayn Rand [1964, 7]; see also Touchstone [2006, 37–38]). According to libertarians, classical liberals, and Objectivists, a person's productivity results in the creation of property (Rothbard 1998, 47; Rasmussen and Den Uyl 1991, 117, 120; Rand, "The Property Status of Airwaves," 1967, 122–23). Production is a (primary) method by which a person acquires property in a free market; that is, by being productive, a person comes to own the fruits of his labor. It would follow that the child is the property of the parents. The child is owned by the parents by virtue of the productive activity of the parents. However, if this is ownership, it is an odd variety of it. Ownership is the right to acquire, use, and dispose of an object. Yet, for the most part, these defining features of ownership do not apply to parents *vis-à-vis* their child. This is ownership that requires *owing* that which is owned.

If the parents' actions do not result in trade, rights infringement, or the ownership of property, what is the result? The result is the creation of a person. As mentioned above in the discussion of the liability case for positive rights to childcare, both reproduction and liability for personal injury result in conditions of helplessness; however, the parents' actions result in the *creation of a person* who is helpless. A person whose actions result in the injury of another creates a *condition* of helplessness, but his actions did not create the person. As Branden (1962, 55) pointed out, the parents create a life, and the life that is created (by its nature) cannot survive alone; therefore the child is the parents' responsibility. Is the positive right to care therefore derived? Parents' actions result in the creation of life. The life of a child follows from the actions of the parents. The rights of the child follow from the life of the child. They do not follow from the actions of the parents. They are inherent in the child. They begin with the child.

Consider the other argument. If it were argued that the parents' actions result in the life of the child, and, therefore, the positive rights to childcare are derived from the actions of the parent, then it would also be the case that the negative rights of the child would be derived from the actions of the parents. That is, because the parents created the life of the child, the rights of the child are derived from the actions of the parents. Positive rights to care require the parents to act. Negative rights require that the parents (and others) observe the right to noninterference. Of course, what negative rights entail for human beings may differ according to stage of development. For infants, they may be limited to not being abused or killed by one's parents or others. What the rights entail in this context is irrelevant to the issue of whether they are derived or not. The point is that if rights are derived from the parents' actions by virtue of having created a life, then whether those rights are positive or negative is irrelevant since both are required for the source of rights—(the development and exercise of) a person's rational faculty. The issue is not whether the rights are positive or negative, but whether they are derived from the actions of others.

I would argue that human rights begin with human life—they are not derivative. As Rasmussen and Den Uyl stated about natural (i.e., negative) rights: "they exist *simply because someone is a human being*" (1991, 81; italics added). This is the case for the positive right to childcare from one's parents. Those who created the human life are responsible for *satisfying* the positive right to childcare, but not for creating that right per se. Rights in this context are inherent in the human being. Thus, this positive right (to care by children from their parents—which is unilateral in nature) is unlike those positive rights that result from exchange or from infringement (which are both reciprocal in nature).

GOVERNMENT

The following subsections will briefly review two arguments for limited government. It will also discuss the inalienability of rights as well as the coercive aspects of government.

Violation of Children's Rights and the Case for Limited Government

Under anarcho-capitalism, adults whose rights have been violated have the option of exacting retribution on their own behalf or paying for privately provided enforcement (Rothbard 1998, 85–96). If they do not exercise either of these alternatives, then their rights are not protected (unless a third party voluntarily does this for them). However, an adult is free to exercise his right not to protect his rights. A child does not have that option.

My case for limited government is based on the rights of children (and those with diminished capacity through no fault of their own) who have been abandoned or abused by their caregivers and have no other outlets for care;

that is, no one will voluntarily take over the care (Touchstone 2006, 184–85, "Rand, Rothbard, and Rights Reconsidered," 2010, 17–19). It would also include protection of the rights of children (and those with diminished capacity as stated above) who have been killed by their caregiver(s). These may comprise a small percentage of the population (and should in a free society); however, it remains the case that under anarchy, the rights of all children in this circumstance would be systematically unprotected.

A child who is abandoned and has no other means of care is necessarily in violation of the law of trespass. Technically, regardless of where he is, he is infringing on the negative rights of a property owner. However, because he is a child, he is not culpable. This situation shares similarities with an insane person who has committed a crime. It was Rand's contention that those who are insane and break the law should not face imprisonment, but be confined to asylums (Berliner 1995, 560). Children as well as adults with diminished capacity (through no fault of their own), who are in a position of having been abandoned or abused by those entrusted with their care and who have no alternative means of care, should have access to nonpunitive care. A government is needed in a situation such as this to provide oversight (at a minimum) (Touchstone, Rand, "Rothbard, and Rights Reconsidered," 2010, 17–19).

By oversight I mean that the government would be in charge of investigation and enforcement related to children and those with diminished capacity who have been abandoned, abused, or killed by their rightful caregivers and for whom no one will voluntarily provide care or seek retribution on their behalf. As a government agency, it would have a monopoly on enforcement and could confiscate the property and/or attach the salaries of those found culpable as well as imprison or execute them, depending upon the crime and on their degree of guilt. The agency would be in charge of securing adequate private care (or providing it, if it were not privately available).

Rights as an Entity

Using the logic that Rand applied to "the organic integrity of an entity," Sciabarra (1995, 145) argued that rights to life and property are a unified whole. For purposes of analysis, they can be isolated epistemologically, but are not separable metaphysically (1995, 145–46). In his discussion of rights, Sciabarra mentioned the rights to life and to property, but omitted the right to retaliate, which is a natural right. Without the right to protect one's life and property, one has no rights.

Sciabarra (1995, 258) noted that Rand's logic did not conform to a strict causal chain. With regard to rights, a person's right to retaliate is not deduced from his right to property, and his right to property is not deduced from his right to life. Rights are reciprocally causative and mutually reinforcing. As I pointed out in "Rand, Rothbard, and Rights Reconsidered" (Touchstone 2010, 13), this is demonstrated in game theory in the Tit-for-Tat strategy in which cooperation is rewarded by continuing to be cooperative with those who are cooperative, and retaliating against those who have defaulted or defected. Tit-for-Tat has been found in repeated games to be a winning strategy for long-range success. It supports the "circular" (in the sense of being mutually reinforcing) nature of rights. "Property is a corollary to the right to life and supports it. Retaliation follows from the right to property. Redress in turn is necessary for the good (life as well as property) to prevail" (Touchstone, "Rand, Rothbard, and Rights Reconsidered," 2010, 10).

By this reasoning, rights form a unity and are existentially inseparable. Thus, the right to retaliation is inseparable from other rights. It cannot be singled out and delegated to the government any more than the right to property can. It's not just their inalienability that makes it impossible to separate them from the individual, it is also their indivisibility from each other.

Children's Rights and Inalienability

A child's rights may be inseparable from his being, but the protection of rights is invested in his rightful caregiver, by virtue of what the positive right to childcare is. A child cannot protect his rights because one of his rights is the positive right to be protected. Thus in the early stage of human development, it may be necessary for a third party (government) to protect the child's rights if his rightful caregiver (who is charged with protecting the child and his rights) is in violation of those rights. The necessity for government in this case is that the rights of these individuals would be systematically unprotected and therefore they would in effect have no rights. (This does not mean that there is no coercive element to government in this regard, as discussed below. The coercive element is not that the individuals in this situation would be prohibited from protecting their own lives, since they cannot. A coercive aspect would exist to the extent that other private individuals and agencies would be prevented from providing protection for them. Of course, the reason that the government would intervene is because those who under normal circumstances would protect the child are the offenders.)

Kelley's Case for Government

There are cases for government other than the one mentioned above. For instance, David Kelley has argued that retaliation should be provided by government because of the private provision of it is impracticable. His is not an efficiency argument, however. In his view the right to retaliate fundamentally differs from the rights of life and property. This follows from the logical inconsistency of having a market in law enforcement agencies, which is predicated upon the enforcement of those laws. By the definition of what a market is (i.e., voluntary exchange), it cannot engage in the exchange of services that are coercive (Kelley 1974, 246–47).

Although Kelley's case has merit, it leaves unresolved the contradiction that, on one hand, rights are an entity and therefore indivisible, and, on the other hand, it is necessary to separate retaliation from other rights and delegate it to government, thereby denying it to the rights holder as such. (That is, the government is not only invested with the authority to protect individuals, but also vested with the right itself.)

Government and Coercion

The presence of government brings with it a coercive aspect. A coercive aspect when government assumes the power to retaliate is that private citizens cannot retaliate on their own behalf. Government would have a monopoly in the provision of retaliatory services. Without government provision (i.e., under anarcho-capitalism), if an adult does not pay for services, he does not receive them. That is an adult's choice. He may retaliate on his own behalf. That is also his choice. However, under government provision, if a person does not voluntarily pay the government (say, through a premium—as suggested in Rand, "Government Financing in a Free Society" [1964, 116–17] and Machan [1975, 271]), he is stripped of the right to retaliate on his own behalf. (A person may defend his life if it is in immediate danger, but a person may not engage in retaliation when there is a delay between the offense and "justice.") This is the coercive aspect of government in this context. It is coercive regardless of the method of payment. The voluntary payment of a premium is exclusionary; that is, non-payers are excluded from receiving protection. A voluntary lottery is not exclusionary. That is, it is possible that a lottery could generate enough revenue to cover the government protection of everyone, so that exclusion of non-payers is no longer an issue. However, a government lottery is coercive in the sense that any government enterprise is coercive—such as a government-run oil company or shoe factory. If a government can run a lottery business, there is no reason to prohibit it from owning and operating any other enterprise.

I have argued (Touchstone, "Rand, Rothbard, and Rights Reconsidered," 2010, 12–13) that because government is coercive, once government takes over protection services, the methods of payment—whether "premiums," lottery tickets, or taxation—must all be coercive, by the nature of what an entity is. Government is coercive by its nature (in this context, because it prohibits private retaliation on the part of the rights holder). An entity has a specific identity. An elemental economic identity is that production equals income.

When a product is produced, income is earned. When government protection services are provided, income is earned. An entity is its attributes and is inseparable from its attributes. Because of the identity between output and income, the attributes that apply to the provision of protective services also apply to income of those who produce the services. By definition, revenue used to pay for protective services must be coercive since the government-provided services are coercive (Touchstone, "Rand, Rothbard, and Rights Reconsidered," 2010, 13–15). There may be more or less coercive methods of payment (sources of government revenue); nevertheless, all have an element of coercion.

As discussed above, when government takes over the right to retaliate for everyone, it is coercive. What then of the very limited case discussed above in which government takes over the retaliatory services and other care (or at a minimum, its oversight) for children who have been abandoned or otherwise abused or killed by their caregivers (as well as others who have diminished capacity through no fault of their own and are in similar circumstances)—is it also coercive? It is not coercive in the sense that it is denying the right to retaliate on the part of the individuals involved. The reason government would take over this function is that these individuals have the right to retaliation; however, by virtue of the source of their (positive) rights (i.e., their limited rational faculty), they cannot provide it for themselves (and their rightful caregivers are the rights violators). That is, when government takes over this function, the individuals are not being denied the right to retaliate on their own behalf because they cannot do it for themselves (by their nature). However, this does not mean there is no coercive aspect to government provision of retaliation even in this narrow context because of the exclusionary aspect. When the government does not allow for competing enforcement, this brings with it a coercive aspect. Even though this case for government is that private individuals or agencies would not supply this function, it is nevertheless coercive because of the prohibitive factor.

As for funding, some or much of the government revenue may be acquired by the confiscation of property of the offenders (those caregivers who have abandoned, abused, or killed those in their care) and/or from an attachment of their salaries. Private donations to government could supply the balance, if needed. If taxation should be required, it is my position that the individuals in the circumstances described warrant protection because their positive right to care is an entitlement, not a gift, and charity by definition is a gift (Touchstone, "Rand, Rothbard, and Rights Reconsidered," 2010, 18–19). That said, government should be the last resort for assuming the actual care of these children. This is partly because government would assume the responsibility for teaching the children. Because government tends to be coercive, it is not in the best position to teach children about freedom. Children are the inheritors of freedom, and are (morally) charged with its preservation and protection once they mature. If they are not taught the principles of freedom and/or they do not see these principles demonstrated, they (very likely) will not have the tools to maintain and defend it.

There are qualifications that apply to government provision even in this narrow capacity. One is that if any revenue is generated through taxation, there would need to be a cap on the tax rate. As a rough guide, the government should not be expected to spend more per child than is spent on average per child by parents. (This is merely suggestive. A more appropriate figure could the median expenditure or even the minimum expenditure for a child by parents.) That amount per child multiplied by the number of individuals in this circumstance (i.e., under government oversight/care) would be the total gross amount of revenue needed by the government. From that would be deducted revenue from all other sources (mentioned above). The *maximum* tax rate would be that total amount divided by the number of tax payers. This tax rate would be expected to be low because very few should qualify for government care/oversight.

Another qualification to government provision is a free country cannot be expected to take in the "surplus" children of other countries—that is, children who are abandoned by other countries. There are practical reasons for this. One is the limited ability to absorb a relatively large number of abandoned children should other less-developed and less free countries take advantage of those that are freer and more economically developed. Another reason involves both rights and pragmatism. When a caregiver abandons a child, he has defaulted on his responsibility, and it is therefore within the legal purview of law enforcement to exact retribution in some form (confiscation of property, fines, and/or imprisonment, for instance). This is a matter of justice (a rights issue), but it also has the effect of deterrence—a practical consideration. If a country was to send its "surplus" children to another country, the latter could not take legal action against those in the other country who have abandoned the children (or could only do so at an expense that could be prohibitive.)

THE RIGHTS OF THE UNBORN

For rights involved with respect to abortion, one of the defining issues for the unborn is what life is—in the sense of whether it is a biological or a metaphysical phenomenon. In Touchstone (2006, 123–24), I sided with the former position. Taking a cue from when life is said to end as measured by the cessation of specific brain wave function, life could be regarded as beginning with the presence of the same brainwave activity (which is about the eighth week of gestation) (2006, 125–26; 2017, 258; cf. Bissell 1981, 28–29). A metaphysical view of death is based on more abstract notions, such as the absence of certain cognitive abilities. The former (i.e., the absence of brainwave activity) is consistent with the medical definition of death. It is biologically based, which has the advantage of being consistent with an ethics and a theory of rights which follow from man's nature (i.e., they are biocentric). This definition of death is also objectively measurable (Russell et al. 2019). The metaphysical definition is more subjective and less quantifiable (and, therefore, also more likely to result in abuse). The argument for the right to life of the unborn is based on the human's rational faculty (in this context, the presence of brainwave activity on which it depends).

There are a number of issues that warrant consideration as they relate to the rights of the unborn. For instance, Hewitson (2001) has examined various economic, social, and legal issues related to a woman providing surrogate reproductive services. One position is that it is within a woman's right to engage in a market for the production of babies. One argument against this is the child has a right to his life and should not be sold in a market. Rothbard (1998, 104) claimed that there is already a market in children at a zero price; that is, adoption. One counterargument to this is that adoption is fundamentally different from selling a child. Selling involves the transfer of ownership. In both cases, selling a child and adoption, an exchange takes place and the child does not give his consent. However, in other respects the two are different. The issue is—what is being exchanged? Ownership is the right to acquire, use, and dispose of an object (Touchstone 2006, 23). In a sale, it is assumed that the child does not have self-ownership.

According to Rothbard, the parent has trustee-ownership rights that allow the child to be sold, but the child retains the right for his person to not be aggressed against. I agree that a child has the right for his person not to be violated. However, I regard the child as having far more rights than did Rothbard. I do not think parents have ownership rights in a fundamental way, as I've mentioned above, because (among other things) it would be ownership in which the parent "owes" the child. I have also argued that the positive right of the child is the fundamental right to care from parents. The market for the buying and selling of children is a market for ownership of a child, not a market for childcare per se. The rights of the child prohibit his ownership. Adoption by its nature does (or should) put the care of the child first because childcare is a positive right of the child.

A counterargument as it relates to surrogate motherhood is that the surrogate is not selling the child, but renting out her uterus to others:

> Pateman, for example, argues that a woman "who enters a surrogacy contract is not being paid for (bearing) a child; to make a contract of that kind *would* be

tantamount to baby-selling" (1988, 212). The contract price, then, is the market-determined price which would be paid for storing an item in a house, which recompenses the owner for the disutility experienced from not being able to use the space themselves, and from having the item in the house. (Hewitson 2001, 236)

An argument against a woman renting out her uterus for the purpose of providing surrogate services in a reproductive market is that when a woman is pregnant, her uterus is no longer hers in the sense that the child is "homesteading"—at least for the period of gestation. The child has a claim on the uterus which prohibits others from renting out the space, so to speak. (The idea that a person would rent the surrogate mother's uterus prior to conception, and, therefore have first claim is problematic in the sense that the "renter" cannot occupy the space. Also, that which will occupy the space is not equivalent to "furnishings," but will be a human with inherent rights—according to the argument above, after the eighth week.)

There are other rights issues related to the unborn as well as children who are born. The market for aborted babies has grown. It has been suggested that there has been a recent push by some state legislators to permit the death of a baby who has survived abortion (Ward 2019). This has nothing to do with a woman having control over her body, since the child is now no longer in the mother's body. However, there is an advantage to harvesting parts from a baby who is still alive and whole rather than dead and dismembered—as is typically the case for late-term abortions (Wetzstein 2015, "Baby Body Parts Testimony Brings Jury to Tears," 2019). There is an incentive for those who traffic in the harvesting and use of baby parts to use this legislation to their advantage. The problem with this, of course, is that it violates the child's right to life (and the positive right to care). The same would apply to the harvesting of organs of the unborn at any time after the eighth week.

In a broader sense, decisions on the organ donations of children who die are usually left to parents. However, it could be argued that because a child cannot give consent, and organ donation has nothing to do with "childcare," such harvesting should be prohibited until a donor has reached the age of consent. This is consistent with the recent "opt out" law in England in which adults automatically become donors unless they explicitly choose otherwise. Among those excluded are children who are under the age of 18 and adults who "lack the mental capacity to understand the changes for a significant period before their death" (Friedman, "All Adults Automatically Organ Donors Unless They Opt Out," 2019). (This aspect of the "opt out" law is relevant to this discussion; however, the law per se is a violation of rights. It assumes that the government owns a person's body unless he opts out.)

Consent is not the only issue insofar as medical research using human organs is concerned. Even for aborted fetuses prior to the eighth week, there are issues involved in harvesting and using the so-called fetal tissue. Typically, these issues are addressed within an ethical context; however, I think there are rights concerns as well. Now that it is becoming possible for researchers to use human and animal tissue to create animals that can have human cognitive faculties (on which rights are based), there are rights issues related to the hybrids and whether researchers should be permitted to create them (Khan 2019; Devlin 2019; Gander 2019; Vibes 2019, "President Trump Ended Ghoulish Contract to Create 'Humanized Mice' Using Aborted Babies," 2019). The rights issue in this context would be that of the "hybrid" instead of the tissue donor. The right would be a "negative" one. That is, a hybrid animal (or animal part) with human faculties should not be created. It has a right not to be produced artificially. This is not an argument per se, but suggests a basis from which an argument might proceed. It is challenging for philosophy to keep pace with technology. Areas in which rights are concerned cannot be solved by simply letting the "market" take care of it. The market assumes voluntary exchange between independent equals. Because of rights (negative *and* positive), trading in humans is prohibited. I think this prohibition needs to be extended to include not only humans but also the artificial creation, production and/or trade of beings (or "parts" of beings) that have human faculties.

Chapter 2

Flourishing

INTRODUCTION

The first section of this chapter discusses the Aristotelian concept of eudaemonia, referred to by Rasmussen and Den Uyl (1991, 72) as flourishing, which they have described as striving toward one's potentiality or excellence. Den Uyl and Rasmussen ("Life, Teleology, and Eudaimonia," 1986, 75) have suggested that Ayn Rand's view is best thought of as a eudaemonistic theory. Like Aristotle and his adherents, such as Norton (1976), Rand, the founder of Objectivism, regarded what she referred to as "life qua man" as a person's ultimate value or end. She viewed productive work as his central purpose and happiness as his moral purpose, and at some level she equated the two (Shelton 1995, 43n73). Norton believed that a person should live in accordance with his daemon, or destiny (1976, 5). Like Norton, Rand saw a person's destiny as being singular, but unlike Norton she tied it more closely to the market. She also linked it more directly to the person's survival (Touchstone 2006, 224–25, 2018, 79, 80n15).

Rand regarded child-rearing as a potentially productive activity, but viewed it as optional (Rand, "Alvin Toffler's *Playboy* Interview with Ayn Rand," 1964, 7, "Of Living Death," 1968, 3). Although reproductivity (child-rearing) is a productive activity, I regard it as sufficiently different from productivity to be considered a separate category and on a par with productivity (Touchstone 2006, 34–36). Because of the importance of parenting in a person's value system, I do not view a person's purpose necessarily as being singular, as did Rand and Norton.

The second section of the chapter deals with Objectivism's Benevolent Universe Premise (BUP) (Peikoff 1976; Rand, "The Ethics of Emergencies," 1964, 48–49). The Universe isn't malevolent or benevolent; it simply is.

But the nature of man is such that he is capable of dealing successfully with the external world. However, this is not guaranteed. The BUP states that if a person thinks and acts ethically then, in the long run, success is to be expected. He may fail, but that is incidental. Man is efficacious. That is, he is capable of dealing successfully with reality.

Aristotle regarded bravery as a virtue, which he thought, like other virtues, is perfected by habituation; which, in the case of bravery means repeatedly facing "alarming situations" (Aristotle 1976, 95). However, if acting ethically results in success, why would bravery be a virtue or even be necessary? The BUP states that success is expected in the long run, but there may be failures in the short term. These are thought to be incidental according to the BUP. Even so, facing a probability of failure requires courage. In some situations, the probability of failure may be high—such as when a parent acts to save his child from drowning. This is regarded as an act of bravery even though it does not neatly fit within the BUP. Even more difficult to explain within the context of Objectivist Ethics (OE), is why a person would choose a career in which he persistently faced a high probability of death—such as firefighting. A rationale for undertaking dangerous professions is briefly addressed in this chapter.

EUDAEMONIA

The previous chapter addressed natural rights. Natural rights for adults are negative; that is, adults have the right to noninterference. Negative rights include the right to life and to property; also included is the right to retaliation if the rights to life and/or property are violated. Negative rights are boundary setting. According to Rasmussen and Den Uyl (1991, 104–105) and to Machan (*Classical Individualism*, 1998, 122), they provide a sphere of moral territory because individuals have moral obligations to fulfill. In the Aristotelian tradition, Rasmussen and Den Uyl saw morality as being primarily realized through self-perfection, or what they called flourishing (1991, 72). Rights are required to give individuals "a context for eudaimonic achievement" (1991, 108).

In Aristotelian ethics, the object of life is that end that is desired "for its own sake" (Aristotle 1976, 63). It is the supreme good. Happiness (eudaemonia) is that end (1976, 73). To arrive at what happiness is, Aristotle (1976, 75) looked to the *proper* function of man (from which he excluded nutrition and growth); which, he said, implies living in accordance with a rational principle. Thus, happiness is an *activity* (Norton 1976, 228). It is living a virtuous life, by which Aristotle meant performing rightly or with excellence—not for a moment, but for a lifetime (Aristotle 1976, 76).

Rand and Life qua Man

According Den Uyl and Rasmussen, one of Rand's significant insights was her observation that only living entities can be teleological (Den Uyl and Rasmussen, "Life, Teleology, and Eudaimonia," 1986, 65–66). Like Aristotle and his adherents, Rand viewed "life qua man" as man's ultimate value (end) (Rand, "The Objectivist Ethics," 1964, 23). Rand distinguished between a value, which is the aim of a living being's actions, and the action that is undertaken to attain or keep the value. Life is the ultimate aim of living beings; however, man is unique in that he has no automatic means of survival. He must learn not only what his aims (values) are but how to achieve them. The actions undertaken to achieve values are virtues. Values (teleology) arise with life and virtues (ethics) arise with man. OE are bio-centric and are rooted in man's nature.

The fundamental fact about living beings is—they face the alternative of life or death. The fundamental fact about humans is—they have no automatic code to guide their actions or to know what their aims are. A human's means of survival is reason (1964, 21). Reason is of epistemological relevance. It does not function automatically. It requires effort. The fundamental ethical decision is to think or not. Reason is man's primary value and rationality is his primary virtue (1964, 25). The nature of being human is that humans are capable of making the fundamental choice as well as other decisions; that is, they have volition. They are also capable of acting on their choices, as long as they are free to do so. Freedom, a sociopolitical principle that arises with the presence of other people, is of relevance to ethics because a person's choice must be uncoerced in order to qualify as virtuous.

As previously stated, Rasmussen and Den Uyl (1991, 105) claimed that natural rights (which are negative for adults) are necessary because humans have moral duties to perform. The basis for rights is man's rational faculty. Rights are necessary so that man may be free to use his rational faculty, because it is his means of survival. It is because of man's life (the value) that rights are required. The actions required to maintain his life are virtues, but man is not limited to acting only virtuously, because he does not automatically know what actions qualify as virtuous. He must learn what they are and in so doing he may make mistakes. Reason is fallible and information is limited and may be imperfect. Man must be free to make mistakes (again, with the qualification that he does not infringe on another's rights) in order to know what he values as well as discover the actions (virtues) to attain them.

If an entity faces no alternative, there are no values. The fundamental value is life—which is only possible for a living being (because of life's contingency). If a being does not have the capacity (rationality) to discover what his choices are and the capability of choice (volition), there are no virtues.

If a person is not sufficiently free to act on his decisions (freedom), he cannot be virtuous. Rand distinguished between virtue and value, action and outcome, cause and effect. Metaphysically, the relationship between man and reality is summarized in Rand's BUP (which may have been originated by Paterson ([1943] 1968, 250–51; Cox 2004, 202), which basically states that man is efficacious (Peikoff 1976; Rand, "The Ethics of Emergencies," 1964, 48–49). The universe is neither benevolent nor malevolent. It simply is. The proposition has to do with man's relationship to the external world. That is, there is a relationship between man's actions and the outcome in the real world that is predictable. Man is capable of achieving his objectives.

The qualifications to this statement are that man is capable of achieving his aims if he acts rationally (i.e., ethically) with the requisite that he lives in a free society. A further caveat is that even if a person acts rationally, there is a possibility that he may not achieve his objective; however, that chance is small. The other qualification is that the proposition applies to the long run. Ethical principles are strategies for long-term success. That is, they result in success if applied consistently within the context of a lifetime. A given ethical action may result in failure, but if consistently followed, ethical principles will yield success.

Productive Purpose

According to OE, virtues are those actions that when followed will sustain one's life (Rand, "Atlas Shrugged," 1961, 121)—if they are consistently followed. Decisions and actions are to be evaluated within the context of a person's whole life. If one's "whole life" is confined to longevity, one's potential life span can be represented by *T*. The BUP recognizes that accidents can happen; however, they have a low probability of occurrence if one acts ethically. Thus, according to my interpretation of the BUP, even if one is ethical throughout one's life, his expected life span would be somewhat less than the potential life span, *T*, because of the possibility of accidents (that are not under the control of the individual and therefore have no ethical implications). Unethical actions can lower the life expectancy further (Touchstone 2018, 68). Not only the expected quantity of one's life can be lessened, but its quality can be diminished as well. (And conversely, living a more ethical life may increase a person's life expectancy and improve its quality.) This is because, like Aristotelians, Rand regarded happiness as inseparable from maintaining (in an ethical way) one's life.

Rand regarded productive work to be man's purpose in life and his moral purpose to be happiness; thus work and happiness are part of the same process, and at some level she equated the two (Shelton 1995, 43n73). The connection between productive work and happiness, from an economic perspective, is based on a chain of events. Productivity (an activity) results in a good (a thing). If a person is self-sufficient, that which is produced is his property which he may consume directly. The result of consuming is utility (satisfaction or happiness). In a market economy, there are more links in this chain. When a product is produced it is sold in the market. In turn, the income generated from the sale can be used to buy goods or services which may be consumed, thus yielding satisfaction. "Consumption" is not confined to expenditures on products. It also includes time spent on leisure activities—such as recreation, either alone or with friends and family. Nonwork time also may be spent improving skills (investing in one's productive capacity). All these comprise a person's life and all make up its totality from the perspective of a lifetime. Even so, Rand isolated productive work as man's purpose. At any point in the chain—from productive work to "utility" (happiness) associated with consumption, it could be said, this is the purpose of one's life. That is, the question is: is man's purpose producing a product or the product one produces or the income that is received or consumption or the satisfaction (utility or happiness) that is generated therefrom? Schools of philosophy have differed based on this issue. To Rand, consuming products, recreation, happiness, and love are the rewards in life. A person's purpose is productive work, in particular, doing it well.

Rand's view on excellence is consistent with the Aristotelian tradition. Excellence (i.e., performing with excellence) is a virtue. Aristotle pointed out that understanding excellence is not the study of what goodness is, but how to become good (1976, 93). He distinguished between moral and intellectual virtues (1976, 91). The latter virtues deal with the arts and professions, although becoming excellent in either involves many of the same principles. A person may be excellent by accident; however, true excellence requires practice. It also requires deliberation (1976, 97). That is, the practice should be deliberate. Aristotle said:

> [T]he causes or means that bring about any form of excellence are the same as those that destroy it, and similarly with any art; for it is as a result of playing the harp that people become good and bad harpists. The same applies to builders and all other craftsmen. Men will become good builders as a result of building well, and bad ones as a result of building badly. (1976, 92)

He also noted that beginning to practice at an early age can make a world of difference (1976, 92). As will be discussed in more depth in chapter 8, as an analogy to a person's life span, one can think of a given task as having a potential length of life if performed perfectly. When a task is first initiated, errors are expected, particularly if the task is a challenging one. Its "expected life span" is short relative to its potential life. However, with studied practice and effort, the number of errors tends to fall, which extends the expected life of the task (Touchstone 2015, 24).

Norton and Destiny

Den Uyl and Rasmussen ("Life, Teleology, and Eudaimonia," 1986, 75) stated that Rand's view is best seen as a eudaemonistic theory that belongs in the perfectionist camp. They believed that David Norton's insights in this regard are more fully expressed than Rand's (1986, 75). Norton (1976, 5) believed that a person should live in accordance with his daemon—that is, his "inner voice," or destiny, which is consistent with Rand's view that productive work is man's central purpose. Norton thought that a person should do well the work that he does well (1976, 232, 233, 311–13). According to Rand ("The Objectivist Ethics," 1964, 26), productive work "means the consciously chosen pursuit of a productive career, in any line of rational endeavor, great or modest, on any level of ability." To Rand, what is relevant from an ethical perspective is neither the extent of a person's ability nor the significance of the task, but that a person fully devotes his mind to his work. Like Rand, Norton regarded a person's reward for doing this as happiness or eudaemonia.

Norton viewed self-worth as emanating from living in accordance with one's destiny (1976, 16). Similarly, Rand ("The Objectivist Ethics," 1964, 25, 27) saw self-esteem (the value) and pride (the virtue) following from productive work. Both envisioned a person's work as the integrating principle of his life. Both viewed it as a single discipline that spanned one's life (Peikoff 1991, 299–300; Norton 1976, 238–39). To Norton, every decision that a person contemplates should be made in relation to one's destiny (1976, 9, 225). Likewise, to Rand ("Atlas Shrugged," 1961, 130), a person should not adopt values that impede his purpose. Similar to Rand, Norton thought a person's nature defines what he should do. By a person's nature, Norton meant what he is uniquely qualified to do according to his specific talents. Rand's view was more generic than Norton's. Although both Rand and Norton thought each person was born with all potentialities, Norton (1976, xi) viewed a person as having an innate destiny. In contrast, Rand ("The Objectivist Ethics," 1964, 28) was inclined to believe that humans were born tabula rasa. Both subscribed to free will; however, Norton (1976, 16) viewed it narrowly as a person's freedom to choose or reject his destiny.

To Norton, it is by specialization that people benefit from what others create by way of fulfilling their inherent destinies. Through what Norton called "the complementarity of excellences" (1976, 10) the right goods would be produced in the right quantities to satisfy the demand for them. Norton claimed that: "[F]or every kind of work that must be done, there are persons for whom that work holds intrinsic rewards, and by whom that work shall be skillfully and lovingly done" (1976, 346). This is the basis for interdependence among people. Interdependence results in "love, the division of labor, and justice" (1976, 275). Rand ("The Objectivist Ethics," 1964, 31) would sum this up as trade, trade, and trade. She viewed trade as the basis for all interactions between adults, whether it is in the spiritual, economic, or social realm. Yet, the "market" for one's talents is largely ignored in Norton's discussion (1976, 311–13, 322–24). According to Norton, if each person pursues his unique calling, there will be the perfect number of workers to tackle any problem. However, the same skill set for garbage collectors—such as strength, endurance, agility, and balance—is also required for mountain climbers. The former is just as honorable, but it offers less excitement and glamour than the latter. I would venture to guess that if each person followed his perceived daemon, most people would find their garbage accumulating.

In a free market, shortages and surpluses are eliminated by the price mechanism. Prices provide the information as well as the incentive to allocate resources where they are in the most demand. Lags in adjustment often occur, but the system functions better than any other alternative. Apparently, there are no prices in Norton's proposed economy. Distribution of goods is based on love—the love of excellence (1976, 317). Scarcity is eliminated by people limiting their desires and by claiming only products that are commensurate with their destinies (1976, 340–41). In order to keep people from claiming a Ferrari when their destiny is something other than race car driving, Norton recommended that a person's loved ones and acquaintances corroborate which goods are consistent with a person's chosen career (1976, 344). It's not hard to imagine that an economy structured along these lines would quickly become unwieldy and invasive. Like Norton, Rand envisioned a man's destiny as singular, but unlike Norton she tied it more directly to the market.

Thomas Kuhn pointed out that many people are mentally imprisoned by conventional wisdom (1970, 58–61). Because of this, those responsible for innovations in art and technology and theoretical advances may not be appreciated by their contemporaries in their respective disciplines. These innovators could be dismissed in Norton's economy, but the same is often the case for a free market. However, under a free market system, a person is free to devote his time and material resources to novel ideas even if they go unacknowledged or unremunerated in his lifetime or ever. The freedom to fail is essential to discovery. Of course, if a person pursues a destiny that is not financially rewarding, he will need some other source of income to sustain him. Unlike Norton, Rand linked a person's destiny more directly to his survival (Touchstone 2006, 224–25, 2018, 79–80n15). If a person has an independent source of wealth, then pursuing a nonpaying destiny poses no problem. (And, according to Objectivism, a person needs productive work even if he does not need a salary, because it serves the psychological purposes of anchoring and ranking his values [Peikoff 1991, 292–303].) However, for those who have no independent source of income and whose destiny is non-remunerative, they will very likely need to engage in paid employment to support themselves while they pursue their calling. If so, a person's destiny cannot be a singular pursuit as both Norton and Rand put forth.

Parenting

The previous subsection discussed the unique singularity of purpose that is each person's destiny as well as its inseparability from excellence, according to both Rand and Norton. I suggested that if a person has a destiny that does not sustain his survival, he will need a separate source of income if he hopes to pursue it. A single overarching career that spans a lifetime around which all other values are to be judged and prioritized would not be possible in a case such as this.

I have also suggested (Touchstone 2006, 18, 242) that a single purpose is not possible for most people because they have parenting obligations. Rand regarded child-rearing as a potentially productive activity, but optional (Rand, "Alvin Toffler's *Playboy* Interview with Ayn Rand," 1964, 7, "Of Living Death," 1968, 3). Unlike Rand, I have elevated reproduction to be separate from and on a par with production (Touchstone 2006, 34–36). Although reproductivity (child-rearing) is a productive activity, it is sufficiently different from productivity to be considered a separate category. One of the distinguishing differences is that parenting is non-remunerative. It is not self-sustaining from the parents' perspective. The parents do not own the product of their efforts. They cannot acquire, use, or dispose of a child as they can with objects of ownership. Because of the importance of child-rearing in a person's value system, I do not view a person's purpose (productive work) necessarily to be singular, as did Rand and Norton.

Because parenting is not life-sustaining from the parent's perspective, it would seem inconsistent to consider taking care of one's child (reproductivity) a virtue, particularly within the context of OE. As will be discussed more fully in chapters 4, 5, and 8, this virtue has little or nothing to do with decreasing a parent's probability of dying—as the practice of other virtues tends to do (either directly or indirectly). (In fact, from the mother's perspective, reproductivity has historically tended to increase that probability.) Reproductivity has to do with life and death, but not with life's contingency. It has to do with life's finality. Reproductivity has to do with replacing one's life. (In terms of the earlier discussion, it would replace the "potential life span," T.) Of course, one person's life does not literally replace another's. As will be discussed in chapter 4, an argument for reproductivity within the context of OE is the replacement of human capital investment with which one has been endowed (Touchstone 2006, 251–54; Touchstone, "Reproductivity, Capital Theory, and Objectivist Ethics," 2010, 229–31).

Within OE, a single purpose serves to anchor a person's value system in order to evaluate and prioritize other values. Having more than one purpose would seem to complicate decisions involving trade-offs between competing values. Attaining a sense of balance may require more deliberation. Also, as will be discussed in chapter 5, rather than prioritizing values on a single scale (which is consistent with both economic theory and OE [Alchian and Allen 1977, 25–26; Becker 1995, 7; Rand 1990, 31]), the presence of children can result in having more than a single scale of values (Touchstone 2016, 47–48).

THE BENEVOLENT UNIVERSE PREMISE AND MAN'S EFFICACY

Implicit in the discussion of a person's destiny or purpose is that a person can choose—that is, he has volition. Choice is inherent in human beings. They can choose and in a very real sense they must choose, because by their nature they have no automatic means of survival. Reason is their means of survival and it is not automatic—it takes effort. However, the ability to choose would matter little, if at all, if values were not achievable. If the results of a person's actions were arbitrary or if they were malevolent, then a person may be able to choose, but the outcome of that choice would be so unpredictable or negative that volition (any choice made or action taken) would be irrelevant.

If the universe is arbitrary or malevolent, then either a person's success is solely based on luck or he is doomed to failure. Unpredictability exists (epistemologically). Failure exists, but a proposition of Objectivism is that it is not to be expected (with qualifications). This is the BUP (Peikoff 1976; Rand, "The Ethics of Emergencies," 1964, 48–49). In fact, as previously stated, the Universe is neither malevolent nor benevolent. But the nature of man is such that he is capable of dealing with reality successfully—although this is not guaranteed. The BUP is the proposition that if a person thinks and acts rationally then in the long run, success is the to-be-expected. Failure is possible, but it is marginal in scope. That is, man is efficacious. The BUP is implicit in the following quote by Aristotle:

> Probably it is not right at all to follow the changes of a man's fortunes, because success and failure do not depend on these; they are merely complements … of human life. It is virtuous activities that determine our happiness, and the opposite kind that produce the opposite effect. (Aristotle 1976, 83)

In OE, virtues are activities that preserve and promote a person's life. If virtues are actions that promote life and if life is a person's ultimate value, why then is bravery a virtue—or even necessary? Why would a person ever be reluctant to act to promote or to preserve his life? Maya Angelou has said that of all the virtues, courage is the most important because without courage a person can practice none of the others. Bravery is needed, in part, because virtues result in *long-term* success. There may be setbacks in the short run. Courage may be needed because there exists a probability of failure. However, this probability is low for virtues, according to the BUP. Aristotle said that we become better at virtues by practicing them: "[I]t is by habituating ourselves to make light of alarming situations and to face them that we become brave, and it is when we have become brave that we shall be most able to face an alarming situation" (Aristotle 1976, 95). Of course in some situations, a person has little opportunity for preparation. A person may have only one shot at standing up for what he thinks is right in the face of opposition. In some cases, not only is there no chance for practice, the risk of failure (death) may be high. A person may have only one opportunity to save his child from drowning. Actions such as this are regarded as acts of courage. Yet they do not seem to fit neatly into the BUP when there is a high probability of losing one's own life; however, they are understandable in light of the greater loss if one failed to act.

It is in some ways more difficult to understand why a person would willingly pursue an occupation in which there is a persistently high probability of death—such as firefighting, for instance. If life is one's ultimate value, why would a person continually risk it? It's true that a firefighter has a greater opportunity for habituating himself to dangerous situations, and, therefore, for becoming brave. However, if simply facing down one's fears resulted in bravery, one might think that, instead of undertaking an arduous profession such as firefighting, playing Russian roulette would suffice. But there is actually more than bravery that is involved in these professions; there is also confidence. Dangerous occupations typically require training—deliberate practice—that improves skills and thereby lowers the risk of failure. Repeatedly playing Russian roulette—assuming one could do so—does not improve the probability of surviving death. Deliberate training and experience where skills are involved result in greater competence; at best, they lead to excellence. This is also usually accompanied by greater confidence. Returning to the earlier discussion of the "expected life span" of a task, deliberate training has the effect of increasing a task's expected life relative to its potential life. The relationship between practice, the reduction in errors, and excellence will be addressed in greater detail in chapter 8.

Chapter 3

Life as the Ultimate Value

INTRODUCTION

According to Objectivism, life (life qua man) is the ultimate value. This is consistent with the Aristotelian concept of eudaemonia. As discussed in the last chapter, eudaemonia means "happiness," which translates into a lifetime lived in the pursuit of excellence (Aristotle 1976, 73; Den Uyl and Rasmussen 1991, 72–76). "Life" has a number of meanings. The first section of this chapter considers two aspects of life: life lived moment to moment and life as a whole—a lifetime. In OE, it is man's potential life as a whole that is seen as the ultimate value (Peikoff 1991, 216–17). That is, it is man's whole life that is of relevance, not life lived moment to moment. A person must think long term to be successful (survive) rather than the range of the moment.

In the second section, I examine the role that life's finality plays in "life" being the ultimate value. Two aspects of life are its contingency and its finality. Life's contingency implies that there is always a probability of dying from moment to moment. Life's finality means that ultimately man is mortal, as are all life forms. The contingency of life can be represented by a probability of dying, r, and life's finality by a potential life span, T. The "expected life span" is given by $PV = \sum_1^T [1/(1 + r)^t]$. The potential life span, T, can be seen as a context for ethical decisions by the effect the pursuit of a more ethical life has on the ratio PV/T. Specifically, if a person chooses to pursue a more ethical life, this has the effect of reducing r and in increasing PV relative to T. The rationale underlying the reduction in r as a result of living a more virtuous life is that, according to OE, virtues are actions that (if consistently followed) tend to promote life. The finite life span, T, provides a context for lifetime decisions. This is contrasted with the life of a being who also faces the probability of early death, r, but is potentially immortal. In relative terms, a potentially endless life provides no context for improvements in ethical behavior. For purposes of illustrating the importance of a finite life (or at least a "limited" one) on ethical decision-making, this discussion isolates only one aspect of life, longevity. Of course, "life qua man" encompasses more than living a long life. If longevity were the only objective, people would not take life-threatening risks. Yet people do undertake such risks, and, in many cases, it is to the benefit of society that they do so. As is briefly addressed, the context for decisions involving risky occupations involves many of the same considerations as those summarized in the simple equation PV/*T*.

The third section addresses the age-old question of whether a person eats to live (life is the ultimate value) or lives to eat ("eat, drink and be merry for tomorrow you may die"). A person needs to consume in order to live, and he needs to be alive in order to consume. The two are not at odds in that respect; however, at the margin, there is a trade-off. A simple example is presented that addresses this question. It concludes that if the emphasis is on "life," a person can have the maximum amount of both life and consumption; whereas, if a person's focus is on consumption, he will likely have a shorter life for a given level of consumption. By thinking long term, in terms of one's whole life, a person can have both longevity and consumption. Even though both are important, by focusing on life, rather than on consumption, a person can achieve both. The balance of this section further examines life as the ultimate value, making the argument by focusing on action rather than value. The emphasis is different than Rand's, but otherwise it is essentially the same case. It also considers what "life as a whole" comprises. In an example presented, which focuses on productivity, a person's human capital is of relevance. However, a person's life is not limited to his productive work. Consumption (broadly conceived) is also a factor. The chapter concludes with a discussion of the relationship between productive purpose and happiness within the context of Objectivist Ethics (OE).

LIFE AS THE ULTIMATE VALUE

As pointed out in the previous chapter, Ayn Rand is credited with the observation that only living beings are teleological (Den Uyl and Rasmussen, "Life, Teleology, and Eudaimonia," 1986, 65–66). It is life that makes values or ends possible. Life makes values possible, but it also makes those things that are not valued possible. Life makes death possible. According to OE, the fundamental alternative for living beings is life or death (Peikoff 1991, 211). However, as Rand pointed out, these are not metaphysically equivalent. Rand (1990, 60) coined the expression "reification of the zero" to represent the fallacy of elevating a "nothing," such as death (the lack of life), to the category of an *existent*. Of the two alternatives, life and death, only life can form the basis for a system of values. A value system deals with actions. Inaction will lead to death and will do so fairly quickly. Death cannot serve as the foundation for a system of values. Eric Mack addressed this line of reasoning, which was one that was put forth by Rand in her argument that life serves as the basis for a code of values; that is, life is a goal worth pursuing (Mack 1986, 134; Rand, "The Objectivist Ethics," 1964, 16).

According to OE, life qua man is the ultimate value. As discussed in the last chapter, the Objectivist perspective can be seen as equivalent to the Aristotelian concept of eudaemonia. "Life" is subject to numerous meanings. The distinction that I make in this section is between "life lived from moment to moment" (i.e., over a period of time) and "life as a whole" (a lifetime). As an analogy to economic concepts, I have likened "life lived within an interval of time" to income. I've also compared a "lifetime" with capital asset value (Touchstone 2018, 61–62). Income is a flow concept. It has a time interval associated with it—say, a year. Similarly, a living being lives from one moment to another—from year to year, for instance. That is, the point of similarity between "life lived moment to moment" and income is that both are flow concepts. Capital is a stock concept. Its value is computed at a point in time. Likewise, a living being's life span is the potential number of time periods (say, years), it may live. Both capital value and a lifetime are stock concepts.

The two concepts of life considered here are in one sense two aspects of life. Life is lived year to year, and the sum of those years is a lifetime. The focus of the year-to-year aspect of life is short term. A being's life span is of long-term relevance. When Rand observed that values arise because of life's contingency (i.e., because a being continually faces the alternatives of life or death), this implies that there always exists a probability of dying from one moment to the next—that is, within the short term. For a living being to achieve any value, it must remain alive from one moment to another. Thus, life must be a value. Because human beings (unlike other living beings) cannot rely on automatic actions to sustain their existence, they must *choose* life. That is, ethics arise with human life. For humans, life is fundamental to the achievement of any other value. King (1986, 111) noted that this would render life an instrumental value, but it does not follow that life is an ultimate value. As a counterargument, it could be said that by choosing to live moment to moment in the pursuit of other values, this ultimately results in choosing one's whole life as a value. However, as I pointed out in Touchstone (2018, 61), the flaw in this argument is that making decisions from the perspective of the "range of the moment" can result in a different life (both in quantity and quality), than one lived based on decisions made within the timeframe of one's whole life. In the following section, I argue that man's mortality contributes to life (as a whole) being the ultimate value.

LIFE AS A WHOLE

In Touchstone (2015) and (2018), I suggested that it is the "finality" of life that is a factor in it being the ultimate value. The contingency of life and its finality can be seen as two distinct aspects of death. A living being that was certain to survive until age *T* and then die, would be mortal, but its life would not be contingent. A being that only faced a probability of dying, would not face the certainty of death. Of course, humans, like all life forms, are mortal. It is due in part to life's finality, or at least its "limitedness," that life is the ultimate value. Although both life's contingency and its finality are inseparable existentially, they can be isolated for analytical purposes, which is an approach I used in Touchstone (2015, 187–89) and (2018, 61–64). As an illustration, I presented two beings, both of whom were assumed to be subject to a probability of early death, but only one who would encounter certain death. Two causes of early death are aging (senescence) and "accidents" (nonsenescence) (Bongaarts 2005, 204). The being who is assumed to be potentially immortal, yet has a probability of early death, would not "age," thus early death would be due solely to accidents. To simplify the illustration, it was assumed that for both beings early death only results from accidents.

There are accidents that stem from factors over which a person has control and others that are not under a person's control. I refer to the latter as "no-fault" accidents. By "no-fault" I mean an accident or mistake that is no fault of the person in question (although someone else may be at fault). Those accidents that are under a person's control have ethical import for the person in question. Because within OE virtuous actions tend to be life enhancing (when consistently followed), pursuit of a more ethical life would tend to lower the probability of dying (other things equal). A virtuous existence can promote both life's quality and its quantity. For simplification, the focus in the illustration is restricted to longevity so as to limit the examination to the role *T* plays in decision-making.

The significance of a finite life with a potential life span, *T*, is that *T* serves as context for decisions of an ethical nature. To put a more ethical life in perspective, the "expected life" of a "being" can be compared with his maximum potential length of life, *T*. For the expected life, the equation $PV_1 = \sum_1^T [1/(1 + r)]^t$ is used, where *r* is the early death rate, or the force of mortality. (The continuous version is $\int_0^T e^{-rt}\, dt$. The value for *r* in the discrete equation is not the same as for *r* in the continuous version.) This equation is a specific counterpart of the general form for the expected life for an asset given in Preinreich

(1938, 220). (Also, see Kurtz [1930] and [Touchstone 2018, 63]. In addition, appendix section "Depreciation and Death" addresses the difference between "present value" and "expected value" as they relate to the expected life span.)

Initially, it is assumed that both beings face the same early death rate, r = 10%, and that the mortal being's potential life span is T = 10 years. Thus, the mortal being, B10, has an expected length of life of 6.145 years. The potentially immortal being, B∞, has an expected length of life of ten years. (The expected life span of B∞ is $1/r$, based on the following: $\int_0^\infty e^{-rt}\,dt = \lim T\rightarrow\infty \int_0^T e^{-rt}\,dt = \lim T\rightarrow\infty\,[1/r\,(1 - e^{-rT})] = 1/r$. See Chiang [1974, 459].) Alternatively, under the assumption that the "no-fault" early death rate is r = 1%, the expected life spans would be 9.471 years and 100 years for B10 and B∞, respectively.

If B10 chose a more ethical life, thereby lowering his early death rate from 10% to 1%, B10's expected life as a percentage of T, would increase from 61.45% to 94.71%. This increase is a gauge of the improvement in expected longevity based on living a more ethical life for the mortal being. Although the increase in B∞'s expected life is larger than B10's in absolute terms, in *relative* terms it has no meaning because in the limit an expected life span relative to an infinite one is zero. (For the expected life relative to T, the lim $T\rightarrow\infty\,[(1/r)(1 - e^{-rT})]/T$ is, applying L'Hôpital's rule, equal to lim $T\rightarrow\infty\, e^{-rT}/1 = 0$ [Touchstone 2015, 189n9].) For the potentially immortal being, lifetime goals have no meaning because no quantifiable life span exists against which they can be evaluated. A more virtuous life may reduce the early death rate, thereby increasing the expected life span; however, regardless of its value, relative to a potentially limitless one, the increase in expected longevity is meaningless. Thus, life would not serve as the ultimate value if it were potentially without limit.

This statement is subject to qualification. The expected life span associated with the "no-fault" probability of early death, the latter of which is assumed to be 1% in this illustration, could be regarded as the best that a potentially immortal being could anticipate. (That is, life has "limitedness," even though it is not finite, per se.) As such, it could be used as a basis (i.e., the denominator) against which an expected life span resulting from less virtuous behavior (in the numerator) could be measured. That is, instead of the potential length of life, T (which is infinite for B∞), the context for "lifetime goals" would be the expected life span for B∞ based on the early probability of dying due to accidental deaths that result from actions that are not under B∞'s control, and which therefore have no moral content from B∞'s perspective.

So, Why Take Risks?

"Life" as a value encompasses more than simply its quantity (cf. Mack 1986, 139). If longevity were the only objective of human beings, they would avoid all life-threatening endeavors. Humans, however, take risks. (In fact, as will be discussed later, they must take risks in order to learn.) Life is a value (the ultimate value) to individuals, and they are also risk takers. These appear to be contradictory. How can they be reconciled?

Economic theory offers an answer; however, economics does not deal in ethics per se. Economics assumes a simplistic rationality on the part of individuals. For instance, it is assumed that given two identical goods, a rational person would choose the one with the lower price, other things equal. From the perspective of economic theory, risk taking is regarded as rational behavior if, in doing so, there is a sufficient return. However, if the focus is solely on monetary return, it would seem that there are occupations that are particularly life threatening, such as firefighting, for which the pay received would appear to be insufficient to warrant the risks involved. To choose such an occupation would not appear to be rational. Nevertheless, there are individuals who pursue these careers willingly (as they must in a free society), and it is to the benefit of society that they do so.

The previous chapter briefly addressed high risk occupations. It mentioned risk reduction as it relates to these careers—specifically, reducing the probability of failure through training (or deliberate practice). As an analogy to the expected life span of a person that is increased by living more virtuously (as discussed hypothetically for the mortal "being" above), a specific task can also be thought of as having an expected life span that can be increased by reducing errors through training. As mentioned in the former chapter, Aristotle distinguished between moral and intellectual virtues. Professions and the arts fall into the latter category; however, both types of virtues, moral and intellectual, can be improved through habit and practice. Occupational excellence is achieved through deliberate practice and experience (Aristotle 1976, 91–92). As I stated in Touchstone (2018, 64): "A life well lived is not simply one in which the risk of death or failure is minimized, but may be one in which a person perfects his skills so as to minimize those risks." The "expected life of a task" as it is related to the reduction of (fatal) errors through deliberate training will be discussed in more depth in chapter 8.

LIFE AND CONSUMPTION

The previous section isolated one feature of life, "longevity," to examine its role in providing a context for ethical decision-making as it relates to a person's whole life. This section presents a simple example that looks at a person's "whole life" from another perspective. Specifically, it considers the trade-off between "consumption" and "life." That is, it addresses the age-old question of whether a person "lives to eat" or "eats to live." The question could be recast as whether a person's purpose is short-term happiness (i.e., satisfaction derived from consumption) or "life" (which in the simple illustration discussed below is equivalent to productive purpose that is expressed as years of a person's life).

Of course, it is necessary that an individual eat in order to remain alive and to be alive in order to eat. Both are needed. At the margin, however, there is a trade-off. The pressure to "eat, drink, and be merry, for tomorrow you may die" reflects life's contingency—that is, there is an ever-present probability that a person may die. Whereas the emphasis on eating in order to *live* is the recognition that it is one's whole life that is of relevance, not simply the "range of the moment." The former underlies what is referred to as "time preference"—that is, individuals tend to prefer a given good now rather than later. The latter is related to the return (due to productivity) that can result from waiting.

This trade-off between consumption and "life" was discussed in an example presented in Touchstone (2018, 64–66). It assumed that there is a single castaway on a desert island, who has a stock of nourishment (hardtack) that could potentially provide him with sustenance for ten years. That is, *T*, the maximum life span, is the potential number of years remaining in the castaway's life once he arrives on the island, which is based on the consumption of provisions available. The rate of yearly intake could be based on, say, the caloric intake necessary to sustain the castaway, which in this example is 1,000 units a year over a 10-year period. Assuming a "no-fault" early probability of dying equal to 10%, the expected life span of the castaway would be 6.145 years. If it is assumed that the discount rate is equal to the mortality rate, then the initial "present value" of the stock of hardtack would be 6,144.45, where the "unit of account" is measured in units of hardtack (Touchstone 2006, 73).

If the emphasis is on consumption, hardtack would be consumed to the point of satiation—that is, as if it had an opportunity cost of zero. It is theorized that a consumer does not typically consume to that point (i.e., where the "marginal utility" equals zero), because there is a positive price to pay and/or there is an implicit cost to bear. In the castaway's case, there is no explicit price, but there is an implicit price (an opportunity cost) that he would incur if he consumed additional hardtack beyond that necessary to sustain his existence. For instance, for any particular year, if he doubled his hardtack intake to 2,000 units, this would reduce his potential life by one year. If he consumed 2,000 units per year for every year throughout his life on the island, his potential life, *T*, would be halved to five years. (In this example, *T* is a function of the stock of hardtack. Typically, *T* would be fixed, or more accurately, fixed for a given PV*t*.) With the increase in the rate of time preference, his expected life would also fall.

By ranking consumption first, his expected life is shortened, while the amount of hardtack consumed remains the same. By putting life first, the castaway can have a longer expected life span as well as consume the maximum amount of hardtack. (If he chose to consume an amount that was insufficient to sustain his life, he would face a shorter expected life, plus he would consume less during his life.) Thus, by focusing on "productivity" in terms of the number of years lived over the course of his remaining life, the person potentially ends up with the maximum longevity and the maximum consumption. Although the example is highly contrived, a generalization can be drawn that there is clearly an advantage to thinking within the context of a lifetime rather than from moment to moment.

Life as a Value and Life's Value

In making the argument that life is man's ultimate value, Rand's focus was on value; beginning with her observation that the concept "value" arises with life. In Touchstone (2018, 66–67), I addressed the same issue with the focus on action. The difference is not one of substance, but of emphasis. In brief, the argument is as follows. Action emerges with life. It is necessary to be alive in order to act. A living being must act in order to be (and remain) alive. For humans, action is self-generated. Ethics arises with human life. Ethics examines how a person should act, given that he is free to choose. Two categories of action are those that promote life and those that do not. Humans do not automatically know which actions promote life and which do not. They are capable (through reason) of learning which do and which do not promote life. They have the ability (volition) to choose the actions they take (and can act on their choices, given the freedom to do so) and can predict with a degree of accuracy what the consequences of their actions will be. Actions that are life enhancing are ethical (with the caveat that they are consistently followed), and those that are not are unethical.

Recall, that the Benevolent Universe Premise (BUP) states that if a person acts ethically, success is the to-be-expected. Failure can occur, but it is incidental. In my interpretation of the BUP, if a person opts to act ethically rather than unethically, the expected loss that corresponds with the probability of failure can be overlooked (Touchstone, 2006, 281–82, "Ethical Principles, Charity, and a Criterion for Giving," 2008, 46, "Economic Decision-Making and Ethical Choice," 2008, 179–80, 2016, 40, 2018, 67). When choosing between an ethical action and an unethical alternative, the probability of success would be greater for the former; however, the return may be larger for the unethical choice. The expected gain (probability of success times the return) may be greater as well for the unethical choice. This may be true even though the probability of success (survival) is lower for the unethical action.

This is why the unethical action may be seemingly appealing. As stated, the probability of failure (death) can be dismissed for the ethical action because it is "incidental." However, this is not the case for the unethical alternative. The probability of failure is larger and cannot be ignored because it is endemic to the action. The magnitude of the expected loss (probability of death multiplied by the loss) is compounded because the loss is not limited to the timeframe under consideration (which for many decisions is short term), but is the value associated with the loss of one's whole life.

An example given in Touchstone (2018, 67) was of a student who has two choices for summer employment—either delivering flowers for a florist or delivering stolen property for a fence. The gains for both are short term. The asymmetry arises in the losses for the two. For the flower delivery job, the loss can be dismissed. The loss for trafficking in stolen goods cannot. The probability of loss (dying) would not be insignificant in the trafficking case, and when multiplied by the value of the person's whole life would yield a sizeable loss. That is, the loss would not be confined to the pay for the summer "job." (When other losses are also considered, such as those related to reputation, legal fees, incarceration, potential future employment, and so on, the expected loss would be even greater.) It is here that a person's entire life (as his ultimate value) gains relevance. The immensity of its loss must be reckoned with. Also to be taken into account is what the loss would comprise. For the student in this example, the loss would be the discounted value of the expected future earnings—that is, his human capital. Although the value of one's human capital is an important aspect of a person's life, it is not all encompassing. It is limited to only one side of life's "ledger."

Purpose: Productive Work and Happiness

The decision discussed in the previous section was related to employment; that is, productivity. Thus, the value of human capital was an appropriate measure to reflect the loss. Measuring the loss in productive output would not be confined to work for pay. Included would be the imputed value of productive endeavors for which there is no explicit payment, such as parenting. The monetary value of human capital is not the *value* of a person's life in the sense of it being what his life is worth. Nor is it to be used as a basis of comparison with other people. Even so, the value of human capital forms the basis for personal decision-making as it relates to such things as investment in education and/or training and the purchase of life insurance.

Although the loss in human capital would be sizeable, it is still limited in scope. When a person suffers an early demise, what he loses comprises more than the value of what he would have produced during his lifetime. Also sacrificed would be the consumption that is forgone. By "consumption" in this context is meant not only consumer goods and services that are purchased explicitly, but also leisure time activities, including time spent with family and friends. For a full accounting of one's loss, a person should reflect upon both sides of the "ledger." Like nonmarket productivity, a monetary value may be imputed to "nonmarket" consumer goods and services. The monetary value, according to Rand, is the objective social valuation (Rand, "What is Capitalism," 1967, 24). However, consumption also has a psychological counterpart ("utility" or satisfaction) that is assigned by the individual (which is measured ordinally).

Although "utility" can be assigned to both productive work and consumption, in economic theory, it is primarily associated with consumption. Economists and utilitarians refer to "utility" as a subjective valuation. (The word satisfaction is often used instead of utility; partly because of the association of utility with cardinal measurement—which most economists now reject.) The sense in which the term "subjective" is used in this context (see, for instance, Hastings 2019) is not the same as Objectivist Leonard Peikoffs's use of the word "subjectivism" in Peikoff (1982, 62)—which metaphysically means that reality is a function of consciousness, and epistemologically means that truth is based in feelings. Although Rand eschewed the term "subjective," the use of the term here is similar to Rand's use of word "judgment" in "What is Capitalism" (1967, 24) as it relates to consumers buying products in a free market. Younkins ("Menger, Mises, Rand, and Beyond," 2005, 347, 350–51) noted that the Austrian economist Carl Menger used the word "subjective" to mean "personal," which bears a close resemblance to the way in which Rand referred to a person's valuation of a good. That is, the individual buyer is the judge of the value of a good in a free market economy, according to Rand ("What is Capitalism," 1967, 25).

Whether income or consumption is measured in monetary units (explicit and/or imputed) or is based on a person's "subjective" evaluation is of less relevance to the employment example in the previous section than whether the framework for decisions is primarily long term or short term. In OE, even decisions whose timeframes are short term (such as summer employment) can have long-term implications and should be made within the context of one's whole life. The focus of so-called "act utilitarians," in contrast, is short-term "utility" or happiness (Yeager 2001, 86, 104–5, 115, 143, 154; Hazlitt 1998, 60). The long range is the focus of "rule utilitarians" (Hazlitt 1998, 13, 21–26, 33–34; Yeager 2001, 62, 85; Touchstone 2015, 179). Like neo-Aristotelians, such as Norton (1976) and Den Uyl and Rasmussen ("Life, Teleology, and Eudaimonia," 1986, 75), rule utilitarians are said to view long-term happiness, or eudaemonia, as the ultimate end. As with Rand's conception of "life qua man," this end encompasses all facets of life—production as well as consumption (broadly defined).

As stated in the previous chapter, there is an economic chain that proceeds from production to income to consumption to satisfaction (utility). The point at which man's "purpose" is located along this spectrum represents a point of departure among philosophical schools of thought. For Objectivists and neo-Aristotelians such as Norton, a person's purpose is productive work. In OE, productivity is man's central purpose, and happiness is his moral purpose. According to Rand: "Existentially, the activity of pursuing rational goals is the activity of maintaining one's life; psychologically, its result, reward and concomitant is an emotional state of happiness" (Rand, "The Objectivist Ethics," 1964, 29; also see Kelley 2015, 72). A variant on the statement that both happiness and productivity are purposes within OE is that both consumption and production are values. However, only productive work is a virtue. A basic accounting identity is that income equals consumption plus saving. An assessment of one's life would consider both the value of his prospective productivity as well as consumption. However, from an accounting perspective, to add income and consumption is to count consumption twice. As an analogy, to regard both producing and consuming as virtues could also be viewed as double counting (Touchstone 2018, 69).

Productive work is the central virtue in OE. When a person meets with an early death, it is his destiny—his potential productive contribution—that is lost. What he would have consumed (his intake) is of value to him; however, what is subtracted from the world is his productive purpose. (OE is an individualist ethics, thus of primary interest to a person is the fulfillment of his destiny. What he contributes to the "world" may be of importance to him, but it is secondary.) Consumption is a value in OE, but consuming is not a virtue. Although egoistic, OE is not a hedonistic philosophy (Mack 1986, 136). Rand's distinction between productive work as man's ethical purpose and happiness as his reward serves to balance output and intake. This is implicit in what I call her "productivity principle," which is essentially the proposition that a person's consumption should not be greater than his income during his lifetime (Rand, "Atlas Shrugged," 1961, 89). Consumption (broadly conceived) is a value in OE; however, Rand recognized that the source of it is productivity. Rand's ethics uniquely ties man's destiny to productive work that in turn provides the wherewithal to sustain his life. Productivity must precede consumption. A person cannot consume something that has not yet been produced. Productivity (or productive activity, which in the broad sense includes "reproductivity") must precede the rewards in life.

Chapter 4

Virtues

INTRODUCTION

Friedrich Hayek and other evolutionary ethicists have suggested that in deriving ethics one should look to social norms because they have stood the test of time, so to speak (Touchstone 2015, 170; Hayek 1973, 43–48; Hazlitt 1998, 13, 72; Yeager 2001, 77). This approach may work in the sense that for a particular society identifying the actions that result in the greatest probability of success might be those that are worth emulating. However, this approach may not be consistent with ethics derived on the basis of that which is consistent with the survival of man qua man. The reason for this is that for man to think and act in ways that promote his survival by virtue of his nature, man needs to live in a society that permits actions and interactions that are consistent with his nature—that is, a society in which he is free to pursue those actions as long as he does not violate the freedom of others. Any particular society under examination may not conform to those requirements. Also, in order to discover the societal conditions necessary to promote the survival of man based on his nature, it is first necessary to identify the ethics on which the society is based. To escape this circular problem, one method is to employ the desert island device. I have argued that Rand used this approach in identifying her cardinal virtues (rationality, production, and pride) and cardinal values (reason, productive work, and self-esteem) (Touchstone 2006, 89; Rand, "The Objectivist Ethics," 1964, 25–26, 32, "The Nature of Government 1964," 107). That is, she examined man alone on an island as a device to determine the primary virtues that would be required to achieve the associated values that would promote man's survival qua man. The first section discusses relatively simple abstract models, which increase in complexity, to address voluntary exchange (the

Objectivist “trader principle”) in a state of nature. The conclusions drawn from these models have ethical implications because their outcomes can result in improvements in the lives of the parties involved in exchange. The section also addresses the evolutionary approach by briefly examining the development of language, and how the imposition of language by agencies onto individuals can have implications for rights and for ethical decision-making.

I have argued that the problem with the “man alone on a desert island” approach in discovering virtues is that it does not allow for reproductivity, which I regard as a primary virtue (2006, 35). That reproduction is a primary value follows from what I call Rand’s “productivity principle,” which essentially states that a person should not consume more than he produces over the course of his lifetime (Rand, “Atlas Shrugged,” 1961, 89). The primary source of a person’s consumption is from the income he earns through productivity. However, a person also may receive an inheritance. According to Objectivism, a person “earns” his inheritance by making it productive—that is, by earning enough to equal or more than equal its value (Branden 1963, 23). In the second section of this chapter, I present the argument that in addition to physical wealth, a person inherits (typically) an investment in his human capital (Touchstone, “Reproductivity, Capital Theory, and Objectivist Ethics,” 2010, 11–13). Consistency would require that a person not only maintain the value of his physical capital, but his human capital as well. The primary way in which a person replaces or maintains his human capital is by having a child and “investing” in that child’s human capital (which is broadly conceived to include the imparting of values and virtues).

DISCOVERING VIRTUES

This section examines two broad categories of discovering virtues. The first is the “empirical” approach, which examines society to find the behavior or behavioral patterns which result in success for most people. The second is the “abstract” approach, which uses models, such as the Crusoe method. The “empirical” method is associated with rule utilitarians, who recommend following traditional societal rules because they have evolved spontaneously and have stood the test of time. Although rule utilitarians advocate an evolutionary approach to rules, they also recommend that the rules that emerge should be validated based on the criterion of eudaemonia. A problem with this approach to the discovery of rules is that the society being examined should allow for rules to emerge based on the free interaction of individuals. However, there may not be a truly free society in existence to permit the observation and discovery of the rules. There is also the issue that it first must be established that a free society is needed as well as what a free society entails.

The Crusoe or desert island approach is an "abstract" method for discovering ethical principles which does not have the drawback associated with the "empirical" approach. This method assumes a state of nature in which a few variables are isolated in order to observe their interaction and to draw a conclusion or conclusions. The conclusions that result can be juxtaposed against reality. If the model fails to account for an essential variable or condition, the model can be modified. To the extent necessary, models that are too simplistic can increase in complexity. To illustrate how relatively simplistic models can increase in complexity, the Objectivist trader principle is discussed in the context of the comparative advantage (CA) model, the prisoner dilemma (PD) model, and the "Tit for Tat" strategy. The evolutionary approach is also discussed specifically within the context of the development of language. The extent to which language is "imposed" rather than permitted to evolve can have implications for rights infringement and for ethical decision-making.

Eudaemonia and Rule Utilitarians

Hazlitt (1998, 14), a rule utilitarian, regarded eudaemonia (happiness) as being the fundamental value on which an ethical system is based and the ultimate value toward which actions are aimed. Both he and Leland Yeager viewed social cooperation as the means for attaining the ultimate value (Hazlitt 1998, 36; Yeager 2001, 289). They both credited Austrian economists Ludwig von Mises and Friedrich Hayek with originating this position (Hazlitt 1998, xiv; Yeager 2001, 13; Mises [1949] 1996, 176). According to Hazlitt, social cooperation brings about the greatest satisfaction for the greatest number of people. An ideal ethical system is one whose rules promote social cooperation (Hazlitt 1998, 127).

Social cooperation means the benefits that emerge from the division of labor—not solely in the economic realm, but also in the social sphere of interaction (Hazlitt 1998, 37; Yeager 1998, xiv). In fact, Mises defined society as the "division of and combination of labor" (Mises [1949] 1996, 143; quoted in Herbener 2005, 163). Cooperation through the division of labor is the most effective method of improving mankind's condition, according to Mises. He related this directly to man's survival, stating that the division of labor is man's preeminent tool in his struggle to survive (Mises [1949] 1996, 176). Hazlitt saw "little harm in regarding [social cooperation] as an end-in-itself, and even in treating it as if it were *the* goal of ethics" (Hazlitt 1998, 36; italics in original). That is, according to Yeager, it is a surrogate for happiness (flourishing) (Yeager 1998, xiv; 2001, 289; Touchstone 2015, 180–81).

Similar to Hazlitt and Yeager, Rand viewed the trader principle as the primary social principle. It is defined as the exchange of value for value between independent equals. Similarly, she saw it as not being limited to economic trade, but extending to communication, friendship, and love. Like Mises, Rand recognized the gains from trade brought about by the division of labor, but her focus was primarily on the voluntary aspect of trade. She identified the trader principle with justice (Rand, "The Objectivist Ethics," 1964, 31–32). Although Hazlitt (1998, 44) regarded cooperation as largely voluntary, he viewed "justice" as adherence to rules of conduct that maintain and advance social cooperation (1998, 13).

Principles Yield Valued Outcomes

According to Hazlitt (1998, 127), ideal moral rules are those that promote social cooperation. How are those rules discovered? Both Hazlitt and Yeager espoused the empirical-evolutionist theory of ethical principles put forth by Hayek along with the utilitarian criterion of happiness (eudaemonia) via social cooperation to assess them (Yeager 2001, 77, 96–97; Hazlitt 1998, 6, 8–9, 72). That is, the principles evolve by an evolutionary process and are "discovered" by empirically observing societal rules and evaluating them by using eudaemonia as the standard. According to this approach, societal rules evolve spontaneously as individuals pursue their self-interests. The rules of conduct that emerge at times may be superior to those deliberately devised (Yeager 2001, 9, 72). The rules need not be limited to ethical standards, but may include cultural institutions, such as money and language (Horwitz 2005, 379, 381). In a broader context, spontaneous order may develop based on rules that spontaneously arise or on rules that are deliberately conceived. Legal rules may be the result of deliberation; whereas ethical rules and customs arise spontaneously (Hayek 1973, 45–46).

Mises also regarded social norms as being the product of an evolutionary process; however, rather than spontaneous, he thought cultural norms as well as ethics, laws, and institutions were all the result of individuals striving to purposively and rationally adapt their actions to achieve social cooperation under the division of labor (Salerno 1990, 26–27). Although Mises ([1949] 1966, 883) may have differed with Hayek, Hazlitt, and Yeager on the issue of spontaneity, they were united in their belief that the social rules that evolved should be strictly observed (Salerno 1990, 31). Although the rules should be subjected to rigorous assessment, once accepted they are worth adherence because they have stood the test of time (Hazlitt 1998, 184–85; Yeager 2001, 153–55).

Hazlitt (1998, 139) cautioned against a robotic acceptance of traditional rules. Although Objectivists use the word "principle" rather than rule (Kelley

1997), they also oppose adherence to tradition "*merely* because it is a 'tradition'" (Rand, "Conservatism: An Obituary," 1967, 198; italics in original). Rand stated: "In a rational ethics, it is causality—not 'duty'—that serves as the guiding principle in considering, evaluating, and choosing one's actions, particularly those necessary to achieve a long-range goal" (Rand, "Causality versus Duty," 1982, 98). Similarly, according to Hazlitt and Yeager, society's rules should be assessed based on the criterion of eudaemonia (Yeager 2001, 77, 96–97; Hazlitt 1998, 6, 8–9, 72). That is, Rand, Hazlitt, Yeager, and Mises advocated the observance of principles because they typically yield valued returns or outcomes (Mises [1949] 1966, 883; Salerno 1990, 31; Yeager 2001, 4, 16, 87, 153, 294; Hazlitt 1998, 57, 73). Objectivists advocate consistent application of principles, as do rule utilitarians, although Rand as well as Hazlitt and Yeager recognized that exceptions may be necessary (Hazlitt 1998, 72, 183–85; Yeager 2001, 87, 92, 94, 151, 155). Both Rand and Hazlitt acknowledged that context is relevant in the application of a principle or rule (Rand, "Causality versus Duty," 1982, 98; Hazlitt 1998, 187; Touchstone 2016, 34–35).

Rule Utilitarians and the Benevolent Universe Premise (BUP)

According to OE, virtues are actions that individuals undertake in order to attain or maintain values or ends (Rand, "The Objectivist Ethics," 1964, 15). However, these are not actions undertaken in isolation. Principles are abstractions. They require consistent adherence. Why should a person consistently follow an ethical principle; or more to the point, why are principles necessary? Wouldn't it be more advisable for a person to act on the basis of the merits of each decision—that is, weighing the benefits and the costs on a case-by-case basis? This is the procedure recommended by "act utilitarians" (Hazlitt 1998, 60; Yeager 2001, 154–55).

There are several advantages to adhering to an established moral code. One is the savings in time and other costs associated with the calculation of the benefits and the costs for each decision a person makes (Hazlitt 1998, 72, 155). By following a rule or principle, there may also be a lower risk of making errors when there is inadequate information. In addition, the general observance of rules allows for a more accurate prediction of the behavior of others. This can reduce transaction costs and uncertainties associated with the coordination and planning of activities. On the flip side, when principles are not consistently observed, the behavior of others is less easily predicted. This may result in less trust in a person's or a business's obligations to follow through on certain promises or contractual arrangements. This can impair the quality of life of individuals as well as erode the social fabric. As Hazlitt (1998, 73) noted, principles "lose their utility" when they are not followed or are only followed sporadically.

Consistency in behavior that is guided by following rules is also related to human nature. Consistent adherence to principles can result in the development of traits or habits whereby virtues become more automatic. Persistently behaving virtuously tends to reinforce emotions that sustain that behavior. Those emotions can fortify ethical behavior when impulses run counter to long-run interests (Hazlitt 1998, 48, 52, 59–60, 72–73, 182; Yeager 2001, 88–89, 175). Conversely, occasional or even one-time instances of acting against principles or a principle can weaken emotions that support virtuous behavior (Frank 1988, 161–62). Making decisions based on principles rather than on a case-by-case basis is also consistent with human nature in that humans tend to think abstractly. Rand stated, "You have no choice about the necessity to integrate your observations, your experiences, your knowledge into abstract ideas, i.e., principles. Your only choice is whether these principles are true or false" (Rand, "Philosophy: Who Needs It," 1982, 5).

If the following of principles leads to success in achieving one's values, then why would anyone ever be tempted to do otherwise? There is a causal relationship between following ethical principles and achieving values; however, it is not what is referred to as a "strict causal change" between action and outcome. An outcome may be *probable*, but it is not certain. Of course, probabilities are not only relevant to decisions involving a particular ethical principle, but also to decisions made on a case-by-case basis. As mentioned, consistent application of principles is advocated by rule utilitarians, whereas a case-by-case approach is recommended by act utilitarians. Hazlitt made the following distinction between the two approaches insofar as probabilities are concerned:

> In *both* cases it is the probable consequences of an *act* that are being judged, but in the first it is the probable consequences of the act *as an instance of following a rule*, and in the second it is the probable consequences of an act *considered in isolation* and apart from any general rule. (Hazlitt 1998, 60; italics in original)

Decisions on a case-by-case basis may favor short-term gains at the expense of long-term interests. Ethical actions have a greater probability in leading to success long range; however, as noted by David Hume and Hayek, success is not guaranteed in the short term. Conversely, it is also possible to act unethically and still succeed. Even so, probabilities favor ethical behavior (Hazlitt 1998, 52, 59; Yeager 2001, 181). Writing on OE, Ronald Merrill essentially summed this up as virtue is the best "way to bet" (1991, 114–15). As observed by Herbert Simon, in a betting situation involving random binary choice, if an event is successful the majority of the time (i.e., the long run), it should be chosen all of the time in order to achieve the maximum outcome on repeated trials (Simon 1959, 260; Touchstone, "Ethical Principles, Charity, and a Criterion for Giving," 2008, 38).

Mises, Hazlitt, and Yeager agree that "probabilistically virtue pays," with the proviso that rules should be consistently followed (allowing for exceptions in some cases) (Yeager 2001, 87, 94, 155, 276, 294; Hazlitt 1998, 72, 79). In essence, the position held by the rule utilitarians discussed above, is implicitly the same as the BUP of Objectivism, which states that if an individual consistently acts according to ethical principles, achievement of long-range success is to be expected. Failure can occur, but it is not to be expected (Peikoff 1976, 51; Touchstone 2016, 35–38).

The Evolutionary Approach to Rules

The evolutionary theory advocated by Hayek, Hazlitt, and Yeager is an "empirical" approach to the discovery of rules and/or principles. (By "empirical" in this context, I mean a procedure in which a society as a whole is examined to discover the ideas or strategies with which most people agree or follow. The rules that most people follow evolve through the voluntary interaction of individuals rather than being imposed.) Essentially it recommends identifying behavioral norms or strategies that result in success for most people. These behavioral norms or patterns are then scrutinized based on the utilitarian criterion of eudaemonia, or social cooperation as its proxy. With this approach to rules, the BUP becomes almost tautological. That is, discover rules that result in success the majority of the time (or for most people); if those rules are followed all of the time, success will be the most probable outcome in the long term. There are a number of assumptions underlying this approach. One is that the person has the freedom to act on his decisions. Even more to the point, an alternative or alternatives may fail to be included in his decision set if certain freedoms of action are lacking in the society. For instance, historically speaking, in a static social system such as feudalism, a person's status and occupation were pre-established at birth, and marriages were pre-arranged. Individual decision-making was thus severely constricted (Touchstone 2015, 194).

An empirical approach to discovering rules can be dependent upon the current social system. The rules that evolve can vary from one culture to another. That is, rules could be relative to a specific culture. To simply observe any existing society might result in the discovery of rules that "work" within that specific culture and legal system, but those norms may not be consistent with those required for man's survival qua man. That is, they may not be in accordance with his nature. According to OE, principles that follow from man's nature and promote his survival are not "relative," but absolute (although they are contextual). To Rand, by nature man is dependent upon reason for his survival. It is not automatic and it is undertaken by choice—a choice that is possible for humans because they by nature have volition. However, they must be free to choose. Man's rational faculty and his knowledge are not infallible (Rand, "What is Capitalism?" 1967, 17). Humans must be free to make errors in order to learn—with the proviso that they do not interfere with the freedom of others (Rand, "Man's Rights," 1964, 93–94, "The Nature of Government," 1964, 108; Rasmussen and Den Uyl 1991, 115). That is, employing an empirical approach to discovering ethical principles that are consistent with man's nature would first require a free society.

However, this raises a couple of issues. One is there may not be a free society in existence to observe so as to discover the rules and/or principles that are necessary in order for man to succeed. Second, how is it known that freedom must be in place (and what freedom entails) in order to discover those principles? Epistemologically, it is necessary to discover the ethical principles that are necessary for humans to succeed before there is a discussion of rights or freedom. This circularity—that existentially individual rights need to be in place before ethical principles can be discovered, and epistemologically ethical principles need to be discovered before there can be a discussion of rights—is problematic, not only for the evolutionary approach to the discovery of ethical principles, but also for other methods as well. One method that could potentially circumvent this problem of circularity has been addressed in the discussion of the cardinal virtues as derived by Rand and of individual rights as illustrated by Rothbard, and that is the desert island device (Touchstone 2015, 193–94).

The Crusoe Model

Hazlitt has advocated for a more widespread utilization of the Crusoe approach in ethics:

> Ethics would be in a more advanced stage than it is if moral philosophers had begun more often with the postulate of the isolated individual and then moved, for many problems, to the postulate of a society of two, three, etc. before jumping immediately to The Great Society. (1998, 380n13)

In chapter 1, I used this device to illustrate an example that supported the non-interference principle and negative rights. That example assumed a two-man society. The desert island device assumes a state of nature which typically describes a highly simplistic setting that abstracts from all but a few variables (e.g., a castaway or castaways on an island) in order to "observe" their interaction, and to draw a conclusion or conclusions. The conclusion drawn may be a generalization that could be applicable to a more realistic setting (such as a larger number of people in a less simplistic environment). In chapter 1, I also used the device to discuss the Primary Social Unit (PSU) and positive rights. The PSU consists of two individuals, neither of whom are men—specifically, mother and child. The Crusoe device is often used to observe (and to draw conclusions based on) the interaction of adult males. The PSU brings attention to one of the limitations of the Crusoe approach, and that is it takes into account only those aspects of human behavior that are isolated for the particular example under investigation.

Of course, this kind of limitation is true for all models. Models are necessarily simplistic in that they isolate those variables that are deemed important for the issue at hand. Models abstract from variables that could affect the outcome of the interaction under consideration; that is, the other variables are assumed "constant." General conclusions may be derived from the model, but they only apply to a more realistic setting if it is assumed that the other variables remain unchanged or their change is so rare or so unimportant as to have no effect. This assumption may be unrealistic if the variables that are assumed constant cannot remain unchanged because they are related or correlated with the variable(s) under consideration, or the assumption may be realistic only for a limited period of time. Some models are static and/or short term in nature. More sophisticated models may introduce more variables, may be long term in nature, and/or may be dynamic. Once a simplistic model is developed, the model may be compared to reality in order to assess whether there are other variables that could have an impact on the variables under investigation, and to question how the variable or variables may affect the conclusions.

Rand ("The Objectivist Ethics," 1964, 25–26, 32) derived cardinal values for OE (reason, productivity, and self-esteem) by using the Crusoe assumption of a single person on a desert island, and, as Rand rightly noted, a person would have to be productive to survive. It is clearly to a person's advantage to produce in accordance with his ability—to engage in such activities as hunting, gathering, fishing, finding, or fashioning some sort of shelter, etc. Rand generalized this principle to a more realistic setting in which man lives in a society. When living among others, a person should produce; however, he is no longer required to be self-sufficient. It pays for him to produce according to his talents (and resources, opportunities, etc.) and to trade with others (who produce according to their talents, etc.) for those things he desires but does not produce. This broader principle is reflected in the OE trader principle.

Modeling the Trader Principle

The trader principle (voluntary exchange) can be illustrated by drawing from the principle of (comparative advantage) CA, as did Rothbard (1998, 35–36).

CA models can be found in most principles of economic textbooks (Gwartney et al. 2006, 371–75). The CA model isolates two parties (which may be two people or two countries) who engage in exchange. The CA principle (attributed to David Ricardo) demonstrates that mutual gains to trade are possible when two parties voluntarily engage in exchange by showing that the payoffs (which are given in units of goods produced by each party) are greater after trade than the payoffs for the original position in which there is no exchange. Although the payoffs are given in units of goods produced and exchanged, there can be mutual gains (in terms of satisfaction or utility) from trade even if "more" units of goods or services are not produced as a result of trade. (Measurement in terms of utility or satisfaction is seen less often in models. One reason for this is that, unlike units of goods, units of utility are not observable. Another is that utility cannot be added across individuals. It is assumed that if a person voluntarily engages in trade, he ends up—or he anticipates that he will end up—in a better position after the exchange than prior to it; that is, he achieves a greater level of satisfaction by undertaking the exchange.)

CA models show how mutual gains *can* result when parties engage in voluntary trade. The OE trader principle describes how two individuals *should* interact; that is, interaction should be voluntary. The leap from *can* to *should* is not a big one because there is "no down side," so to speak. The CA illustration shows a win-win situation for both parties. It is a more realistic model than the single-man desert island approach in that it shows how voluntary interaction can benefit both parties when a person lives among others.

The prisoner's dilemma (PD) is a game theory model that shares the "mutual gains from exchange" feature of a CA illustration, but introduces an incentive for each party in the exchange to "cheat." In the CA model, each player faces greater gains after trade than before with no other considerations. However, in exchange there are typically incentives to cheat. The PD model assumes a state of nature in which there is no government and no governmental means of enforcement. It also presents a payoff structure for exchange which includes not only payoffs before and after exchange but also payoffs for cheating. If a player decides to engage another player in trade, each player faces either two courses of action—to follow through on his end of the bargain or to cheat. Each person's respective payoff for cheating exceeds the payoff each would receive if both parties followed through on trade. That is, for each player the dominant strategy is to cheat (Frank 1988, 31). However, if both parties cheat, both end up in the original position in which they are worse off than if they had followed through on trade. This is the dilemma. Both would be better off if both followed through on trade than if both cheated, but it is not clear which of the possible four outcomes will prevail—that is, whether neither will engage in trade, both will follow through on trade, or one player will cheat on the other.

Two methods of cheating are to default and to steal. In a default, both parties agree to an exchange and then one party reneges. Either the customer reneges on paying once he has received the product (good or service) from the seller, or the seller reneges on supplying the product once he has received payment from the customer. A default is possible when there is either a delay in payment for a product or a delay in delivery of a product. In a broader sense, cheating can take other forms of theft in which an overt or implied threat of force is a factor. This can occur when two parties agree to a simultaneous exchange of a product for money and then one of the parties robs the other. There can also be theft through stealth—the thief steals the product of another without the victim's immediate knowledge.

One "solution" to the dilemma is for a player only to entertain trading with a potential trading partner (whether a person or a company) who has a reputation for honesty. If a potential trading partner has a reputation for honesty, then that knowledge can reduce uncertainty, and therefore can increase the likelihood of trade. However, a reputation is based on what is known about a person by observing (or having information about) his behavior. There may be "golden opportunities" to cheat (i.e., when a person has almost no chance of getting caught). For instance, a person could be tempted to cheat on a one-time exchange in which there is no possibility of encountering the other party again. A reason not to cheat even when there is a golden opportunity is based on findings concerning human nature. It "pays" for a person who desires a reputation for honesty to be honest even when there is no opportunity for him to be caught if he cheats. It has been found that when a person caves into short-term impulses to cheat this tends to erode the emotions necessary to sustain him in the future in instances in which submitting to those impulses would not be to his advantage (i.e., there is a likelihood of getting caught). In order to sustain those emotions, a person needs to be honest even when there is a golden opportunity to do otherwise (Frank 1988, 91). (Many people who are in prison have impulse-control problems [1988, 161].) It follows that if a person has a reputation for honesty, he is very likely honest. Of course, in a relatively large economy, there is an increased likelihood of anonymous trade—that is, trading with partners for whom reputations are unknown. This increases the likelihood of default.

"Tit for Tat" and the Principle of Reciprocity

On the assumptions that trade is anonymous and repetitive, it has been found that a PD model using a retaliatory strategy called "Tit for Tat" results in the greatest success (overall score) when compared with a number of other exchange strategies (Axelrod 1984, 31). "Tit for Tat" is regarded as a strategy involving proportional retaliation because a player cooperates with a partner who has been cooperative on the previous trade and retaliates against a party who has defaulted on the previous trade (1984, 118). The conclusion that proportional retaliation is a winning strategy is based on a model with simplistic assumptions; yet it is consistent with Rothbard's principle of proportional justice (Rothbard 1998, 86). One of "Tit for Tat's" simplistic assumptions is that the game is played for small stakes. Thus, retaliation only involves a player refusing to engage in future trades with a party who has defaulted on a previous exchange. This kind of "proportional" retaliation would be inadequate for exchanges of significant value. (Rothbard's principle of proportional justice, which could be called "two eyes for an eye," takes into account the value of that which has been sacrificed by the victim as well as damages [1998, 88].)

The PD is more realistic than a CA model because it accounts for incentives to cheat. However, the PD is limited because it does not take into account the "cost" of cheating. "Tit for Tat" does allow for a cost—in the form of retaliation. Thus, even with incentives to cheat, "Tit for Tat" has been shown to be a winning long-run strategy. That is, default does not pay *if* victims of default respond by retaliating. The principle that trade *should* be voluntary is strengthened because not only is it consistent with the virtue of productivity found in the one-man Crusoe model, but also it "pays" in the long run when living in a society. However, one of the reasons it results in success is because retaliation *should* be undertaken in the case of cheating. (Furthermore, retaliation *should* be proportional.) That is, a rule of always engaging voluntarily in exchanges with others results in success if others also follow this rule. Adherence to the rule reduces uncertainty—which has the advantage of reducing other costs and further increasing exchange possibilities, which in turn can result in even more success (in terms of greater satisfaction and/or a greater number of units of goods or services). Of course, there may be those who do not follow the rule. In addition to the principle of voluntary interaction (i.e., the trader principle), the principle of retaliation is also necessary in order to achieve long-term success. The two combined principles—that is, of voluntary interaction and of retaliation, form the principle of reciprocity. (Although reciprocity usually is defined as the interchange of mutual benefits, Axelrod [1984, 119] described it as responding in kind to the action taken by one's opponent on the previous play; i.e., cooperating with cooperators and retaliating against defectors.) The principle of reciprocity is a broader principle than the trader principle because it includes a response to coercive interaction.

"Tit for Tat" can be seen as an ethical principle for exchange. The reasons given above for not cheating (which are not comprehensive) involve an understanding of the trader principle through abstraction (employing models), empirical observation, and knowledge of human nature (specifically, impulsive behavior) based on scientific findings. However, any one or all of these require the willingness and the ability to reason and to acquire knowledge. Reason takes effort and it is not infallible. Knowledge can be imperfect. There are those who refuse to put forth the effort that reason requires. According to OE, this is unethical (Rand, "Atlas Shrugged," 1961, 127, 78–79). Of course, a person who refuses to think may nevertheless act in an ethical manner—perhaps by accident. It is also possible for a person to make an error in reasoning even when he puts forth the effort. This, according to OE, is not, or is not necessarily, a lapse in morality from the person's perspective (Touchstone 2018, 76n3). For those people who are unethical and cheat on an exchange, retaliation is necessary in order to have long-run success, as "Tit for Tat" demonstrates. In addition, retaliation is required in order for a person (who cheats because of faulty reasoning) to learn. This discussion has focused primarily on abstract reasoning. However, another method of learning is trial and error. In the case of an error, there needs to be a corresponding consequence, otherwise the wrong lesson will be learned. A person who cheats needs to experience retaliation directly. A potential cheater needs to observe that retaliation is a consequence that cheaters have experienced. This informs his decision of whether or not to cheat. The threat of retaliation should not be the primary reason that a person does not cheat on an exchange, but it serves as a reason. (It may provide a potential cheater with a reason not to cheat on an exchange and, because reason is not automatic and takes effort, it may afford him further time to discover other and better reasons not to cheat.)

Other reasons for not cheating on trade that were not considered in the discussion above involve rights. In the CA and PD models, ownership rights are assumed implicitly; that is, each party to an exchange owns that which is traded. At best, these models lend support to the rights to property in a state of nature, but they do not establish rights per se. Cheating on trade violates the noninterference principle, a principle which subsumes the rights to life and to property as well as the right to retaliation. In repeated plays of a PD, it was found that retaliation is necessary so that exchange results in long-term success. Retaliation also has a deterrent effect in that it informs potential cheaters about the consequence of their actions as well as provides a disincentive to cheat. In addition (and more importantly), retaliation provides justice for victims of cheating by compensating them for rights violations. Enforcement of rights violations is not an issue in "Tit for Tat" because retaliation is merely a refusal to trade in the future with a defaulter. (That is, there are other aspects of the trader principle that are not addressed in this discussion.)

Models and Their Limitations

The Crusoe device can be used to address rights, including property rights, as did Rothbard (1998, 29–50). In addition to the Crusoe method, game theory has been used to deal with the establishment of ethical principles in a state of nature. Game theory models also have been used to describe the spontaneous establishment of conventions in a state of nature. The convention that is established is regarded as "arbitrary" in the sense that more than one solution is possible (Sugden 1986, 33; Touchstone 2018, 80n16). For instance, the convention "drive on the right-side of the road" has been established in the United States. However, the alternative convention, "drive on the left-side of the road," could have been established instead. In some cases, once a convention is accepted, as in this case, it has the force of law or is enacted into law because failure to follow the convention could threaten the rights (life or property) of other drivers. One feature of conventions is that even if they are not enacted into law, once established, they may be difficult and/or costly to change. This is true even if a convention is suboptimal.

In some cases, game theory "convention" models have been used to establish "property rights" in a state of nature. Rights are not conventions. There is no alternative to the establishment of ownership as a "right" (Sugden 1986, 70–78, 93–103; Touchstone 1995, 68, 2006, 82, 2018, 80n17). "Convention models" are inappropriate for establishing rights; however, they can be vehicles for demonstrating ways in which property may be assigned in a state of nature. An example of this is the "equality game." The "equality game" may describe how property is divided, but it is not prescriptive (Sugden 1986, 102–103). One flaw in its use as a prescriptive tool is that the outcome of the game (equal division of property) is predicated on the premise on which the game is based (see Hayek 1973, 80).

Models can be "normative" in the sense that the outcome can result in principles or strategies of behavior that have ethical import when the objective or standard of evaluation is one that is consistent with life qua man. In the models discussed above, CA, PD, and "Tit for Tat," the objective of the "player" is to improve his life long term by acquiring more goods—which is consistent with eudaemonia. Not all models have as their objective (or as the criterion on which they are based) the long-range preservation or improvement of a person's life. Thus, the rules or strategies that emanate from them would not be ethical principles. Some models are ostensibly descriptive and/or predictive but may have normative implications.

In some quarters, modeling has garnered a bad reputation, and at times deservedly so. Criticism is warranted when models result in sweeping generalizations and/or are used to justify intrusive actions of government that infringe on rights. This has been the case for models that are variations on Malthus's population model. Malthus's insight was brilliant in its way. Combining the conditions that land is fixed in supply, a food supply grows arithmetically, and a population increases exponentially can result (other things equal) in population eventually outstripping its ability to sustain itself leading to its collapse with eventual repetitions of the pattern (Malthus [1803] 1963; cf. Barnett and Morse 1963, 51–58). The model is predictive, but in a normative sense, the prediction is one that would be preferable to avoid. Although the Malthusian prognosis did materialize in some countries to some extent, it was and is not inevitable (Barnett and Morse 1963, 199; Johnson and Bennett 1980, 48). In fact, quite the opposite occurred in the west for countries that were relatively free. The population is at less than replacement in most western countries. There are a number of reasons for this. One is an increased standard of living has been accompanied by an increase in the cost of rearing children. Additionally, there has been an increase in opportunities for paid employment for women coupled with scientific advances in birth control.

With the advent of the computer, more complex variations on the Malthusian model have predicted similar dire consequences due to population growth, but also due to pollution, limited resources, and, more recently, climate change (Murphy 2019). The dismal predictions associated with the first and second Club of Rome reports (Meadows et al. 1975; Mesarovic and Pestel 1976) have not come to pass—particularly in western countries. This is primarily because of technological advances (which are not subject to prediction, and thus limit any predictive model that is potentially affected by changes in technology). In free markets, as a resource becomes scarcer, its price rises, which automatically encourages conservation as well as the substitution of less expensive alternative resources, and also provides an incentive to innovate and to make discoveries. When models' predictions are at serious odds with reality, it is not reality that is brought into question, but the models.

The false predictions of the Club of Rome reports led economists to re-examine their models in light of what had actually transpired. Among ideas that were challenged was the notion of "limited resources." "Limited resources" is a bit of a misnomer in the sense that what is considered a resource is also a function of technology. For example, oil was not considered a resource but a nuisance before the advent of the internal combustion engine. It was acknowledged that the total elimination of all pollutants is unnecessary since relative low levels can be absorbed or otherwise handled by the environment. However, it was also recognized that a lack of ownership in air, water, and animals (particularly migratory) can lead to overuse or over-harvesting. These problems can be dealt with by prudent laws and/or regulations.

These models have been used (whether purposely or not) to provide governments with the rationale to use legislation and regulation to incentivize and/or dis-incentivize behavior. This has led in some cases to bloated bureaucracies which ostensibly have devised rules and regulations to manage behavior in order to avoid a catastrophe, but in effect has resulted in a greater amassment of power by the state and less freedom for individuals. Natural rights are few. Positive laws should be designed to protect rights, not infringe upon them. Ironically, prescriptively, it was found that more freedom (not less) and better definitions of property rights (not more infringement of rights) lead to a slower growth in population (or, even to negative growth), more conservation of resources, more innovation, a higher standard of living, and (with prudent legislation) less pollution. Models and all abstractions need to be derived based on reality, and whenever it is evident that they are in some sense at odds with reality, they need to be re-evaluated based on real-world findings.

Language and the Evolutionary Theory

Like natural rights, virtues are also limited in number. In her list of all of man's virtues, Rand included seven ("Atlas Shrugged," 1961, 128; cf. Aristotle 1976, 127–42, 149, 163, 171, 203). Social rules, on the other hand, tend to be numerous by comparison. According to rule utilitarians, people should not only follow ethical rules (because they have survived an evolutionary process), they should adhere to social rules as well, such as rules of etiquette (Hazlitt 1998, 9, 75–80). In addition to etiquette, social norms include conventions and customs. These are behavioral rules to which "most people" adhere. "Most people" need not be the majority within a country, but could be the majority within a (smaller) geographic location (see Hayek 1973, 47). The "majority" needn't be geographically based, but may apply to a community of people that is united by their philosophy, religious affiliation, profession, or social status, for instance.

Following social norms is not (necessarily) what people should do, but it is what they tend to do—otherwise they would not be norms (in the descriptive sense). It is because people tend to follow social rules, that behavior is predictable to some extent. Following social rules does not guarantee success, survival, or acceptance by others, but it may. Following norms also avoids the repercussions of not following them. That is, cultures have methods of "enforcing" social norms. Depending upon the rule and upon the culture, the consequences of not following a social norm may be virtually nonexistent or could be quite costly. Some of the most challenging ethical questions from the individual's perspective are those decisions that involve what action to take when a societal norm is at odds with an ethical principle, particularly when not following the social norm could be costly.

The evolutionary theory encompasses not only ethics, but other social institutions. For instance the theory also extends to language. According to Hayek (1973, 10, 74), Hazlitt (1998, 9, 355), and Yeager (2001, 8–9, 259), language is an institution that tends to evolve gradually over time.

Language, like customs and other social norms, is relatively more spontaneous in its development than it is deliberately devised. Laws, in contrast, tend to be deliberately constructed, according to Hayek (1973, 46). Language is epistemological in nature, not ethical—although it has normative implications. In an elemental sense, language is the usage of words. According to Rand, "Man retains his concepts by means of language" ("The Psycho-Epistemology of Art," 1975, 17). Words are perceptual symbols that designate concepts (Peikoff 1991, 98). To Rand, reason is concept formation (Rand, "Faith and Force," 1982, 62). Concepts are abstractions; however, they are rooted in reality. Objectivist epistemology distinguishes between valid and invalid concepts on the basis of whether or not they are reality based. Invalid concepts are words that have vague, contradictory, and/or erroneous definitions (Rand 1990, 49). Thus, the criteria on which concepts are evaluated are somewhat different than for ethical principles. However, language and its development can have serious implications for rights and for ethical decision-making.

The evolutionary theory describes how language has developed, and also could be viewed as advocating that an evolutionary process is how language *should* develop. That is, for the most part, language should develop by the voluntary interaction among people; a non-coerced "bottom-up" process, rather than one that is top-down and authoritarian. (By "top-down" in this context, I mean language imposed by agencies onto individuals.) This is not to say that deliberation (i.e., giving careful consideration, being unhurried and, being aware of consequences) is not involved or should not be involved in the development of language. The key point is that its development should be the result of *voluntary* interaction. (In Objectivist terminology, it should develop in accordance with the trader principle). The reason it should be voluntary is that concept formation is an important aspect of reason, and humans must be free to reason because it is their tool of survival (Rand, "The Comprachicos," 1975, 227). This does not mean that the voluntary development of language will not yield errors. Reason is not infallible and humans may make mistakes. In fact, they must make mistakes in order to learn. Mistakes are not eliminated by a top-down authoritarian approach in any event, since it is still humans who devise and impose the language—only fewer of them. Experts in given fields provide significant input into language formation (for instance, in the medical definition of death as established by the American Academy of Neurology [Russell et al. 2019]). However, if language were exclusively a top-down process, it would impede man's ability to think, to learn, and to survive.

Of course, laws are encoded in language and some definitions are enacted into the law. According to Hayek, it is likely that early uses of language were to communicate established codes of conduct:

> [M]an became man and developed reason and language while living for something like a million years in groups held together by common rules of conduct, and … one of the first uses of reason and language must have been to teach and enforce these established rules. (Hayek 1973, 74)

According to Yeager, ancient laws "recorded" law rather than being established by legislation:

> Ancient Romans and the English shared the concept of law as something to be discovered more than enacted (Leoni 1961, cf. Rothbard's 1972 review) … . In discovering and announcing the law, judges were more like spectators than actors; they resembled grammarians *recording* language or statisticians *recording* economic activity. (Yeager 2001, 259; italics in original)

Hayek (1973, 82–83) made a similar observation. The U.S. Constitution's First Amendment enacted the right to freedom of expression. The amendment protected the voluntary interaction that (if observed) would allow language to evolve in accordance with the evolutionary theory advocated by rule utilitarians. (It also provided for the freedom to use one's rational faculty—which is necessary for man's survival qua man, according to Objectivism.)

Whether implicit or explicit, laws use definitions. These definitions may be those that are commonly used (i.e., lawmakers simply record definitions that are traditionally accepted), or they may be imposed (a top-down approach). For example, in some cases, laws that apply to females differ from those for males (for instance, laws related to abortion apply to women). Laws in the United States have implicitly assumed definitions of "male" and "female" based on traditional usage. More recently this has changed in the United States as well as in some other western countries. In forty-eight states in the United States, a person can change the sex shown on his birth certificate (based on the genetic definition) to a different one (based on other criteria) (Lefler and Shorman 2019). California has passed legislation that penalizes (with up to one year in prison) workers at long-term health care facilities who fail to use correct gender pronouns (Boorman 2017). In New York City, a fine of as much as $250,000 can be imposed on an individual who uses the wrong gender pronoun. The New York City Commission on Human Rights (NYCCHR) has established thirty-one genders (Touchstone 2017, 242; Beamon 2016; NYCCHR 2016). In Canada, a father was gagged and convicted of family violence for referring to his daughter (who was undergoing hormone treatment) as a girl (Keenan 2019). In the United Kingdom, a female Catholic journalist is potentially facing two years in prison for using the wrong gender pronoun (Evans 2019). Have laws simply encoded new concepts of sex or "gender" that have emerged or evolved through voluntary interaction, or are the laws imposing "top-down" definitions?

As Hayek pointed out:

> The spontaneous order arises from each element balancing all the various factors operating on it and by adjusting all its various actions to each other, a balance which will be destroyed if some of the actions are determined by another agency on the basis of different knowledge in the service of different ends. (1973, 51)

A case could be made that new definitions of sex and gender have not "bubbled up" based on *balanced* forces in society, but have been assigned by institutions that serve ideological ends not necessarily understood or shared by those on whom they have been imposed. For instance, new definitions of sex and gender have been recommended via organizational codes of conduct by agencies such as the American Psychological Association (APA) (2012, 11; Touchstone 2017, 247–48). Universities, libraries, and other institutions of learning have adopted new definitions as well (e.g., see Volokh [2016]; Gockowski [2016]; Goldfarb [2019]). Some professors in the United States have been forced out of academia for failing to use the new terminology and/or definitions or for issues related to the definitions ("Univ. of Louisville to Faculty: Express Your Views at Your Own Risk," 2019). A British doctor lost his position when, in response to a hypothetical question posed by his supervisor, he replied that he would not call "any six-foot tall, bearded man 'madam,'" if the (fictitious) man requested it ("British Medical Doctor Fired Because He Believes Gender is Fixed at Birth," 2019). In Scotland, a 17-year-old student has been expelled from school and not permitted to complete his education because he claimed that there were only two sexes (Christian 2019). (A GoFundMe account was set up on the Internet to raise money—which it did, approximately $2,000—so that the student could continue his education at another school; however, reportedly, the fund was shut down and the money returned to donors because the account violated some unspecified terms [Friedman, "Teen Who Said There Are Only Two Genders Expelled from School," 2019].)

Free speech is necessary for the development of language. However, some of the institutions that have adopted these codes are private or quasi-private. There is a question of the extent to which an institution has a right to impose language it deems "polite," and at what point the imposition of such codes violates the right to free speech. There is the argument that a private agency has the right to impose any speech code it chooses since the employee and/or customer is free to work and/or shop elsewhere. (However, in some instances, an agency may be in violation of honoring an agreement with its employees and/or customers, if it fails to live up to the terms.)

The newer definitions have not only affected speech but also action. A case in point is the effect it has had on girl's and women's sports. Increasingly, so-called "biological" girls now compete in sports with those who are not. Because males in general tend to have some *unalterable* physical characteristics that give them an advantage, female athletes have been losing competitive titles (Knox et al. 2019; Morton 2019; Miller 2017). In addition, in contact sports, there is also greater physical danger for females who compete against biological males than against biological females (Desanctis 2019; Helen 2019). It could be said that adult females are not "forced" to compete. Entering competitions is voluntary. At this point, if biological females banded together, they could create alternative venues (outside of academics) for competing among themselves if they did not want to risk losing titles and/or sustaining injuries by entering the established competitions. However, the Equality Act, which has been passed by the House of Representatives, would change that ("H.R.5—116th Congress," 2019). Although the Equality Act would not require males and females to be treated as identical (for purposes of competitive sports or other purposes), it would establish that there could be no distinction under the law between biological females and biological males who "identify" as females.

The rights issue is a more difficult one in the case of children, who in some instances do not have the "volition" to choose to the extent that adults have, because they do not have the rational capacity of adults. Thus, they may be more susceptible to coercion than adults are. In most instances, children also do not have the freedom to choose the institutions in which they learn or compete. Some have faced or fear retaliation if they complain about changes in rules (Ellington 2019). It is questionable whether children should be used in social experimentation of this kind (Richardson 2017). The same could be said of children who "agree" to permanently change their sexual identity through surgery, chemical procedures, and/or hormonal treatment (Heldt 2018; Cordell-Whitney 2017; Showalter 2019; Jacob 2019).

Currently, the Department of Education is looking into a complaint by high school girl athletes in Connecticut who must compete against biological boys who subjectively identify as girls. The NCAA transgender policy, which applies to colleges, requires that males take hormones that suppress testosterone for at least a year before competing with girls ("The Feds Investigate Connecticut Athletics for Letting Boys Compete in Girls' Sports," 2019). One problem with applying the NCAA policy to high school students is that it encourages children to take hormones when they still may not have developed the rational capacity to make that choice (and the guidance needed to make an informed choice keeps changing [Kirkup 2020]).

The "gender" issue has many contradictions. On the one hand, transgenders are regarded as a separate gender. That is, gender is no longer regarded as binary. Laws are currently being enacted to require quotas based on that "belief" (see, for instance, "Judicial Watch Sues California over Gender Quota Mandate for Corporate Boards," 2019). Yet in sports, rather than having competitions based on the various gender categories (and recall in New York there are thirty-one of them [NYCCHR 2016]), gender is still regarded as binary, so that biological boys who identify as girls may compete against girls. It is unfortunate that children are being subjected to adults' confusion on this issue (Blake 2019; Huber 2019). One proposed solution is that in the case of children, sports competitions (outside of private venues, which can make their own rules) should be open to anyone. Biological males would have the advantage in most cases.

As mentioned, the criteria that apply to language are not the same as those that are used to assess ethical principles. Concepts, according to Objectivist epistemology, are based in reality. I have addressed the distinction between "sex" and "gender" in Touchstone (2017, 247–54). The definition of "sex" is scientifically based on the presence of either an XX or XY chromosome make-up. (There are also a small percentage of individuals with DSD (divergence sexual development), whose sexual definitions are based on phenotype rather than genotype.) At the present time, "gender" does not rise to the level of a concept. For instance, the definition of the NYCCHR relies solely on what a person feels or what is in his mind. "Although there are other definitions of gender, this is the most pernicious because it solely resides in a person's mind" (Touchstone 2017, 250). It is not based on physiology or on behavior nor does it correspond to anything in external reality. A person's opinion about himself is part of reality because his mind is part of reality, but opinion is not the basis for a concept ("Male Prisoners Self-Identifying as Trans for 'Perks,'" 2019). A concept is a generalization, which means there must be two or more existents in reality. Because a person's gender resides in the mind of a person, it could be unique to each person, and therefore potentially unlimited in number.

At present, "gender" is an invalid concept. An invalid concept is one that has a vague, contradictory, and/or erroneous definition. "Gender" is vague. For example, the University of Oregon lists six personal pronouns groups: he, him, his; she, her, hers; they, them, theirs; ze, hir, hirs; co, co, cos; per, per, pers ("Using Pronouns," 2019). According to an article by Walden (2019), one of the "BBC Teach" films claims there are more than 100 genders and *Facebook* lists 71. As mentioned, the NYCCHR has established thirty-one genders. As previously noted, the concept, "gender," is contradictory. In California, a law has been enacted that requires gender quotas for Corporate Boards based on the belief of the legislators that there are more than two genders ("Judicial Watch Sues California over Gender Quota Mandate for Corporate Boards," 2019). Yet, in competitive sports, NCAA transgender policy insists that there are only two—thus, under specified conditions, biological males who identify as females *are* females and can compete as females. In other words, there are no transgenders, there are *only males and females*. This is example of what Rand ("Philosophical Detection," 1982, 22n*) called "concept stealing"; which is when a concept [gender] is used while simultaneously denying an earlier concept [sex] on which it is logically dependent.

Because the codes of conduct discussed above are established at the institutional (macro) level, yet have an effect at the individual (micro) level, these are examples of what Hayek referred to as "unbalanced forces." The institutions that are establishing the new language are agencies that are serving different ends from many of those on whom the codes are imposed. The enforcement of specific words (related to sex and gender) has not been confined to the private agencies (such as the APA) or to the governmental agencies who have established the codes, but has extended to other private organizations and companies. At this time, in the United States, the private enforcement of what is deemed "acceptable" speech is more onerous than enforcement by the government. (Although the word "censor" applies to government enforcement of speech, in the discussion below, I use the term to apply to speech enforcement by private agencies.) The Southern Poverty Law Center serves as an advisor to Internet media giants (Facebook, Twitter, Google, and Amazon) concerning hate speech and hate groups. The media companies, in turn, use the information to police (edit, suspend, expel and/or otherwise punish, or put at a disadvantage) those who are of a certain political, philosophical and/or religious persuasion (Hasson 2018). Mastercard has been pressured by another nonprofit organization (Color for Change) to cut off funding to journalists for their views. Banking institutions, such as Bank of America, also have reportedly been involved in cutting access to accounts of those who have opinions with which they disagree (Johnson 2019).

Societal Rules vs. Virtues

Although freedom of speech is protected in the U.S. Constitution, a document has little meaning if a populace does not value the freedoms it was designed to preserve. People preserve freedom; pieces of paper do not. Although the Constitution applies to the relationship between the government and citizens, in order for the free speech to be preserved, those in the private sector must regard it as a value worth preserving. Polls indicate that younger people in the United States value freedom of speech less than have other generations. Universities may bear some of the responsibility for this trend. It is, after all, the universities who prepare future teachers as well as educate many of those who work in government, in the media, and in corporations. One way of dealing with rights violations is for a person to take the issue to court ("California Professor Vindicated after Termination for 'Dangerous' Conservative Views," 2019). This, of course, is very costly when pursued by a single individual, and is why there are many who opt not to do so. It is typically not as costly for the opposition since they consist of institutions with much vaster resources at their disposal (Raul 2019).

Aside from rights issues, there are some very tricky ethical issues, both from the philosopher's perspective and from those who are not philosophers, of how to negotiate between a person's principles and speech codes that he perceives as coercive. A science professor's job may be at risk if he chooses to eschew definitions of sex that to his thinking are at odds with reality because he adheres to definitions of sex that are genetically based. Does he lose his job out of principle or cave into the speech requirements? Some professors, such as Canadian Jordan Peterson, have been forced out of academics for adhering to their principles (Weatherbe 2016). Rand (1943) in her fiction has shown how a person of integrity maintains it. He does not yield, even if it means quitting a job or even ending a career. Of course, in the short run, this may not be a viable option for some people.

There may be ways in which a person may be able in some way to preserve his principles even if he thinks that he otherwise may be compromising them in a short-term situation. He may choose to engage in some other avenue or forum to promote or to preserve his values. Even this route may not be available. In some instances, even nonwork activity can cause a person to lose employment (Kabbany 2019). In those cases in which a person is edited or "censored" on an Internet platform, an alternative is to create a competitor to the company. This, of course, can be quite costly. Although not a victim of blacklisting himself, because of the "censorship" that Jordan Peterson perceived to be taking place on Patreon, he is creating an alternative free-speech platform called Thinkspot ("Jordan Peterson Launches Anti-Censorship Site Thinkspot" 2019). Creating an alternative social media platform, does not always guarantee that it will be able to operate freely without being "censored" or forced to close down. Parler, which is a free-speech competitor to Twitter, claims to have been censored by Apple, and potentially could be removed from Apple's App Store if it does not comply with a ban on "offensive speech" (Heyes 2019).

Interestingly, legislative efforts at the federal level to curtail Internet technology companies from editing ("censoring") speech has been met with resistance by those conservative and libertarian organizations who are funding recipients of those very tech companies. To the extent that this has happened, it is not surprising. A similar strategy was employed, for instance, in the private sector by companies to discourage unionization of a company's workers. In an attempt to silence key employees who were considered to be union sympathizers and influential over other workers, a company would promote them to higher paying positions. (Much of the legislative controversy involves Section 230 of the Communications Decency Act which exempts tech companies from liability for the content that is posted on their platforms because of their neutrality. An argument by free speech advocates is that the companies should lose this exemption if they fail to be neutral (which is, of course, the basis for their exemption); that is, if they perform as publishers/editors of information [Smith 2019]. According to Day [2019], an amendment to Section 230 requires that tech companies edit their content for material that could affect their users' "well-being"; however, the companies are supposed to allow for political diversity. An alternative view is that Section 230 advances free speech on the Internet [Brown 2019].)

The problem here insofar as the "evolutionary theory of language" is concerned is that the "forces," to which Hayek referred, are not "balanced." As the countervailing power model demonstrates, there is power in numbers. The theory of countervailing power typically applies to a single "seller" (a monopoly) comprised of what were formerly a number of unorganized workers confronting a single "buyer" of labor services (the monopsonist). The typical classic example of countervailing power is a single company in a company town that is confronted with bargaining with a union that has organized its workers. At one time, company towns were not that uncommon. The company owned the town and employed most or all of the workers in the town. At times the company provided shelter for the workers and paid them in scrip that could only be redeemed at the company store. Even if they were many in number, individual workers had little bargaining power against the company. If the workers organized, they could then bargain as a group—which, of course, would tend to balance out the power between the bargaining entities.

Educators, athletes, parents, and other individuals who regard their freedoms as being abridged and/or who think their principles are being compromised could be significant in number. (Of course, anyone who values freedom is affected by rights infringements even if he has not been directly involved). However, they have little power as individuals. Power must be organized. There may be potentially many who would like to band together to counter institutions that impose codes with which they disagree, but they may be dispersed and unorganized. In such cases, leadership is required. Of course, good leadership is rare, and when it emerges it is at risk in the sense that it is a target for neutralization by opposing forces. ("Neutralization" may take the form of nothing more than doxxing a person and/or his family, which can involve publicly listing a person's residence, his family member's residence(s), or his children's school locations [Parke 2019].) Unfortunately, unlike the company town scenario, there is not simply a single "agency" (to employ Hayek's term) imposing "acceptable" language; nor is there only a single agency that is enforcing it. At present, there are a number of agencies all of which have a single (or similar) purpose—to silence those with whom they disagree (politically, philosophically, and/or on religious grounds). In order to have countervailing power, a group or a number of groups would be required to balance these agencies. Of course, the problem with establishing any counter-group is that once established, if it continues to function, it may eventually stray from its intended purpose. It may even be overtaken by those it intended to counter. Group dynamics may not come under the purview of philosophy, but it is a major force in reality.

The focus of ethics is the behavior of the individual. As an aside, one implication to this very brief discussion on language is that there is a "civic" side to ethical behavior. By "civic," I mean activity that deals with rights and ethical principles as they apply to "governance"—although it may not be confined to government per se. There is a civic side to life that, as the saying goes, "a person ignores at his own peril"—or, at least, possibly at the peril of his values. A person has not only a destiny (or, as discussed earlier, perhaps more than one destiny) to pursue in life, he also has other demands that he must address.

In the discussion of man's purpose, it was pointed out that Rand as well as David Norton along with some other neo-Aristotelians regarded man as having a single purpose. I pointed out that if a person has a child, he has more than one purpose. Life becomes more complex, because he must balance his time, thought, resources, and energy between the two purposes. This discussion indicates that there is also a civic side to life that may draw on a person's resources as well. Of course, Aristotle addressed civic virtue. His view of citizenship emphasized the duties of the citizen more so than his rights (Aristotle 1982, 531–39). The point here is that a person may have to devote some of his time to preserving values that he finds are being threatened. The next section will delve further into parenthood as an ethical purpose of a person's life.

REPRODUCTIVITY: A PRIMARY VIRTUE

As Rand pointed out, the cardinal virtues in OE—rationality, productive work, and pride—are achievable by a man alone on a desert island. OE is an individualistic ethics, and the desert island device exposes the primary virtues required for a person's survival. Alone, it is not possible for a person to pursue a parasitic lifestyle and survive (Rand, "Atlas Shrugged," 1961, 127). Productive work is a moral necessity. OE is grounded in human nature. For humans, as for all living creatures, life is the ultimate value. It would seem to follow that reproduction would be a cardinal value in OE, because it is required in order for life's continuance. Yet, in OE, reproduction is considered morally optional (Rand, "Of Living Death," 1968, 3; Merrill 1991, 103, 121, 1997, 86–89; Walker 1999, 112–15). Even though procreation is required to sustain life, it is not needed to sustain an individual's life, and it is a person's own life that is the ultimate end in OE. Reproduction is seen as being potentially productive in OE, but it is one career among many that a person may choose (Rand, "Alvin Toffler's *Playboy* Interview with Ayn Rand," 1964, 7).

I regard reproductivity (child-rearing) as a productive activity, but to be categorically distinct from productivity. In OE, the purpose of productive work is primarily to preserve a person's own life. A person owns the product of his labor. Ownership is the right to acquire, use, and dispose of an object. A parent cannot (ethically) own his child in the full sense of the word. He has no right to use or dispose of the child in any way he chooses. In economic theory, child-rearing is regarded as productive in that it is viewed as a human capital investment. However, it is an investment in which the return primarily goes to the child, not the parent. To the parent, it is non-remunerative (Touchstone 2006, 9, "Reproductivity, Capital Theory, and Objectivist Ethics," 2010, 225). For the most part, child-rearing is unilateral from parent to child. These differences I think are sufficient to justify assigning reproductivity to a category separate from productivity within the context of OE.

I have argued that reproduction is a primary value. That is, it is essential to a person's existence. It is one not achievable by a man alone on a desert island, because it requires interaction with another person (at least for the time necessary to conceive). Thus, in contrast to the contention of OE that other people are not fundamentally a part of reality (Peikoff 1991, 252–53), others are (or at least another person is) fundamental, not only metaphysically but also ethically. (And, of course, as the PSU analysis demonstrates, at least one other person is needed for the development of every living person to attain adulthood since humans are born dependent and remain so for a number of years [Touchstone, 2006, 34].)

When a person lives among others, being self-sufficient is no longer required in that a person no longer has to rely on himself to produce everything required for his existence. He can specialize and trade with others—which can yield enormous benefits. In OE, the trader principle—that is, the exchange of value for value between independent adults—is the primary (and only) social principle. It is not limited to the economic sphere, but extends to the communication of ideas and to friendship and romantic love (Kelley 1996, 24–25; Peikoff 1991, 236–37). Living in a society, also allows for the possibility of what I have referred to as forced unilateral transfers (theft, murder, assault, and so on) (Touchstone 2006, 39). It is possible for one person to be parasitic upon another for his existence. Parasitic behavior of this kind is unethical because it fails to achieve success long term, where success is life qua man (Peikoff 1991, 219).

It follows that, according to OE, a person should "never seek or grant the unearned and undeserved" (Rand, "The Objectivist Ethics," 1964, 27). Voluntary unilateral transfers are acceptable under some circumstances in OE, but in most instances should be avoided. It is acceptable to receive charity in an emergency, but (because misfortune is a metaphysical exception) it should be limited in scope and duration (Rand, "The Ethics of Emergencies," 1964, 47–49). Acceptance of an inheritance is ethical in OE, with the qualification that the heir should make it productive (Branden 1963, 23). (See Sacks [2019] for a comparison of the Hebrew words for inheritance, *nachala* and *yerusha/morasha*. The former stands for something that is automatically passed down from generation to generation. The latter requires positive action in order to acquire legitimate title. An example of the former would be a hereditary title. The latter would be akin to the inheritance of a company, which requires "hard work if the business is to continue to be worth something." Although they are not identical, the Objectivist view of inheritance is more in keeping with the latter view of inheritance.) According to Peikoff, in this context, "productive" means that the recipient should work to increase the worth of the estate (Peikoff, 1991, 391). Drawing on Adam Smith's account of productivity (Adam Smith, [1776] 1937, 639) as well as the tenet of economic theory of keeping the value of capital intact, (Simpson et al. 1951, 263), I've interpreted productivity in this context to mean that, at a minimum, the heir should attempt to maintain the monetary value of the bequest.

From Rand's standpoint, a person is an economic drain if he earns less than he consumes, whether he is on the dole or makes millions (Rand, "Egalitarianism and Inflation," 1982, 132). In economic parlance, a person is said to trench on his capital, when his consumption exceeds the interest generated by his capital. Accordingly, a person is an economic drain if he spends on consumption all of the earnings from his employment and also trenches on his inherited wealth (the principal). In monetary terms, the amount that can be consumed, and still maintain the value of a capital asset (i.e., not trench on its value), is called standard income, which is equal to the interest rate multiplied by the initial capital value (Fisher [1906] 1965, 110, 116, 1930, 6). The present value ($PV) of the asset would be given as $\$PV_t = \int_0^T Y_t\, e^{-\rho t}\, dt$, where Y_t is the income in year *t*, ρ is the interest rate, and *T* is the life of the asset. This assumes a constant rate of interest as well as no other unforeseen changes in the market (Fisher [1906] 1965, 396–97). This also assumes that a sinking fund is set aside yearly to accumulate interest at the same constant interest rate. The sinking fund is: $SF = \$PV(\rho)/(e^{\rho T} - 1)$ (Allen 1967, 240). At year *T*, the sinking fund will have accumulated to equal the initial present value of the capital asset. For example, based on the discrete versions of the above equations, for a constant annual Y of \$1,000, $\rho = 10\%$, and $T = 10$, the initial \$PV would equal \$6,144.45, standard income would equal \$614.45, and the per year sinking fund contribution would equal \$385.55.

Once the heir has successfully maintained or increased the value of his bequest, he has "earned" it in a moral sense. Then to whom does he bequeath it? The traditional answer is family, but to Rand, family is no more than a cultural institution (Sciabarra 1995, 349–50). I stated in "Reproductivity, Capital Theory, and Objectivist Ethics":

> In her article on patents, Rand indicated that once their duration had lapsed, their legitimate heirs were those who could keep them viable by making them productive [Rand, "The Property Status of the Airwaves," 1967, 132]. To extend this idea by way of analogy, those who should inherit property should be those who can best make it productive. "But who produces the producers?" (Touchstone 2010, 228)

In terms of a person's inheritance, the focus in OE is on physical capital. However, a child also receives from his parents' (and/or others) an investment in his human capital. To Rand, a person is "self-made" in his wealth as well as his soul (Rand, "Atlas Shrugged," 1961, 131). ("Soul" to Rand meant consciousness.) Rand, of course, was referring to an adult. A person is born tabula rasa, insofar as the content of his consciousness is concerned (Rand, "The Objectivist Ethics," 1964, 28). Until a child has matured, his education and nurturance are to a large extent the responsibility of his parents. This care would contribute to the child's physical, mental, and ethical development—in economic terms, his "human capital."

Until he becomes an adult, a child is entitled to at least minimal care by his parents. However, when he has reached adulthood, he is not ethically obligated to repay his parents for the basic care he has received from his parents while he was a child. A person may give assistance, financial and otherwise, to his parents, but he is under no obligation to do so if it is overly onerous (Branden 1962). (Of course, a person is obligated to repay his parents for education and other loans as well as other kinds of assistance that were incurred during his adult years.) As I have stated, if an adult child repaid his parents for the full investment in his human capital, the parents' benefit would be twofold. A parent would receive full re-payment for his contribution to his child's human capital investment as well as have received the investment in his human capital by his own parents (Touchstone 2006, 251).

Even though child-rearing is potentially productive, it would seem that parenting is primarily a one-way venture. It is not self-preserving. Thus, a case for parenting would appear to be difficult from the perspective of OE. To the extent that a person is "obligated" to have a child, I have argued that it is based on the replacement of the investment in a person's human capital by his parents (Touchstone 2006, 252, "Reproductivity, Capital Theory, and Objectivist Ethics," 2010, 229–31). Investment in human capital can be regarded as equivalent to a bequest of physical capital in that both enhance the income earning potential of the recipient. To the extent that a beneficiary of a physical estate should maintain its value, the recipient of human capital investment should also keep its "value" intact. As with physical capital, if a person spends all of the income received from the investment in his human capital and fails to set aside a sinking fund to replace it, he in effect would trench on the value of his human capital. Of course, humans own themselves, thus there is (or should be) no capital market for humans. A sinking fund is neither set aside nor is it required, because for humans a child is his replacement capital, so to speak.

What I have termed the "productivity principle" in OE is that a person's earnings must at least cover his consumption over his lifetime if he is to avoid being an economic parasite. As mentioned above, the principle as stated does not explicitly take into account maintaining the value of his inheritance. The productivity principle should account for not only inheritance of physical capital, but also the replacement of human capital investment. To do that, a person would have to earn not only sufficient income for his consumption (and to maintain his physical inheritance) but also earn enough to replace the spending on his human capital by uncompensated parents and/or others.

From an investment perspective, having a child may seem self-sacrificial because it is not the investor who receives the return. Prospectively, it may appear to be irrational. It must, however, also be understood retrospectively (Touchstone 2006, 255, "Reproductivity, Capital Theory, and Objectivist Ethics," 2010, 233). Rand noted that production must take place before consumption (Rand, "The Fountainhead," 1961, 80). However, from the point of view of a human life, consumption precedes production for several years. Of course, someone must be producing in order to provide for a child during his development, and that is typically one's parent or parents (Touchstone 2006, 255). As with the incentive structure that underlies the PD, there is a temptation on the part of an adult to default on maintaining one's human capital by not having a child. Once an adult has received the "investment" in his human capital by his parents, there is no enforcement mechanism to pay back that investment by having a child and investing in his human capital. The only "enforcement" is a moral one; that is, for a person to regard keeping one's "human capital intact" as a responsibility in the same way that "earning one's keep" is a responsibility or maintaining the value of one's physical inheritance is a responsibility. (It appears that in many developed countries parents are, in fact, defaulting by not having children (or enough children) since births are less than replacement in most of these countries [*SPSS* 1999;

The Economist 2007].) Although having a child and "investing" in that child is the primary way in which a person would keep his "human capital intact," as with physical capital, this investment can be more broadly defined to include other outlets. For example, a person may unilaterally invest in another person or other persons or he may leave a bequest to an institution that is engaged in teaching or otherwise passing on knowledge and/or values to others (Touchstone, "Reproductivity, Capital Theory, and Objectivist Ethics," 2010, 234).

A defining characteristic of capital is that it must take physical form. Rand called a machine a "frozen form of a living intelligence" (Rand 1957, 1064). Humans also embody "living intelligence." Like machines, humans are tangible. Unlike machines, humans have volition. They embody the living intelligence that creates the machines. Also, unlike machines, humans also value and have values. Moral principles are intangibles. "Virtues and values cannot *be*, unless they are embodied" (Touchstone 2006, 257; italics in original). They come alive when they are embodied in humans, and they can only be transferred to other humans, not to physical objects. When a human being dies, his virtues and intangible values die with him. To the extent that a person values his principles, he would want to keep them alive—it would be in his self-interest to do so. That is, by keeping his values alive, he is keeping alive the best that is within himself, so to speak. In order to keep his values alive, they must be embodied in another or other human beings.

Of course, a person cannot be forced to keep his human capital intact anymore than he can be forced to take care of himself. However, by taking into consideration his life as a whole, instead of accounting solely for the adult stage, it would be the ethical thing to do. Maintaining one's ethical and other intangible values beyond one's own life by maintaining his human capital could be regarded as unilateral if one only focuses on his adult stage of life. However, when one takes into account his whole lifetime, it can be seen as reciprocal in that the person is keeping intact that which has been given by uncompensated others. "As such, it is not a gift one is giving; it is a value one is maintaining" (Touchstone 2006, 258).

The argument that has been made thus far is that reproduction is a value. As I pointed out in Touchstone ("Reproductivity, Capital Theory, and Objectivist Ethics," 2010, 235), it would seem to be derived from the "productivity principle" when viewed within the context of a person's entire life—that is, reproduction (like consumption) is derivative. Rand said of production: "Men have been taught that the highest virtue is not to achieve, but to give. Yet one cannot give that which has not been created. Creation comes before distribution—or there will be nothing to distribute" (Rand, "The Fountainhead," 1961, 80). Production is a prerequisite for consumption. However, re-phrasing Rand's quote, it likewise could be said: "That which is valued is not reproduction but a person's own life. Yet a person cannot live unless reproduction has taken place. Without reproduction, there would be no life to live." Reproduction, so it would seem, is primary (Touchstone 2006, 35). It is necessary in order for a person to eventually achieve maturity so as to take "ownership" (i.e., full responsibility) for his life. Reproduction precedes production, which precedes consumption.

Although reproduction is required for a person to come into existence, it is not needed for a person's continued existence. However, it could also be said that if a person has another source of income (say, an inheritance), it is not necessary for him to be productive. Yet, according to OE, a person should be productive, regardless of whether he is independently wealthy or not. Even if a person's physical needs were met, being productive satisfies a psychological need (Peikoff 1991, 301). The same could be said for reproduction. It may not be needed to preserve a person's physical existence; however, it is needed to satisfy a psychological need. One that is more fundamental than productivity, since reproduction is a pre-condition for production. Based on this line of reasoning, it would follow that, like productivity, reproductivity would be a cardinal virtue (Touchstone 2006, 36, "Reproductivity, Capital Theory, and Objectivist Ethics," 2010, 236).

Chapter 5

On Giving

Decisions under "Certainty"

INTRODUCTION

According to Objectivist Ethics (OE), the fundamental alternative is life or death. However, as Narveson (1998, 97) has pointed out, for many decisions that people face "'life or death' just isn't where it's at." The future always entails a degree of uncertainty. Risk is based on the probability of an outcome for a given action. For many decisions, the risk of failure (death in this instance) is so low (and the probability of survival is sufficiently high) that probabilities can be ignored. These are decisions under "certainty," which are the kinds of decisions considered in this chapter. This chapter continues with a look into virtues. Virtues are actions that if pursued consistently sustain a person's life long range. Thus it would be expected that the probability of death would be low. However, the decisions considered in this chapter involve virtues that are "unilateral"; that is, the primary recipient is someone other than the decision maker. Unlike the purported purpose of virtues, these virtues are not life sustaining for the decision maker per se since he is not the direct beneficiary. However, the decisions in this chapter are not those in which the decision maker is taking an action on behalf of someone else for which the probability of his dying is imminent. There is another sense in which the decisions in this chapter are "certain," and that is, they are based on rules of thumb that primarily use historical data. That is, the figures are known (or can be known). Of course, the actual figures would not be confined to the rules of thumb; the latter serve merely as guides or baselines.

In OE, productivity is a cardinal virtue. OE is an individualistic ethics. Rand derived productivity as well as the other cardinal virtues by isolating a single man on a desert island and determining what actions he would need to take in order to survive. When man lives among other men, the primary (and only) social virtue in OE is the trader principle (Rand, "The Objectivist Ethics," 1964, 31–32). There are rule utilitarians who also regard this as the primary social principle and identify it with eudaemonia (Hazlitt 1998, 14). Chapter 1 examined reproductivity (childcare) in a state of nature in a two-person model (the PSU). The previous chapter argued that reproductivity is a productive activity, but reproduction is separate from production and is a primary value. Although childcare appears to be unilateral, when considered in a global or an intergenerational context, it is consistent with the trader principle (broadly interpreted). This chapter returns to childcare and also addresses charity. Charity is unilateral in nature but, similar to childcare, also can be seen as globally reciprocal.

Life is finite. It has been argued that there is not simply one purpose to life, but multiple demands. One of the challenges in life is balancing these demands. This chapter presents broad guidelines related to childcare and charity; that is, it considers a heuristic for charitable giving as well as a rule-of-thumb for expenditures on one's child. It also argues that these expenditures can be seen as separable from those for oneself—that is, each can be ranked on a separate scale from that for oneself.

CHILDCARE AND CHARITY

In the previous chapter, it was argued that reproductivity (childcare) is a productive activity; however, it is sufficiently different from productivity to warrant a separate category. Reproductivity appears to be unilateral from parent to child, and it is, in the sense that the primary beneficiary is the child and the child is under no obligation to repay the parent for basic childcare expenditures. It also is inconsistent with the trader principle since it is not trade between independent equals. However, from an intergenerational or global perspective, reproductivity is reciprocal in nature. This is in part because it fits into the "productivity principle," which essentially states that a person should not consume more than he produces within his lifetime. This principle not only applies to the income from a person's "labor," but also to his inheritance; that is, if a person is a recipient of a bequest, he should maintain or increase its value. Objectivist Branden (1963, 23) acknowledged this about a person's physical capital, but I extended the idea to the investment by one's parents in his human capital (Touchstone 2006, 251–54, "Reproductivity, Capital Theory, and Objectivist Ethics," 2010, 229–31). In order to maintain the value of that investment, a person would have a child.

Unlike childcare, many if not most people have not been direct recipients of charity. Based on the rationale underlying reproductivity that is founded on maintaining one's inheritance, it would seem to follow that a person would be under no moral obligation to give to charity. This is basically Rand's position about both charity and reproduction; that is, a person is under no moral obligation to do either. According to OE, having a child is optional. The following sums up Rand's position on charity:

> My views on charity are very simple. I do not consider it a major virtue, and, above all, I do not consider it a moral duty. There is nothing wrong in helping other people, if and when they are worthy of help and you can afford to help them. I regard charity as a marginal issue. What I am fighting is the idea that charity is a moral duty and a primary virtue. (Rand, "Alvin Toffler's *Playboy* Interview with Ayn Rand," 1964, 10)

Objectivist Peikoff has stated that even a "tinge of self-denial" is a sacrifice, and therefore is not ethical (1991, 232). Charity doesn't correspond with the defining features of a virtue, which is an action that, if consistently followed, promotes a person's life long term. Charity primarily benefits another or others. To persistently give away one's income to others would not be self-preserving. In fact, it would be quite the opposite.

Additional rationales have been given for giving to others within the framework of Objectivism. For instance, Kelley (1996, 50) has argued that benevolence is "nonspecific investment" (i.e., undertaken without an expectation of a direct return) in the potential of other people. The motivation for giving is not based on another's suffering, but is self-interested. Even though, like Rand, Kelley thought giving to others should be marginal, he elevated benevolence to a major virtue (1996, 53). Tibor Machan's focus was on generosity, which he considered one of the many benevolent virtues. Unlike charity, which can require deliberation, generosity may involve discernment but is spontaneous. It includes activities such as giving a gift, offering counsel, and being tolerant (Machan, *Generosity*, 1998, 1–2, 23).

My case for charity is similar to the case for reproductivity except that it is more general. It is analogous in that it argues that most people receive an "inheritance" or a benefit for which they have not paid or have not paid in full—that is, value has not been exchanged for value. Although most people may not have received charity from others, they are net beneficiaries in other ways. For instance, most people have benefited from advances in basic knowledge, as well as from inventions and other creative works, without having paid or having only paid in part. "There is an 'inheritance' of knowledge with which most individuals are endowed" (Touchstone, "Ethical Principles, Charity, and a Criterion or Giving," 2008, 45). Because there are no property rights in basic knowledge and only limited property rights in inventions and other creative works (e.g., patents and copyrights), the originators have not been compensated or fully compensated for their work. And, of course, most of the benefactors are dead and cannot be paid for that reason. For those who are "net beneficiaries," a debt is outstanding, so to speak, and it cannot be expunged. Also, as Paterson ([1943] 1968, 306) pointed out, an inheritance of freedom is bestowed on all those who are born and reside in free countries. Freedom is a right, but it is not free. Free people owe a debt to all of those who have established and preserved their freedom. These benefactors, many of whom are no longer alive, are owed a debt that cannot be paid. Because of an inheritance of knowledge and liberty, over the course of a lifetime a person very likely will have "consumed more than he has produced." It would not, therefore, be a sacrifice to give to charity (Touchstone 2006, 326–28, "Ethical Principles, Charity, and a Criterion or Giving," 2008, 45–46).

Charity: Where Does One Stop and You Begin?

In "The Right to Welfare and the Virtue of Charity," Den Uyl (1993) sought to examine whether there is an inclination to reduce charity to an aspect of justice, and, if so, to question whether this endangers the existence of charity as a distinct virtue. An example of the reduction of charity to justice was Lawrence Becker's argument in his book *Reciprocity* (1990). Charity is warranted, according to Becker, because individuals have been recipients of positive externalities. According to Den Uyl (1993, 222), Becker's case for charity is oriented toward the recipient. Den Uyl's case for charity is self-directed, stemming from the classical model of self-perfection (1993, 202).

My case for charity shares features with Becker's; however, it is not other oriented. The justification supports the idea that giving need not be self-sacrificial because (or more accurately, when) a person has been a net beneficiary in the senses discussed above; that is, because a person has benefited from others whom he has not paid. The rationale underlying the case that charity is not necessarily self-sacrificial is based on a "global" notion of reciprocity. However, that does not reduce charity to bilateral trade or to justice. Charity is not an exchange between independent equals; it is primarily unilateral. The primary beneficiary is the receiver of charity. Just as it was argued in the last chapter that reproductivity is a productive activity, yet it is sufficiently different from productivity to justify a separate category; it is also the case that, just because the rationale for charity is based on the idea of "global" reciprocity, charity is nevertheless sufficiently different from reciprocity ("justice") to warrant a separate category.

Den Uyl's concern with the reciprocity argument is that it offers no limit to giving to others. He pointed out, based on the reciprocity case, "each of our lives could be perpetually mortgaged to whatever someone's conception of our obligation to reciprocate might be" (1993, 223). The same criticism applies to my argument as I have presented it thus far. That is, it provides no guideline insofar as how much to give to charity is concerned.

In his book *With Charity toward None* (1972, 227–28), O'Neill's interpretation of the Objectivist position on charity would suggest that no amount of giving is justified. This is not the case, of course. Rand was not critical of charity per se, but of altruism, which essentially she described as always putting others' needs and desires above one's own (Rand, "Atlas Shrugged," 1961, 144). Kelley (1996, 50) said of altruism that it "offers no principled guidance on how to draw the line" between oneself and other people. Of course, a strict reading of Rand's view of altruism is that it is a moral doctrine in which other people should receive *all* of a person's income, time, and other resources—which, of course, is suicidal. To avoid suicide, a person would survive by living with the guilt that whatever he does consume is at the expense of someone else.

Mueller (2010, 193) acknowledged that the pursuit of giving on an extreme scale could be suicidal. Similarly, Machan (*Generosity*, 1998, 3) recognized that charity could be self-sacrificial. Ludwig von Mises ([1949] 1996, 241) pointed out that the boundary between expenditures on oneself and those on charity is not always discernible. Concerning this boundary, Hazlitt said:

> [T]his is one of the unsettled problems of ethics. There will be those who think that the only obligation of the individual is not to transgress against others; and there will be those who think that his obligation to help others is practically without limits. There will be still those who take an intermediate position.
>
> Probably no exact boundary can be drawn, and no exact rules can be framed, concerning the extent of our duties to others. In such duties there will always be a twilight zone, shading off from what is clearly imperative to what is clearly quixotic and in the long run harmful. (Hazlitt 1998, 106–7)]

A Rule-of-Thumb for Charitable Giving

According to Rand, misfortune is not the norm in life; it is marginal. Those in need should be a relatively small portion of the population, particularly in a free society. However, as Rand ("The Ethics of Emergencies," 1964, 48–49) and Den Uyl (1993, 222) have noted, another's need cannot be the (sole) justification for giving. In percentage terms, even though the number in need may be relatively few, a single individual cannot give so much as a modest amount to each of them.

Rather than a percentage of the people who are in need, another way of addressing giving to others is based on the percentage of one's income (and/or time and/or other resources at one's disposal). Productivity is principled behavior because it sustains a person's existence. If charity was considered equivalent to productivity, then spending an equal amount of time (and other resources) on charity might appear to be justified. If charity were deemed more important than productive work, then spending more than half of one's resources on charity might be in order. "More than half" is a vague guideline. As a long-run strategy, continually spending more and more on charity relative to one oneself would not result in long-run success.

I have proposed a rule-of-thumb for charitable giving based on my interpretation of the BUP, which essentially states that if a person acts rationally, success is the expected outcome and misfortune is unlikely. Because survival is the gauge of success, then in elemental terms, this means that if one is ethical, he can expect to survive. However, a probability of death is always present, even if one acts rationally. For any given year, an individual's expected income is the probability of survival multiplied by income for the year plus the probability of dying multiplied by zero (because if he dies he earns—or more accurately *receives*, since he is dead—nothing). In the event that the individual survives the year, the difference between his actual income and his expected income is a result of "good fortune," or is a bonus, so to speak. Because, according to my reading of the BUP, it is "accidental" or "incidental," that amount can be given to charity without being considered "self-sacrificial." This applies solely to monetary contributions.

Charity also can take the form of volunteer work. Donating one's time may be substituted for monetary expenditures (Touchstone 2006, 343, "Ethical Principles, Charity, and a Criterion or Giving," 2008, 47–48). Other qualifications also apply. If a person has had a particularly difficult year because of personal or family health or financial difficulties, he has experienced "bad fortune" and may be in no position to contribute to charity. A person may also be relieved of contributing if he is already paying the equivalent amount via taxes for government transfer payments. This is, of course, only a rough guideline, but it helps to put giving in perspective for those who may be tempted to "give until it hurts."

CHARITY AND CHILDCARE EXPENDITURES ARE SEPARABLE

Gloria Zúñiga distinguished between actions that are strictly economic and those that are moral. The decision to buy either a black suit or a blue suit is strictly economic. Deciding between buying a hat for oneself and giving to the poor has both economic and moral significance. Given that a person's income and other resources are limited, only one of these two expenditures may be undertaken. She stated the following:

> Frequently, in fact, we may find that judgments that are beneficial from an economic self-interested perspective are also wrong from a moral perspective. Having a new hat would be economically beneficial for me since it would add a nice accessory to my wardrobe. However, from a moral perspective, it might be seen as a frivolous choice in light of my knowledge of someone's need for food. Since economic judgments involve a set of considerations that are orthogonal to those involved in moral judgments, there is no necessary relation between economic value and moral value. (2005, 139)

Here again is the altruistic prescriptive as Rand defined it, that morally, others' needs are above one's own. If buying a hat for oneself is frivolous relative to giving to someone in need, then (since there are more people in need than a single person's resources to satisfy them) other people's needs would tend to outrank one's own (except for the most basic requirements for living).

Zúñiga stated that, given a limited budget, one expenditure must be chosen over the other—that is, they are substitutable in that there is a trade-off between the two. Yet, she also suggested that economic and moral decisions are somehow separable. The latter view is inconsistent with the prevailing perspective on how spending decisions are made. Ludwig von Mises envisioned all goods arranged along a single preference scale (Mueller 2010, 165). Mises said: "Acting man … chooses between various alternatives, no matter whether they are to be classified as material or ideal. In the actual scales of value material and ideal things are jumbled together" (Mises [1949] 1996, 233). This view is not unlike the prevailing outlook in economic theory that sees economic and ethical expenditures ranked ordinally along a single scale of preferences (Alchian and Allen 1977, 25–26; Becker 1995, 7). Similarly, Rand regarded values as arrayed on a single scale much like the view held by economists. Her position was:

> Degrees of intensity can be and are measured approximately, on a comparative scale. For instance, the intensity of emotion of joy in response to certain facts varies according to the importance of these facts in one's *hierarchy* of values; it varies in such cases as buying a new suit, or getting a raise in pay, or marrying the person one loves. (1990, 31; italics in original)

It would seem that, since an individual must budget his income, time, and other resources, and because by opting for one choice, he necessarily forgoes another (the highest-valued alternative), then all alternatives would be arranged on the same scale. However, I contend that decisions concerning charitable expenditures are (or can be) separable from expenditures on oneself, and that there are (or can be) separate preference scales for the two categories of expenditure. I also maintain in the next subsection that expenditures for one's child are separable from expenditures on oneself (and from charitable expenditures).

In the discussion above, I presented a heuristic for charitable giving based on the previous year's income multiplied by the probability of dying. This gives a rule-of-thumb amount that can be spent on charity for the year. As such, it can be separated from potential spending on oneself and one's family, and thus does not compete directly with those expenditures. By so doing, charitable expenditures can be ranked on a preference scale separate from the preference scale(s) for other expenditures.

Because the preference scales are separable, a decision maker does not regard a potential charitable donation as directly lowering his utility (i.e., being a "sacrifice" in the Objectivist sense). The source of the decrease in utility experienced by the person who donates to a charity is for the highest-valued alternative charitable contribution that he forgoes within his ranking of charities, instead of the highest-valued alternative expenditure for himself (and/or others)—which is the case when all expenditures are ranked on a single scale (Touchstone 2016, 50–51). Because charitable expenditures are separable from those for oneself, they are not directly substitutable. In this way, "economic" and "moral" decisions are independent, in a way in which Zúñiga implied.

A Baseline for Spending on Children

The decision of whether or not to have a child is unlike the decision of whether or not to work for pay. The decisions arise from different considerations. Decisions on spending on one's child are also (to some degree) different from those on oneself (or others). The argument for having children, which is based on maintaining the investment in one's human capital, can allow for the separation of childcare expenditures from other expenditures similar to the way a sinking-fund allocation is separable from other expenditures out of the revenue generated from physical capital.

As a guide to the amount to spend on one's child, a starting point would be the amount that a person's parents had expended on his human capital. This would include not only spending on basic education, but also for sustenance. This amount (accounting for inflation) would serve as a starting point for the estimation of a "sinking fund" amount. The sinking fund amount would function as a rough guide for the minimum annual expenditure for one's child.

The sinking fund amount based on the value of a person's human capital (i.e., based on a person's discounted lifetime income) may be thought of as a better guideline than one based on one's parents' expenditures. However, the former is derived from an "expected" figure that results from not only the parents' expenditures, but a person's own investment as well. There are times in which this figure can be distorted, as it would in, say, the case of Jeff Bezos. The sinking fund on his human capital would exceed (in almost any conceivable circumstance) the amount that should be spent on a child's human capital development. In an instance like this, if a parent wanted to provide for an inheritance for his child beyond a reasonable human capital investment, it could take the form of physical capital.

Not all expenditures on one's child are separable in this way. This amount serves as a rule-of-thumb (Touchstone 2016, 47). To the extent that the expenditures budgeted for one's child are separable, they could be ranked on a separate scale from the scale(s) for the parent's other expenditures. That is, all of the potential expenditures arrayed on the scale would be solely for the child. The expenditures for the child would not compete or be substitutable for the parent's spending for himself. This would apply particularly for a child's basic expenditures.

> Since the ranking of the potential expenditures for the child is on a *separate scale*, the parent no longer sees the expenditure on his child as directly *reducing his own utility*. To the extent the parent experiences a reduction in utility when he purchases something for his child, it would be for the value of what the amount of money he spends could buy—that is, for the highest-valued alternative expenditure on *his child*, not for the highest-valued alternative expenditure for *himself*. (2016, 48; italics in original)

Insofar as who makes the spending decisions on the child, it could be predominantly one parent or a joint decision by both parents. As the child gains maturity, his opinion should be taken into account in some cases. There are some children whose special needs require more attention. At a minimum, the amount should be enough to provide one's child with at least a minimal education and subsistence.

As I mentioned in Touchstone (2016, 48), in an economically advanced society, in many cases, the issue is not the minimum amount to spend, but putting a cap on the debt the parent or parents will incur. In the event a parent's spending is significantly greater than the sinking fund amount on the value of his own human capital, he may be risking his ability to sustain himself (and others). That is, spending on one's child would be directly competing with that for oneself. If this spending poses a serious risk to the parent or other family members, the parent may need to explore other avenues, such as charity or grants.

An advantage to separating expenditures for charity and for children from those for oneself is that they are not in direct competition with potential expenditures for oneself. This is not unlike how people who have a business and a household keep their accounts. By keeping them separate, family and business decisions are not mixed together. With separate preference scales, a parent may avoid the temptation of paying for a gym membership fee for himself rather than an equivalent amount that is needed for his child's dental work, since the expenditures would be on separate "accounts." As mentioned, having a separate guideline also is helpful when dealing with what may be a more prevalent problem for a parent, which is when to say no to expenditures on one's child. The examples given here have been on monetary expenditures. Time is also a scarce commodity. Decisions on spending time with one's children are somewhat different because the parent typically must work for pay as well as provide childcare. Children are by nature dependent and require supervision. At those times when the parent cannot be physically present, adequate supervision must be provided (2016, 53). Of course, there are times in which a parent must decide between work and being with his child. This type of decision will be addressed in the next chapter.

Chapter 6

On Decision-making under Uncertainty

INTRODUCTION

The last chapter continued with a discussion of virtues. Virtues have been defined as those actions that if pursued consistently tend to promote life qua man. The last chapter considered decisions under "certainty." Of course, the future is always uncertain. However, the decisions under consideration were those in which the person was not "risking his life" in the sense of imminent physical peril. The probability of death was so low that it could be ignored. The virtues considered in the last chapter were "other-oriented," specifically, those related to charity and childcare. Because they are primarily other oriented, they do not directly support the life of the decision maker—which, of course, could be life threatening if carried too far. They are nevertheless virtues because they are consistent with reciprocity broadly defined. Although these virtues may be "justified" based on other arguments, the focus was on global reciprocity.

According to economist Becker (1995, 7, 13), economic theory applies to all aspects of human decision-making. Similarly, according to Alchian and Allen (1977, 26), there is no distinction between moral values and "trinkets in the marketplace." It is true that "life" forces individuals to choose. In economics, scarcity demands that a person choose among alternatives. In ethics, the fundamental choice is between life and death. The ultimate scarcity is one's own life (his time). In that sense, there is a commonality among all decisions—whether strictly economic or ethical in nature. However, the last chapter argued that some decisions *can be* "separable" from others. This separability would at least apply to some basic expenditures of money and other resources related to decisions that are other oriented. The rationale underlying the separation is two-fold. The first is that the categories for which the separations apply (i.e., children and charity) warrant the money and resources expended (based on global reciprocity). The second is that by separating these expenditures, they do not directly compete with decisions related to oneself. The considerations that underpin these decisions are (or can be) somewhat different from those for oneself.

This chapter will continue with ethical decision-making. It will consider, among other things, situations in which the probabilities of expected loss cannot be ignored. The focus is primarily on the loss of one's life. The first section discusses ethical decisions in general. The second section considers decisions between an ethical action and an unethical alternative. The third section examines decisions among competing values. The fourth looks at ethical decisions for which the expected loss cannot be ignored.

VIRTUES AS STRATEGIES FOR SUCCESS

For decisions that take uncertainty into account, probabilities become relevant. As a clarification, Frank Knight made a distinction between risk and uncertainty. According to Knight, risk applies to decisions for which a given action has more than one outcome and the probabilities are known or can be estimated. Uncertainty is concerned with decisions for which an action has more than one outcome and the probabilities are not known or estimable (Baumol 1977, 458). In other contexts, such as in risk management, uncertainty pertains to situations in which probabilities are calculable. When I refer to uncertainty, it will be decisions in which probabilities may or may not be known or estimable. I regard probability to be epistemological in nature in that knowledge of the future has an element of uncertainty.

The BUP acknowledges the stochastic in the decision-making process. For a given ethical action, either success or failure may occur with probabilities associated with each alternative. The BUP states that if a person consistently acts ethically, then success is expected in the long term. Failure may occur, but the probability is low, and thus can be ignored. Ethical principles can be regarded, insofar as making a decision is concerned, as conforming to a "strict causal chain." That is, even though probabilities may be calculable, they can be ignored. In this way, ethical principles are similar to conventions. Once a convention emerges, it results in a pure strategy (Sugden 1986, 35–56; Touchstone, "Economic Decision-Making and Ethical Choice," 2008, 177–78). Once "driving on the right-hand-side of the street" is established, that is the only action that is acceptable. (Although conventions may permit exceptions under some conditions, such as allowing a driver to pass another vehicle when there is no oncoming traffic in the opposite lane.) By following a convention, a driver does not have to calculate the probabilities for each alternative every time he sets out to drive his car. By observing the convention, he is more likely to have "success" (i.e., to arrive at his destination safely). Similarly, following virtues is a strategy for success. Generally speaking, calculation of probabilities is unnecessary and success is expected.

CHOICE BETWEEN AN ETHICAL AND AN UNETHICAL ALTERNATIVE

The economic approach to decisions recommends calculating the gains and losses for every alternative a person faces. This is much like the approach advocated by act utilitarians. For instance, each time a driver approached a red light, he would weigh the gains and losses for each alternative—where the alternatives are either to observe the red light and stop or to dismiss it and continue driving through the intersection. Rand cast the fundamental alternative as a choice between life and death (Rand, "The Objectivist Ethics," 1964, 21; Peikoff 1991, 209)—between a value and a non-value. Ethical actions are life affirming and unethical actions are not. Yet, decisions are typically not cast as choices between life and death. Decisions are seen as the choice between two or more alternatives, each of which has probabilities of survival and death associated with it. Many times a person faces more than two alternatives. For instance, a person who is considering going to college may have several colleges from which to choose. However, economists see the opportunity cost of a choice as being the highest valued alternative that is foregone. In that sense, a person may be seen as ultimately choosing between two alternatives.

Rand saw a decision as a choice between one alternative that is ethical and another that is not. Those decisions are fundamentally either-or. Economic decisions are often portrayed as involving a trade-off between goods; that is, goods (whether economic or moral) are "marginally substitutable for each other" (Alchian and Allen 1977, 26). However, as Peikoff pointed out, an individual cannot sacrifice a given amount of a virtue to attain an increment of a vice and remain virtuous (Peikoff 1991, 264, 273). An example of this kind of either-or decision was given in chapter 3 in which a person was deciding between an ethical course of action and an unethical alternative. Specifically, it involved a student choosing between two summer "jobs." Both were delivery positions—one for a florist and the other for a fence of stolen property (Touchstone 2018, 67). Based on my interpretation of the BUP, for the ethical job, the expected loss (the probability of dying multiplied by the monetary value of the loss) could be ignored, because when a person acts ethically, loss is the not to be expected. This is not the case for the unethical action; that is, the expected loss cannot be dismissed by virtue of what unethical activity is—that is, it does not promote life long range. Furthermore, even though the gain is confined to the anticipated salary for the summer, the loss is based on the entire value of a person's human capital (the discounted value of income earned over the person's entire life). The expected gain is based on the income for the working period during which he would survive—in this example, the summer. However, if the person dies, he does not merely lose the income he would have earned during the summer, but also the income he would have received for the rest of his life. In "Economic Decision-Making and Ethical Choice" (Touchstone 2008, 178–80), a more general example was presented for a decision between an ethical choice and an unethical alternative. In most cases, other losses associated with the unethical alternative would also be higher (such as those related to incarceration, legal fees, reputation, etc.) In any case, because of the asymmetry involved in the losses for the two alternatives, the ethical alternative would be chosen. For this reason, it is unnecessary to actually perform these calculations. The unethical choice would not appear as an alternative in a rational person's decision set.

CHOICE AMONG ETHICAL ALTERNATIVES

When choosing between two productive (i.e., ethical) career paths, a person would compare the net discounted value of expected lifetime earnings for the respective occupations. Other aspects would also be taken into consideration. (For example, the amount of travel may differ for the respective fields, which could be an advantage or disadvantage depending upon a person's tastes.) However, the expected loss would be ignored, because success is the to-be-expected insofar as the probability of dying is concerned. There may be other probabilities with corresponding losses that may be taken into account, however (Touchstone, "Economic Decision-Making and Ethical Choice," 2008, 181).

Most of the decisions in life are between or among competing values. Although production and consumption are both values in OE, productivity is a virtue and consuming is not. It would appear that productive work would have the ethical edge. This is true not only of productive work, but also of saving. Saving (when it is invested) is productive (Rand, "Egalitarianism and Inflation," 1982, 131–32; Touchstone 2006, 246). Of course, Rand saw productivity as the purpose of life, and happiness as the moral purpose. I regard what I call Rand's "productivity principle" as a rough guide for balancing productivity and consuming; that is, consumption should not exceed income over the course of a person's life (Rand, "Atlas Shrugged," 1961, 89).

The difficulty of applying the principle is in the details—the day-to-day decisions. For instance, a person may have to decide between attending an unexpected and urgent business meeting and spending the day on a recreational outing with his family (Touchstone 2006, 366). These are not always easy decisions. At times, a person (depending on the urgency and other circumstances) may have to defer one of the activities relative to the other. For instance, in this case, if the person thought that missing the meeting would put his job (and therefore his ability to take care of himself and his family) in jeopardy, he very likely would opt for the meeting. In this case, the expected losses would have to be taken into account in his decision, and the expected loss of his livelihood would very likely have the greater weight.

Although consuming is not a virtue per se within the context of OE, there are virtues associated with consumption. As Rand ("The Sanction of the Victims," 1982, 6) pointed out, "the spending of money is a grave responsibility." The purchase of goods is an affirmation in a number of respects. One is that it signals the producer and other potential producers that this product is desirable. Rand spoke of affirmation in *The Fountainhead* in an exchange between Howard Roark and Gail Wynand:

> [T]he ability to say "Yes" or "No" is the essence of all ownership. It's your ownership of your own ego. Your soul, if you wish. Your soul has a single basic function—the act of valuing… . In this sense, everything to which you grant your love is yours. (1943, 582–83)

Of course, ownership involves more than admiration. As I pointed out in Touchstone (2006, 218): "Action is required, and purchase is that action when it comes to material goods." By actively purchasing a good, a buyer is providing the wherewithal (via income) for this producer to continue supplying the product as well as the incentive (through potential income) for potential producers to enter this business. Purchase literally provides the means by which not only the product, but also the producer survives.

In some cases, an individual is less mindful of how his "savings" are allocated within his portfolio because he is one step removed from the decisions—that is, in one way or another the decisions are assigned to someone else. If a person has a diverse portfolio which consists of investments in companies that produce goods some of which are at odds with his principles, then (to the extent that a person is aware of how his savings are invested and can have input into those decisions) they (like his consumer decisions) should also be guided by his ethical principles.

Although it cannot be explored in any depth in this discussion, a note on boycotts and other forms of economic pressure is relevant here. At present, the political left increasingly has been using boycotts and the threat of boycotts to put pressure on companies and organizations to achieve a variety of objectives—such as firing people with whom they disagree or stopping the publication or the selling of books, etc. (for instance, see Aviles 2019; Spencer 2019). This is not exclusively a tactic of the left; however, currently the left tends to be more organized and effective than the so-called "right" insofar as boycotts are concerned. The left also has used proxies to pressure corporations. This tactic is described in Saul Alinsky's *Rules for Radicals*. The proxy tactic was discovered in 1967 when it was realized that a boycott would be ineffective against Kodak. The objective was to acquire proxies from Eastman Kodak stockholders on behalf of an organization in Rochester, New York called FIGHT (Alinsky 1989, 170). The proxy tactic also led to the discovery of other political maneuvers (1989, 181). Putting economic pressure on corporations by acquiring and using proxies is not a method that has been used by organizations that are "right leaning." I am not advocating the use of "Saul Alinsky" tactics per se. However, a person would be justified in not buying a product if the company were supporting a position or policy that was at odds with a person's principles (for instance, if the company was contributing to a non-profit organization that actively lobbied against the second amendment.) If this is acceptable for a single person, then it would likewise be acceptable for an organized group of like-minded people to refrain from buying the product. In general, collective tactics would be acceptable in those instances in which a person, in a defensive posture, is attempting through organized means to encourage private companies or other organizations to refrain from activities that violate individual rights. Of course, the difficulty in utilizing these countermeasures is that a civic-minded organization must be in place to coordinate the efforts. This kind of activity is related to the civic responsibility that I discussed in chapter 4.

CHOICE BETWEEN ETHICAL ALTERNATIVES: WHEN THE EXPECTED LOSS CANNOT BE IGNORED

Based on my interpretation of the BUP, when a decision involves a choice between an ethical course of action and one that is unethical, the probability of dying (and the associated expected loss) can be dismissed for the ethical choice, but it cannot be overlooked for the unethical alternative. For these decisions, calculation of expected gains and losses is not required. When decisions are limited to ethical alternatives (such as choosing between two productive careers to pursue) or to alternatives that have little ethical content (such as choosing between two suits to purchase), the expected losses (related to dying) can be ignored in many cases. The expected losses can typically be disregarded for ethical actions because, according to the BUP, success is the to-be-expected and loss is the not-to-be-expected.

The BUP acknowledges that for particular situations, following the ethical course could result in a significant loss. These circumstances would tend to be unusual over the course of an individual's life. For example, in order to rescue one's child from drowning, a person may willingly risk his life. In this situation, the parent's probability of dying and the corresponding loss could not be overlooked in making the decision. If a person's life is his ultimate value, how is risking one's life justified? Rand ("The Ethics of Emergencies," 1964, 45) addressed this question within the context of OE. A person may risk his life for another if he thought his life would be unbearable without that person.

There are some professions in which individuals put their lives at risk on a continual basis—such as firefighters, police officers, and combat soldiers. In some cases, a person may go "beyond the call of duty," such as when a soldier throws himself on a grenade to save his comrades. Unlike a parent risking his life for his child, a soldier may risk his life for fellow soldiers, some or all of whom he does not know personally. Would this be rational? I addressed this in Touchstone ("Economic Decision-Making and Ethical Choice," 2008, 182–85) and (2006, 303). According to my interpretation of the BUP, in the grenade example, either choice that the soldier made could be justified. If a person clearly thought the action would end his life, he would be justified in not taking the chance. (In a more general sense, this assumes, of course, that the situation is one in which the soldier has the discretion to make a choice. In many cases, the choice of risking one's life is the first one—the voluntary decision to enter combat. After that decision, the soldier oftentimes must observe the orders of his superiors—unless it is an unlawful order.) Of the two, the more difficult choice to explain is choosing to risk one's life when there is a high probability of death.

I have likened this kind of decision, theoretically speaking, with the decision to buy life insurance (Touchstone 2006, 285, "Economic Decision-Making and Ethical Choice," 2008, 187–89). A person may opt to purchase life insurance even though the expected value with the policy is less than the expected value without it—that is, he may choose to accept an "unfair bet." In part, the reason for the willingness to buy insurance under this condition is that a person is "born at risk" in the sense that his death is certain. The uncertainty is its timing. The person's original position (without insurance) is one of uncertainty (and disequilibrium). A person may be willing to undertake a "fair bet" (i.e., one for which the expected values in each state are equal) or an unfavorable one (as described above), because either of these may be preferable to the initial position (Ehrlich and Becker 1972, 627). By opting to buy insurance, the person ends up in a position of "certainty."

When insurance is actuarially fair, the expected monetary values are equivalent for each state facing the individual. However, under the assumption of risk aversion (diminishing marginal utility), the expected utility with insurance is greater than the expected utility without it. To illustrate, if it is assumed that the probabilities of survival (π_a) and death (π_d) are both 50% and the estimated value of an individual's human capital is \$100,000, then in the original state (no insurance), the expected value of his human capital would be \$50,000 = ($\pi_a \times$ \$100,000 + π_d x 0). The cost of one-term policy for full coverage (assuming an unloaded premium) would be \$50,000 = $\pi_d \times$ \$100,000. Thus, if he insured his life and lived, the value of his human capital less the premium would be \$50,000. If he died, the face value of his policy (\$100,000) less the premium (\$50,000) would be \$50,000. Thus, the expected value in the insured state would be \$50,000 = ($\pi_a \times$ \$50,000 + $\pi_d \times$ \$50,000). That is, when insurance is actuarially fair, both the expected values of the uninsured and insured states are identical (\$50,000).

Now, if the person's utility function is assumed to be $(V^{1-\rho})/(1-\rho)$, where ρ =.5, then in the uninsured state, the person's expected utility would be [$\pi_a \times$ (\$100,000)$^{.5}$/.5 + $\pi_d \times$ 0] = 316.23, and in the insured state his expected utility would be [$\pi_a \times$ (\$50,000)$^{.5}$/.5 + $\pi_d \times$ (\$50,000)$^{.5}$/.5] = 447.21. Thus, even though the expected *values* are equal in both states, the expected *utility* is greater in the insured state. Opting for insurance would result in greater expected utility even though the expected values in both states are identical.

Now, if it is assumed that the premium is loaded (say, by a flat value of \$10,000), then if the person was insured and he survived (assuming, for comparison purposes, he remained fully insured), the value of human capital (\$100,000) less the premium (\$60,000) would be \$40,000. If he died, the face value of the policy less the premium would be \$40,000. Thus, the expected value of the insured state would be \$40,000. The expected value of the uninsured state would remain at \$50,000. The expected value in the uninsured state is greater than in the insured state because insurance is not actuarially fair (i.e., the premium is loaded). The expected utilities of the uninsured and insured states would be 316.23 and 400.00, respectively (under the assumption that the person remained fully insured). Thus, even though insurance is actuarially unfair, a person may still opt to purchase insurance because the expected utility with insurance exceeds the expected utility without it.

Although the life insurance framework may lend some understanding to the kind of theory that underlies decisions of this nature, it is not presented to suggest that individuals actually make these kinds of calculations when it comes to risking their lives. It is presented to make the point that life is finite. Associated with every action a person takes is some probability of dying. However, there is no probability that a person will never die. That is, the insurance example reminds us that all humans are born at risk. Our deaths are inevitable, and it is this inevitability that may account for why some people might be willing to risk their lives and it may be rational for them to do so.

That inevitability alone explains nothing. What is also relevant is that there is a "bequest motive." The insurance example assumes a bequest motive on the part of the prospective buyer, but it does not offer a reason for a bequest motive. The motive seems obvious for most insurance buyers. Many policy holders have family members who may survive the insured person, and they feel responsible for them. For instance, they may have minor children, who would be left in a state of dependency if they died. Therefore, they would want to provide for them even beyond the termination of their own lives.

How does this relate to the soldier who is willing to risk his life in the situation described above? There could be a number of reasons why a person would willingly join an army to engage in combat. Among them could be a desire to defend his country. The concept of "country" comprises a number of things, not the least of which may be the principles on which it has been founded or for which it stands. If a person thought those principles were at risk, that could weigh into his decision. According to Rand, one person may be willing to risk his life for someone else if he thought his life would not be bearable without that person. An individual may think similarly of a principle, such as freedom. That is, he may risk his life if he thought the principle was in sufficient jeopardy, and if he thought life would be intolerable without it.

Like humans, principles have lives. If threatened, they must be defended. Defense is not limited to tacit acceptance. At times, it may also extend beyond the written or spoken word. There are instances in which physical response is required. It sounds contradictory to state that, on the one hand, a person's ultimate value is his life and principles are actions that sustain one's life, yet, on the other hand, a person might willingly risk his life to preserve a principle or principles. People rationally value their lives, but one doesn't merely live for the range of the moment. A person values the entirety of his life—as an integrated whole. The future is important to a person—not only his future, but beyond his existence. At the core of why a person would be willing to risk death is the concept of identity. A person's identity is how he thinks and how he acts. It comprises his values and his virtues. They are embodied within him. Virtues are actions that are undertaken in order to attain a value or values. Central to identity is consistency. "A person may act on his principles even when he faces death because by acting consistently he is preserving his identity" (Touchstone 2006, 305).

In response to the last statement, it could be said that once a person is no longer alive, he no longer has an identity. This presumes that legacy is unimportant to the individual. A person's virtues die with him, but his principles need not. Like humans, principles are mortal. They risk dying if they are not preserved. However, unlike humans for whom death is an inevitability, the death of principles is merely a possibility. If a person were confronted with the possibility of losing a principle if he does not risk his life to save it, he might choose to risk his life. "By risking his life to preserve a principle, he acts to keep alive the best within himself. Furthermore, that which he values most has the potential for immortality, even though he does not" (2006, 305). Risks of loss are not confined to loss of one's life, of course. For instance, whistleblowers often face the loss of their jobs. They may also risk having a livelihood in their professions because of blacklisting and other forms of backlash (O'Neil 2019). There are serious consequences to following one's conscience, and they cannot be dismissed. Ethics does not require that a person risk it all in order to preserve a principle, but the discussion above at least provides a rationale for why a person may do so.

Chapter 8 will address some of the other considerations involved in why a person may risk his life. It is confined primarily to professions for which there are risks involved—that is, by the nature of their professions, the individuals repeatedly face the risk of death or failure.

Chapter 7

On the Concept of Probability

INTRODUCTION

This chapter will propose a new definition for the concept of probability. In my view, there is a foundational element missing in probability theory. What is lacking is an overarching definition of the concept of probability; one sufficiently broad to subsume the commonly used definitions of probability (with qualifications). There are several theories of probability. Three of them are the Subjective (STP), Classical (CTP), and Relative Frequency (RFT) theories of probability (Crovelli 2012). Although each of these theories has its proponents, each of the definitions in these theories suffers from limitations.

Subjectivist probabilities are estimated by observing behavior, particularly in making wagers (Weatherford 1982, 10, 221, 223). There is evidence that people do ascribe their own probabilities to events, but these can be at variance with outcomes based on relative frequencies underlying those events (1982, 238–39). The CTP, which assumes equiprobability, is inadequate in handling probabilities such as those for unbalanced dice and those based on actuarial tables. CTP is based on analytic propositions that are said to be logically true a priori (1982, 62). Purportedly, they are verified by laws of logic and mathematics, not by experience (1982, 191, 205). If proven, they are regarded as certain (1982, 192, 208), but they say nothing about external reality (1982, 126, 205). RFT probabilities are based on actual rates of occurrence of some characteristic found in the external world (1982, 8). RFT probabilities are synthetic propositions. They are considered "contingent"; that is, their properties cannot be known a priori (1982, 201). They are regarded as neither confirmable nor falsifiable (1982, 205, 208), as such they are subject to the same disadvantage as all empirical statements as never being certain (1982, 125).

The first part of this chapter will give an overview of the analytic-synthetic dichotomy within the context of the Objectivist view on concepts. In the second part, three definitions of probability will be discussed. In the third, the proposed definition of the concept of probability will be presented as it relates to "orthodox" theory. The fourth part will overview Bayesian theory and how the proposed definition applies to probability within that framework. In the fifth will be a discussion of computer learning systems, in particular principal component analysis and adaptive resonance theory as they relate to the proposed definition.

ANALYTIC-SYNTHETIC DICHOTOMY

The split between conceptualization (which is internal) and perception (of external reality) is reflected in the rationalist-empiricist dichotomy. The Rationalists regard logic as the source of knowledge and tend to minimize experience. The Empiricists view experience as the basis for knowledge and largely dismiss logic (Peikoff 1990, 112). The logic-fact dichotomy is incorporated in what is called the analytic-synthetic (A-S) dichotomy (1990, 117). The A-S theory separates propositions into two categories: the analytic and the synthetic (1990, 90).

According to Objectivist Leonard Peikoff, analytic propositions are tautologies or definitions in which the predicate of the proposition is said to repeat the subject (1990, 91). They are a priori, and, except for some minimal experience needed to establish their concepts, are independent of and provide no facts about reality (1990, 93, 107). Analytic statements are not verified empirically (1990, 108), but by analyzing the concepts that are contained therein (1990, 90). If validated, they are necessary; they must be logically true (1990, 92, 106). Unlike analytic statements, a synthetic statement is a synthesis of two concepts—the subject with a new predicate, the content of which is not subsumed in the subject. Synthetic propositions are a posteriori statements of fact pertaining to external reality. It is on the basis of empirical facts, not logic, that such statements are refuted (1990, 91–93). They cannot be proved and are said to be contingent. They "*happen to be* true—but they do not *have to be* true" (1990, 92; italics in original). They can never be certain. All that can be claimed is some degree of probability.

The A-S dichotomy offers two alternatives. If a proposition is proven, it provides no information about reality. If it is about reality, it is incapable of being proven (1990, 93–94; cf. Weatherford 1982, 205).

Concept Formation: Objectivist View

According to Objectivist epistemology, a concept is formed by cognitively isolating two or more existents that share similar characteristics that differentiate them from other existents in reality and mentally integrating the existents into a single unit that is assigned a perceptual symbol (i.e., a word) (Peikoff 1990, 97–98). The essential characteristics, or essences, on which concepts are based are contextual. They are derived on the basis of all the available information pertinent to the existents at the time the concept is formed. Unlike Platonic and Aristotelian philosophy, Objectivism regards the essences as epistemological not metaphysical (1990, 102; Younkins, "Menger, Mises, Rand, and Beyond," 2005, 337, 369–70). The concept *means* the existents in reality that the concept subsumes, and it encompasses *all* of the characteristics of the existents (Peikoff 1990, 98). This includes all of the characteristics known at the time the concept is formed as well as those yet to be discovered. Concepts are open ended, as is all knowledge (1990, 99). That is, unlike the position of many philosophies, Objectivist epistemology does not limit concepts to its defining characteristics. This is the reason why a given concept can have different definitions depending upon context (1990, 103).

A-S Dichotomy and Objectivist Epistemology

According to Peikoff, the A-S dichotomy suffers from both epistemological and metaphysical errors. One of the main *epistemological* errors is that Objectivists see no basis for making a distinction between analytic and synthetic propositions (1990, 100). This is because the view of "concept" held by most conventional philosophers is not correct (1990, 106). To Objectivists, analytic propositions cannot be validated, as conventional philosophers suggest, merely by an analysis of its concepts separate from reality. Concepts are formed and validated by observing reality. For the analytic proposition: "Man is a rational animal," the meaning of the concept, "man," is not "rational animal," but all of the existents in reality that are subsumed by the concept. For a synthetic proposition such as: "A man has only two eyes," (1990, 100) the predicate, "only two eyes," is said by conventional theory to provide new information that is not included in the subject "man." However, according to Peikoff, the subject "man" encompasses all men, including all of their characteristics, both known and the yet to be known.

The distinction that is relevant, according Ayn Rand, is between *metaphysical* facts and *man-made* facts. By metaphysical, she means facts inherent in the nature of that which exists. A metaphysical fact is that the earth is orbited by a single moon. Man-made facts are those that result from the application of human action (Rand, "The Metaphysical Versus the Man-Made," 1982, 27, 1990, 110). A man-made fact is not metaphysically necessary. For instance, that the United States has fifty states is a man-made fact. Even so, it is and remains necessarily *true* as long as man does not alter it (Rand, "The Metaphysical Versus the Man-Made," 1982, 28, 31, 1990, 111).

Concepts of Consciousness

A concept *means* the existents in reality that are mentally integrated in the concept's formation. This is the link between epistemology and metaphysics. A concept, for example, "chair," is formed by observing concretes with similar characteristics. The concretes are grasped at man's perceptual level of consciousness. A higher-level concept, such as "furniture," is a more abstract concept. Higher-level concepts subsume lower-level concepts. Furniture subsumes not only chairs but other structures as well (Rand 1990, 22).

There is a category of concepts called concepts of consciousness that pertain to the product of man's mental processes. For instance, the sciences of physics and chemistry would be examples of this category of concepts. These concepts do not refer to physical existents in reality, but to the products of the abstract thought that are related to the scientific disciplines. A subcategory of concepts of consciousness is concepts of method. These concepts "designate systematic courses of action devised by men for the purpose of achieving certain goals" (1990, 35). Infinity is a concept of method. Infinity is not a concept of units that exist in reality. It is an epistemological/mathematical device that is used to achieve certain computational ends. Its meaning is limited to those contexts (1990, 305).

THREE DEFINITIONS OF PROBABILITY

Subjectivist Theory of Probability

According to Roy Weatherford (1982, 9), the trajectory of the theoretical development of the Subjectivist theory of probability (STP) is from Frank P. Ramsey to Bruno de Finetti to Leonard J. Savage. Crovelli (2012, 164) credits Augustus De Morgan with articulating the subjectivist interpretation several decades prior to that of de Finetti. Weatherford gives the definition of subjective probability as "the degree of belief of a given person in a given proposition" (1982, 9; cf. Crovelli; 2009, 6, 2010, 15). According to adherents of the theory, "objective probabilities" do not exist, or, at a minimum, they have less significance than do subjective probabilities (Crovelli 2012, 163–65). Personal or subjectivist probabilities are estimated by utilizing Behavioristic methods; that is, by observing behavior, particularly in betting situations (Weatherford 1982, 10, 221–25). Both experimental psychologists and decision theorists have designed methods for estimation which involve conducting a series of small wagers and comparing results (Winston and

Albright 1997, 406–409; Kruschke 2011, 28–29). However, there are no set rules for adjusting subjective probabilities (Weatherford 1982, 224).

One advantage of subjective probabilities is that they can be used for initial probabilities, which permits expanded use of Bayes' Theorem (1982, 225–26, 232). One of the chief criticisms of STP is that it confuses opinion with fact. It's true that differences in odds are real, and these are based, to a large extent, on differences in opinions among people (1982, 238; Jetton 1994, 12; Chou 1969, 124). However, it is also the case that some probabilities are more accurate than others, as in the case of the toss of a balanced coin. In such a case, it would be an error to give the odds as 4 to 1 (Weatherford 1982, 239; Mises [1951] 1968, 164–66).

Classical Theory of Probability

The Classical theory of probability (CTP) defines probability as a fraction, the numerator of which is all of the cases that fit a given description and the denominator of which is the total number of equipossible alternatives (Weatherford 1982, 6–7, 26). The CTP identifies probability with chance (Chou 1969, 121). The calculus of probability is the same for all major theories. One of the chief differences among the theories is the calculation of initial probabilities (Weatherford 1982, 28). Early investigations into probability dealt with games of chance, such as throws of dice. Each side of a (balanced) die has an equal probability of turning up when the die is tossed. Thus, the initial probability for a given side is 1/6. From observations of this kind, James Bernoulli devised the rule for initial probabilities, often referred to as the Principle of Indifference, an expression that refers to John Maynard Keynes' suggestion that "*alternatives are always to be judged equiprobable if we have no reason to expect or prefer one over another*" (Weatherford 1982, 29; italics in original). This a priori proposition formed the basis for most of the early theorems in probability theory.

Relative Frequency Theory

Relative Frequency theory (RFT) defines probability as the limit of the relative frequency of an attribute in a random collective (Chou 1969, 123–24). It is the limit of the ratio of the presence of an attribute in one infinite class in another infinite class (Weatherford 1982, 6). (As pointed out by Jaynes [2003, 166], the appropriate calculation is the limit of the ratio, not the ratio of the limits [cf. Weatherford 1982, 149].) In addition to Richard von Mises, Hans Reichenbach is also credited with being chiefly responsible for developing the theory (Weatherford 1982, 148; Mises [1951] 1968, 169, 1957, 11–22, 28; Howden 2009, 3n4; Crovelli 2009, 3n2). Ludwig von Mises advocated a theory of probability that was essentially the same as his brother's (Mises [1949] 1996, 105–18; Crovelli 2009, 2–3; cf. Howden 2009, 2n1). (Ludwig von Mises also advanced the notion of "case probabilities" (Mises [1949] 1996, 113–15; Crovelli 2010, 6; Howden 2009, 6; Hoppe 1997, 71.)

RF theorists take the position that the theorems on which probability theory is based are analytic; however, a probability per se is a synthetic statement that is empirically derived (Weatherford 1982, 9). RFT probabilities can be only approximations. The true RFT probability cannot be known because of the problem of infinity; that is, the limit of the series must be reached for the probability to be known (Weatherford 1982, 131–32). As the number of observations increases, the relative frequency tends to become increasingly stable (1982, 148). The question that arises is how many observations are sufficient (1982, 159). A strict adherence to the RFT definition would indicate that no RFT statement can apply to any finite group of observations (1982, 148, 169–70). Furthermore, any finite RFT value would be consistent with any limit if one did exist. Any ratio based on a finite sample is always insignificant relative to infinity. Thus, *any* relative frequency based on a finite group of observations is compatible with any limit for an entire series (1982, 202). If upon repeated trials, empirical observations fail to conform to relative frequency predictions, this does not refute the theory (1982, 200). Thus, RFT probability statements can neither be confirmed nor refuted.

If a limit does exist, it includes all occurrences of all the events that have ever existed—for instance, all red giants relative to all stars till the end of time. There is only one such value, which is constant and immutable (1982, 177–78, 216). Since limits cannot change, Richard von Mises acknowledged that all that can be changed are estimates or beliefs about what the actual probabilities are (Weatherford 1982, 178; Mises [1951] 1968, 172). If it is possible to ignore the philosophical objections associated with a limit being embedded in an empirical definition, the greatest virtue of RFT probabilities is that their calculation reflects characteristics exhibited in the external world (Weatherford 1982, 160, 168, 185, 205; Jetton 1994, 24). RFT is capable of handling not only probabilities associated with balanced dice and other games of chance but also unbalanced dice. It addition, RFT can estimate probabilities related to mortality and other actuarial risks and can deal with scientific statistics as well (Weatherford 1982, 209, 218).

Relative Frequency vs. A Priori Probabilities

RFT probabilities are advocated because they are based on actual rates of occurrence of some reality-based characteristic found in the external world (1982, 8). In RFT, knowledge of probabilities is synthetic. RFT probabilities are empirically based (1982, 193, 201; Carnap 1945, 522). They are only known a posteriori (Weatherford 1982, 157, 192). They are "contingent"; that is, their properties cannot be known a priori. RFT probabilities are neither confirmable nor falsifiable (1982, 201, 205, 208). They are subject to the same disadvantage as all empirical statements "in being sometimes false, often unknown, and never certain" (1982, 125).

Unlike RFT probabilities, which are empirical and contingent, CTP probabilities are based on abstract, analytic propositions that are logically true a priori (1982, 62). The logical statements or equations on which the theorems are deduced are empty in the sense that they are unrelated to the external world (1982, 192). A priori probability statements are verified by laws of logic and mathematics, not by experience (1982, 191, 205). If proven, they are "certain" and "necessarily true" (1982, 192, 208); however, they provide no information about the world (1982, 126, 205; Carnap 1945, 522).

Three Epistemological Categories

This subsection will briefly review theory, prediction, and empirical findings ("reality"). It is not meant to be definitive or comprehensive. Its purpose is merely to provide a framework for a later discussion of the proposed definition of the concept of probability within the contexts of these three categories.

Theory endeavors to uncover relationships that are universally true or generally true under given conditions. One definition of theory is that it is a set of coherent propositions. Propositions are statements that describe relationships among concepts (Zikmund 1997, 24). Theory is often advanced by the development of theoretical models. Models are built by isolating a number of relevant concepts. A theoretical model may take the form of a proposition or propositions that state relationships between or among concepts that are true, given certain conditions or constraints.

In some cases, concepts can be translated into variables, and the models can be transformed into algorithms or equations that hold under certain conditions. In turn, algorithmic models may be applied to real-world situations, including what may be expected to happen in the future. This is the predictive aspect of epistemology. Prediction often incorporates both theory (models) and empirics (data). For example, for a generic theoretical economic model, prediction would use empirical (ex ante) data to estimate the coefficients of an equation in which forecasted data is inserted into the variables. The predictive model is designed to approximate real-world occurrences against which ex post empirically derived values are compared. Predicted values may not equal ex ante results. If there is a significant difference between the model prediction and the outcome, it could be the result of a poor model (for instance, it may have been misspecified), or the data used to estimate the coefficients of the model may have been inadequate, or data used as input for the variables of the model may have been in some way lacking, or there may have been an unexpected occurrence (sometimes referred to as an exogenous "shock") that would not happen under ordinary circumstances, or there may be some combination of these.

The ex ante figures are "approximate" (i.e., they approximate ex post values) in part because typically they are based on models that take into account only those variables that reasonably can be expected to be of relevance. However, there may be other variables that could affect the outcome. The relationships described by the theoretical and predictive models are based on certain assumptions. Among these assumptions are that some variables remain constant. That is, it is assumed that some variables that could affect the outcome of the relationships of the variables that are isolated in the theoretical context do not change. One of the contexts, for instance, could be the time period under consideration. Some variables reasonably may be assumed to remain constant for a given period of time. Other variables that either are held constant or omitted altogether may include a vast number that could affect the outcome of the relationship(s) of the variables under consideration, but would be very unlikely to occur under most circumstances or would be impossible to predict (e.g., an innovation).

Prediction is the link between theory and the empirical results (reality). Theory aims for universal truths that may exist within constraints. Theory may take the form of models; however, a predictive equation may not mirror its theoretical counterpart. In economic theory, some theoretical equations may be more complex than the predictive counterparts (or vice versa). In most cases, predictive economic models are more specific (to product, industry, time period, etc.) than the theoretical model. For example, the predictive variables tend to be more specific than the concepts that they represent. Predictive equations may only replicate reality in a very narrow sense. For instance, in tracking radar, a second-degree polynomial equation can be used to approximate the curvature of the earth (Keene and Varnado 1964, 6).

Theoretical models abstract from and simplify reality. Even a mathematical concept as basic as counting involves abstraction. Counting (i.e., addition) is fundamental to the theory of probability as well as to its application. The assumption underlying addition is "likeness" of the entities that are counted. This assumption is fundamental to the CTP definition. CTP applies to games of chance. All sides of a die are assumed to be identically alike except for the numbers attached to them. If in reality all sides are not equal due to biasness, the CTP definition fails to predict adequately. For example, if side 6 is weighted more heavily than the other sides, and 1/6 is used to predict the outcome for side 6 for a large number of tosses of the die, the outcome will very likely not equal or be close to 1/6. The assumption on which the sum in the denominator is based is violated because all sides are not alike (Weatherford

1982, 6–7, 26). When categories are somewhat dissimilar, one does not abandon the arithmetic of addition; another approach to probability (prediction) may be used—for instance, the RFT.

The RFT approach can be useful in predicting proportions for an unbalanced die—that is, when there is variation between or among categories. It reframes the "category" as being based on the number of tosses rather than the number of sides and can work well so long as "other things remain constant." The RFT approach is also useful in prediction for cases in which there are variations within a given category or for a given concept. As the saying goes, "You can't add apples and oranges." And, at times, you can't even add oranges and oranges. For instance, an owner of a grocery chain might predict for each store the proportion of oranges that are expected to be unsold (and disposed of). His predictions could be "off" because oranges were assumed to be identical. If the prediction is "wrong," this does not mean that the rules of addition should be abandoned. Nor does it mean that the concept of "orange" needs to be re-defined. It may mean that oranges need to be categorized by an attribute that in some way fits the context—for example, by freshness (age), size (weight), or type (Valencia, navel, etc.), etc.

The RFT approach can be useful for prediction for unbalanced dice or for actuarial tables. However, the RFT suffers from the conceptual problem of incorporating the concept of infinity in its definition of probability. Infinity does not exist in reality. In the real world, counting is possible, but counting to infinity is not. Reality cannot bend to conform to theory—which is what the RFT definition of probability appears to require. The remedy to this problem does not involve abandoning infinity as a theoretical concept. Infinity is useful within the context of the theoretical rules of probability. Nor does it mean abandoning the relative frequency approach to prediction. As will be discussed below, when a probability is seen as a predictor (a proportion used to predict), the concept of infinity can apply because prediction is a bridge between theory and empirical results. Infinity cannot apply to empirical results, however.

In the next section, the proposed concept of probability is presented and will be addressed in relation to the three epistemological categories mentioned here. Also discussed with regard to the proposed definition will be the concept of infinity and how it relates to the three categories.

PROPOSED DEFINITION OF THE CONCEPT OF PROBABILITY

This section presents my proposed definition of the concept of probability. The concept is discussed in the context of examples based on "orthodox theory," which, according to E. T. Jaynes, is based on the rival schools of thought of R. A. Fisher and of J. Neyman and E. S. Pearson (Jaynes 2003, 492). The Neyman-Pearson school is associated with confidence intervals and hypothesis tests, which enter into the discussions that follow.

Probability theory and its application are utilized by humans to deal with aspects of uncertainty as they apply to the future. My view is that one of the foundational elements that is lacking in probability theory is an overarching definition of the concept of probability; one that is general enough to encompass many of the existing definitions of probability and their applications (with qualifications). I propose the following definition of the concept of probability: a proportion (or a range of proportions) that is used to predict a proportion that measures the presence or absence of a characteristic or event that is of an either/or nature. By "predict" I mean a value that is used to estimate another value, one that is typically not known at the time of prediction. The terms "estimate," "predict," and "forecast" have specific meanings in given contexts and are sometimes used interchangeably. By estimate I mean that an ex ante proportion(s) is/are used to predict an ex post proportion(s). Within the confines of the proposed definition of the concept described above, the former proportions are probabilities and the latter proportions are not. Ex post means "after the fact." Usually, the actual or "ex post" proportions are not known at the time of prediction. In some cases, to "test" how well a predictor predicts, it will be used to estimate an "ex post" value that is already known. Nevertheless, the primary purpose of predictors is to estimate values that are unknown at the time of prediction.

In the binomial example discussed below, "probability," *P*, is used to designate the percentage of a theoretical distribution out of all possible outcomes that corresponds to a particular outcome or a range of outcomes. The *P* values are theoretical "probabilities." (Conventional theory refers to these as probabilities; however, they would be considered probabilities under the proposed definition only if they were used in prediction. Quotation marks are used to indicate conventional usage.) The "probability," *p*, is used to denote the proportion of a specific characteristic that is present in a collective, such as the proportion of white balls out of a total number of balls in a population, *N*. As mentioned below in the binomial example, this *p* value is equal to the expected value of a theoretical distribution. The expected value is often employed in prediction, and when it is, it is a probability. However, I also use *p* to represent the proportion of a specific characteristic that is present for a given trial (sample), *n*. (Below, I attach additional notations to *p*, depending upon the context, to add clarity.)

When a proportion is used in prediction, it is a probability, whether it is used in a theoretical context or in the prediction of an actual proportion.

Rather than modifying the word "prediction" by the qualifiers "theoretical" and "actual," when I use the word prediction, I mean the use of proportions in the prediction of an *actual* proportion unless stated otherwise. Under the proposed definition, the probability is a proportion used in prediction. If it is not used to predict, it is not a probability. To clarify this point, Weatherford indicated that according to the frequency definition, to claim that *the probability of a star being a red giant is 0.02* would require observing all red giants relative to all stars until the end of time. That is, in an infinite sequence of observed stars, the proportion of red giants would approach 0.02 in the limit (Weatherford 1982, 181). Of course, this kind of *empirical* observation is not possible; however, if it could be undertaken, .02, or 2%, would not be a probability as Weatherford suggested insofar as the proposed definition is concerned. This is because at the end of time there would be no need to predict the future proportion of red giants. The value, .02, which would be known, would be a proportion, not a probability.

With regard to the proposed concept, relative frequencies can be utilized as probabilities, whether derived within a theoretical context or based on empirical data. Theoretical probabilities (i.e., proportions used to predict "future" proportions) based on infinity do fit within the proposed concept. An example below presents a theoretical binomial distribution, which is a limit for a distribution based on theoretical relative frequencies. Relative frequencies based on actual data may also serve as probabilities as discussed below. However, the proposed concept is not limited to the frequency definition. For example, the frequency definition rules out probabilities based on continuous distributions as well as irrational probabilities (Weatherford 1982, 59), which the proposed concept does not.

The proportion need not be a "good" predictor. If it is used to predict, it is nevertheless a probability. In general, a concept may have various definitions depending upon the context. There are many definitions of probability, any one of which may have some utility in given a context. For instance, although subjective probabilities may be at odds with probabilities that are based on empirical evidence—such as relative frequencies, individuals do *act* on subjective probabilities, as behavioral studies indicate. There may be better or worse approaches to probability theory and application. Nevertheless, individuals under some circumstances may not choose the better or the best methodology for decision-making. This may be because the individuals are not rational, or it may be because they do not have the time or resources to employ the best method and must rely on the "best" given the constraints. The proposed definition of the concept of probability is not one that advocates a "best" theory of probability (cf. Jaynes 2003, 420). It is descriptive, not normative.

Example Using the Binomial Distribution

In the following, I examine how the proposed definition relates to a binomial distribution problem. After that, I also relate the proposed definition to an example involving the normal distribution. Both of these distributions are commonly employed. The normal distribution has unique properties; for example, the next subsection dealing with confidence (prediction) intervals is specific to the normal distribution (Jaynes 2003, 199, 210, 214, 240–41).

The following is a typical example using the binomial distribution which will provide a framework for discussing the definition of the concept of probability that I have proposed. It assumes a population, *N*, of 5 balls, one of which is white and the others black. A sample size, $n = 3$, is assumed. Because it is assumed that there will be replacement during sampling, the population size in effect is infinite. The number of possible samples (sample outcome combinations) of sample size three is $2^3 = 8$. It is further assumed the event of interest is the number of white balls per sample. Each ball is equally likely to be chosen in a sample.

The probability, *P*, that *X* white balls out of *n* will be selected, where *p* is the proportion of white balls and $(1 - p)$ is the proportion of black balls is given by the formula (Shao 1976, 222, 237; Chou 1969, 146):

$$P(X;n,p) = \binom{n}{X} p^X (1-p)^{n-X}$$

$$\binom{n}{X} = n!/\left[X!(n-X)!\right].$$

In order to clarify the concept of probability that I have proposed within the context of existing theory, in the following I specify the population proportion as *pp* (which was shown formerly in the above equations as *p*), the sample proportion as *ps*, the population proportion when used as a probability as *ppp*, the sample proportion when used as a probability as *psp*, the actual population proportion as *ppa*, and the actual sample proportion as *psa*. The probabilities, *ppp* and *psp*, are ex ante values. The actual values, *ppa* and *psa*, are ex post.

The sample proportion, *ps*, values are 0/3, 1/3, 2/3, and 3/3, for which the respective theoretical "probability" distribution, *P* values, are 0.512, 0.384, 0.096, and 0.008. That is, the "probabilities," *P* values, are the percentages of the 8 sample outcome combinations for which there are, respectively, 0, 1, 2, and 3 white balls out of a sample of size $n = 3$ (Shao 1976, 237–38). For instance, the *P* value of 0.096 indicates of all the 8 sample combinations of sample size 3, the proportion for which there are 2 white balls is 9.6%; where *pp*, the proportion of white balls in the population, is 1/5. (When a proportion is expressed in percentage terms, it is specified with the percent sign, %. It is otherwise expressed as a decimal or a fraction.) That is, there are 3 sample combinations for which it is possible to draw 2 white balls out of $n = 3$ balls: WWB, WBW, and BWW. The associated "probability" of these 3 sample combinations out of 8 in total is: $P(2; 3, 1/5) = 3!/[2!(3 - 2)!](1/5)^2(4/5)^{3-2} =$ 0.096. The outcome of *ps* = 2/3 has a low relative frequency (*P*) and would be relatively unlikely to occur for a given sample. However, 2/3 is still an outcome that would be consistent with the theory.

In theory, on repeated trials, the "expected outcome" would be 1/5 and is equal to the proportion of white balls in the population, *pp*, which is (0/3)(0.512) + (1/3)(0.384) + (2/3)(0.096) + (3/3)(0.008) = 0.20. The *ppp* of 1/5 can be used as a predictor of the proportion of white balls in a sample (*psa*) selected from the population. However, when the sample size is small, the *ppp* will not be a good predictor of the sample proportion (*psa*). In this example, *ppp* = 1/5 is not a good predictor of *psa*, because for $n = 3$, there is no sample for which it is possible to have an outcome (*psa*) of 1/5 or 0.20. With a sample size of 3, 0/3 is the proportion of white balls that has the highest percentage of occurrence, *P*, equal to 51.2% for the 8 possible sample outcome combinations. The *ppp* of 0.20 becomes a possible predictor of the *psa* with a larger sample size. For $n = 10$, the sample proportion, *ps*, = 2/10 occurs with a *P* of 30.2% of the distribution, which is the largest percentage for that distribution (Chapman and Schaufele 1970, 323). For $n = 20$, the sample proportion, *ps*, = 4/20 occurs with a *P* of 21.82%, which is the largest percentage for that distribution (Shao 1976, 243).

As *n* increases, the proportion of the distribution, *P*, becomes smaller for the sample proportion = .20. However, the proportion of the distribution becomes larger for a given interval; that is, for a constant error, *E*. For example, for $n = 10$ and an *E* of 0.20, the interval 0.20 ± (2/10), or 0 through 0.40, corresponds to a percentage of the distribution equal to 96.6% (Chapman and Schaufele 1970, 323). For $n = 20$, the interval is 0.20 ± (4/20), which corresponds to 99.0% of the distribution (1970, 326; Shao 1976, 243). The advantage of a larger sample size, *n*, is that, if the population proportion is known, then it (*ppp*) plus and minus an error, that is *ppp* ± *E*, becomes a better predictor of the sample proportion, *psa*, in that the error becomes smaller for a given percentage of the distribution. What this example also illustrates is that if the population proportion, *pp*, is unknown, then the sample proportion, *psp*, becomes a better predictor of *pp* for a given *P* (in that *E* decreases) as *n* increases.

As the sample size, *n*, increases, the closer the binomial distribution, which is discrete, approximates the normal distribution, which is continuous (Shao 1976, 247). An advantage of using the standard normal distribution in prediction is that it is a single distribution that does not change with sample size.

Normal Distribution and the Proposed Concept

For a binomial distribution, a "probability," P, can be calculated for a single outcome, *ps*. In the case of a normal distribution, the "probability," P, is calculated for an interval of outcomes (*ps* values), not for a specific outcome (a single *ps*). A probability interval (a proportion $\pm E$) can be used in prediction, where E corresponds (for a given n, as explained below) to a percentage of the distribution, P. A typical value for the percentage of the distribution is 95%. The 95% is the "probability," P, associated with the interval estimate.

A standard normal distribution is a theoretical distribution that has a population mean, μ, of zero and a standard deviation, σ, equal to one. The population, N, is assumed to be infinite. When dealing with proportions, the relevant distribution is the sampling distribution (Zikmund 1997, 462–64). The sampling distribution is a theoretical distribution based on a population, N, from which samples of size n are drawn, and approximates a normal distribution as the sample size, n, increases. A sampling distribution is relevant, because it is necessary to have a collective in order to compute a proportion.

When the population proportion, *pp*, is known, *ppp* can be used to predict a sample proportion, *psa*. Typically, a test is performed after the sample of size n is taken to find if *psa* is significantly different from *ppp* for a given percentage of the distribution, say 95%. An error, E, is added to and subtracted from *ppp* to obtain a confidence interval (critical limits), and if the *psa* falls within the limits, then it is concluded that there is no significant difference between *ppp* and *psa*. The E for the interval is equal to ZS_p, where Z is the number of standard errors from the population mean for the standard normal distribution. For example, a Z-value of 1.96 corresponds to approximately 95% of the distribution. S_p is the standard error of the proportion (Zikmund 1997, 577). S_p is a function of n and is approximated by $\sqrt{[p(1-p)/n]}$ (for n of 100 or greater), where the p value in the equation for S_p is based on the sample proportion, *psa* (Shao 1976, 316, 334, 336).

Another way of expressing this result is that if the *psa* is found to be within the interval, then the probability interval could be said to have been a "good" predictor, given the criteria on which the prediction was based. However, the problem with this statement is that the interval for *ppp* relies on sample results—specifically, to compute S_p. To use an "interval approach" in *prediction* using *pp* would require using the population proportion, *pp*, in the equation $\sqrt{[p(1-p)/n]}$ instead of *psa* (Shao 1976, 316–17). The closer *pp* is to .50, the larger the prediction interval will be (Shao 1976, 336; see Chapman and Schaufele 1970, 114).

The sample size, n, must be decided upon before the sample is taken, and therefore before the sample proportion, *psa*, is known. The equation $n = Z^2(p)(1-p)/(E)^2$ is often used for a simple random sample (Zikmund 1997, 475).

When determining the sample size, n, the E that is chosen is based on a judgment call. In the case in which the population proportion, *pp*, is known, the value of p in the equation for n would be based on *pp*. A rule of thumb that is employed for checking whether the sample size is too small is (1) multiply n by *pp*, and (2) multiply n by (1 – *pp*). If either (1) or (2) is equal to 5 or less, then n is too small for the standard normal distribution test (*Z*-test), in which case a *t*-test could be used (Zikmund 1997, 578).

Often the population proportion, *pp*, is not known. Thus, the population proportion (*ppp*) cannot be used to predict the proportion for a sample (*psa*) taken from the population. However, once the sample is taken, the sample proportion (*psp*) can be used to predict the population proportion (*ppa*). The *psp* is the probability in this case. An interval of *psp* ± *E* can be used to predict the *ppa*, which, as mentioned, is not known at the time of prediction. For instance, suppose *psp* is used in to predict *ppa*, the proportion of white balls within a population of white and black balls, and the *pp* is unknown. In calculating the sample size, *n,* when *pp* (the proportion of white balls) is not known, a proportion of 50% may be chosen as a rule of thumb. (The reason 50% is often chosen is because of all the possible proportions, it will result in the largest sample size.) Assuming that an E of 5% is acceptable, the n would be equal to $(1.96)^2(.5)(1 - .5)/(.05)^2 \approx 384$ for a random sample with replacement. If the *psp* were 85/384, then the population proportion (*ppa*) would be expected to fall within $0.22 \pm 1.96\sqrt{[(0.22)(0.78)/384]}$, or an interval of 0.178 to 0.262, with 95% probability.

This interval can be checked against the actual population proportion of white to total balls (*ppa*) if and when available. Suppose the population, $N = 5$, is the number of white and black balls that are in a bin from which the sample was drawn. In this case, the *ppa* of white balls to total balls is easily discovered by simply looking at the balls in the bin. If there were one white and four black balls in the bin, then it could be said that the probability interval, *psp* ± *E*, was a "good" predictor of the population proportion of white balls in that *ppa* of 0.20 fell within the interval.

If instead of 85/384, the *psp* had been 19/384, or approximately 5%, then that would be a very unlikely occurrence and not reflect the *ppa*. As mentioned before, a result such as 19/384 is theoretically possible, although unlikely given the assumptions underlying the distribution. However, if one of the assumptions was violated, there could be some other reason for the "unlikely" outcome. In that case, the sample proportion, or probability, would be capturing something in addition to the attribute color. If, say, the white ball was the size of a ping pong ball and the black balls were the size of basketballs, then it might be less likely to select a white ball from a bin one-fifth of the time on repeated trials. That is, there would be some other variable, size, that is affecting the outcome. A truly random procedure would require that all balls be exactly the same except for color. In this case, color is related in some way to another variable, size. Size is biasing the selection process. Because color and size are related, size cannot be assumed the same for all colors. Therefore, the interval (*psp* ± *E*) would be a poor predictor of the proportion of white balls in the population (*ppa*).

The question is—what is the objective of the prediction? If the objective is to predict the proportion of white balls in the population of $N = 5$, then the *psp* will be a poor predictor if the balls vary in size. However, if the objective is to predict future sample proportions (based on draws from the bin), the *psp* may be an adequate predictor so long as other things that could affect the outcome do not change. In cases for which a number of variables affect the probability, one method of handling this is collecting and sorting frequency data by reference class when this is possible. For life insurance, the relevant reference, or risk, class has to be identified in order to predict future death rates (proportions) based on known relative frequencies (Weatherford 1982, 160).

Infinity and the Proposed Concept Definition

As discussed, infinity has been problematic for the RFT. Infinity is a theoretical and not an empirical concept. Of the three epistemological categories considered here—theory, prediction, and actual results—the concept of infinity applies to the first. It can also have a place in prediction because the latter can involve theoretical constructs or algorithms which utilize the concept of infinity.

The concept of infinity is utilized in probability theory in a number of contexts. One includes the assumption of an infinite population—for instance, when it is assumed that there is a finite population, *N*, and there is sampling with replacement. Another is the assumption of an infinite sample size, *n*. In the binomial distribution example considered above, the "probability" of white balls (based on the proportion of white balls out of five balls) is 1/5. Given $n = 3$, the theoretical distribution using the combinatorial approach is based on an infinite population on the assumption of sampling with replacement. The expected value of the distribution is .20. As *n* increases, the binomial distribution approximates a normal distribution.

Because in practice, prediction utilizes aspects of theory, the concept of infinity is routinely used in prediction. For instance, for a game of chance, say, in predicting the proportion of sixes in repeated tosses of a die, the predictor (i.e., probability) reasonably could be based on the proportion of sixes out of the total number of sides of a die; that is, 1/6, under the assumption of a balanced die. For cases in which *pp* is unknown, *ps* could be used to predict *pp*. Whether *pp* is known or unknown, an error, *E*, can be added or subtracted from the proportion used for prediction (probability) to arrive at a prediction interval for the actual proportion under consideration. For example, if *pp* is unknown, the error, *E*, could be added to and subtracted from *psp* to arrive at a prediction interval for *pp*. For the standard normal distribution the *E*, equal to ZS_p, would be expected to decrease with an increase in *n* for a given *P*. The *Z*-value is dependent upon the proportion of the distribution, say *P* = 95%, that is selected. That distribution is theoretically based on the concept of infinity.

The actual value, *pa*, is finite. It is a proportion, not a probability (unless and until it is used to predict another proportion). And once *pa* is arrived at, it is known. The actual value is what it is. Similarly, with repeated trials, a relative frequency distribution based on actual data can be constructed and may be compared with a theoretical distribution. The theoretical distribution is based on an infinite population (where for a binomial distribution a finite population, *N*, is assumed to be sampled for a sample size *n* with replacement, or a normal distribution is approximated as *n* increases). The actual relative frequency distribution is based on actual data at a point in time, which may be collected over a period of time, but not an infinite time period.

True Probability and the Proposed Concept Definition

In conventional theory, the "inherent" or "true" probability is the value that the *observed* relative frequency approaches as *n* increases (Jetton 1994, 3; Weatherford 1982, 170). Within the context of the proposed concept, the idea of a "true probability" is solely a theoretical abstraction. It is a value that exists under certain assumptions. For instance, in the example described above, the number of white balls as a proportion of the total number of balls in the population is 1/5. For a theoretical binomial distribution, for a given sample size, *n*, the expected value of the "probability" distribution will equal 1/5. The "true probability" exists in theory, and it is equal to 1/5. The "true probability" is one for which the probability (proportion used to predict) equals the proportion based on the outcome of a repeated (infinite) number of trials.

More to the point, in the case of simple probabilities, by which I mean a probability for which an event can be "described by a single characteristic," the "true" probability would be one for which the proportion of a characteristic within a population, *N* (which would be the proportion that is used in prediction), equals the "long-run" proportion for the event (the expected value of the distribution of samples of sample size *n* with replacement). The probability would be identified with chance. Returning to the die example, for a die, the percentage of a characteristic within the population would be the proportion of, say, sides of a die that are "six" out of the total number of *sides* of a die; which is one out of six. The percentage based on the event would be the proportion of tosses that are "six" out of the total number of *tosses* of a die; which in the "long run" would be 1/6. The "long run" in this case means an infinite number of tosses. As has been mentioned, infinity is a theoretical concept that applies in this context.

In the case of application, a proportion of a characteristic of a population may be used in some cases as a predictor for the proportion based on the frequency of an event. This is usually justified in predicting games of chance, for instance, tossing a balanced die. That is, the proportion of sixes out of the total number of *sides* could be used to predict the actual proportion of *tosses*. Unlike theory, in the prediction of actual proportions, there is no "true" underlying long run (where long run is infinity) proportion that is the "true" probability. The proportion used to predict is the probability, not an estimate of the probability and the actual proportion is what it is—a proportion, not a probability.

In cases in which there is an unbalanced die or in other cases in which it can be reasonably assumed that the proportion of a characteristic of a population (e.g., one side of a die—say, a six) would not equal (because of bias) the proportion based on the frequency of an event (tosses of the die), then the predictor (i.e., probability) may be based on the relative frequency for a finite group of events (tosses). For an unbalanced die, the predictor would be capturing not only the relative percentage of sixes on a die, but also the weight associated with that side of the die. That is, there is more than one variable at play and the probability is capturing both. Beyond games of chance, relative frequencies are often used in prediction. (As discussed later, for cases in which historical data is lacking—as, for instance, in utilizing Bayes' Theorem for initial or prior probabilities—equiprobability is often assumed. Bayesian posterior probabilities are a weighted combination of the prior probabilities and the likelihoods.) For example, actuarial tables based on historical data are used to predict mortality rates. Although prediction employs theoretical constructs, such as theoretical probability distributions, prediction is separate from theory. A probability (based on a relative frequency) used to predict an actual value is a predictor or estimator of the actual proportion; it is not an estimate of the probability. As such, it can be a better or worse predictor; however, unlike in theory, as stated previously, in the real world there is no "true" underlying long run (i.e., infinity) proportion (relative frequency) that is the "true probability."

The actual value, *pa*, is a proportion, not a probability (unless and until it is used to predict another proportion). Whether the actual proportion can or will be calculated is another issue. It may be too costly or technically difficult to calculate. There are also proportions ("probabilities") that are used to estimate or predict values (for instance, expected values); however, in the future, collection of the data to calculate the actual proportions is not undertaken because it is not needed, or the data is collected, but it is for a purpose that is unrelated to its use in the estimation of the expected values. For example, "probabilities" of dying and surviving taken from an existing mortality table may be used by a person to calculate his expected income (in order to make a decision on, say, how much life insurance to purchase). One of the purposes of mortality table figures is to predict future death rates. That is, they are probabilities from that perspective. However, within the context of this specific decision, once the decision maker has made his decision, he may be uninterested in what the future proportions actually are and whether data on them is actually collected. Nevertheless, the proportions that he used in the estimation of his expected income may still be regarded as probabilities based on the proposed definition. They are proportions used in prediction of future proportions. Whether or not in the future they are calculated is not relevant to their purpose. In most instances, whether they are regarded as probabilities (i.e., proportions used to predict future proportions) or are simply regarded as proportions is clear from the context for which they are utilized.

BAYESIAN ANALYSIS

The previous section dealt with "orthodox" theory as it relates to the proposed definition of the concept of probability. In this section, the focus is on the Bayesian theory. The foundation of Bayesian theory is Bayes' Theorem, which is an equation that follows from the rules of probability; specifically, it is derived from the definition for conditional probability (Kruschke 2011, 53). Typically the way in which Bayes' Theorem is presented is to point out that in research it is often the case that the probabilities that are available based on relative frequencies are not the probabilities that are desired. The desired probabilities can be attained through the application of Bayes' Theorem. The problem is that to utilize Bayes' Theorem it is also often the case that information that is needed for the equation (i.e., prior probabilities) is unavailable.

For instance, it may be known that for a deck of ten cards, the proportion of kings that are black and the proportion of queens that are black is 50%, respectively. These proportions are called likelihoods. It would be preferable to know the proportions of all black cards that are kings and queens, respectively. These are termed posterior probabilities and are not known. Bayes' Theorem can supply these; however, information that is required to utilize the theorem to calculate the posteriors is typically unavailable—the prior probabilities. The assignment of values to prior probabilities is a source of controversy in Bayes' theory.

One of the ways of approaching Bayes' Theorem is to present a simple example in order to provide a basic understanding of the equation itself. This is done in the following two examples. The first example continues with the deck of cards previously mentioned. It assumes that the priors are known. In a second example on drug testing, the priors are based on previous research. These posteriors are then compared with posteriors based on uninformed priors. In a third example, the focus shifts to distributions and how distributions change with more information; particularly, the change in the posterior relative to the prior. The balance of the discussion in this section will be related to that aspect of Bayes' theory; that is, distributions and how they change with knowledge. Probabilities based on Bayesian theory will be discussed within the context of the proposed definition of the concept of probability.

The Bayesian Equation: A Tabular Approach

In this subsection, table 7.1 will be used to illustrate Bayes' Theorem. That is, the values in column 5 (C-5) are based on the Bayesian equation:

Posterior probability = (Prior probability)(Likelihood)
/ sum[(Prior probability)(Likelihood)].

This equation is usually presented using probability notation; however, for a simple problem, it may be more easily understood using table entries. Based on the column numbers shown in table 7.1, the Bayesian equation can be re-written as:

C-5=(C-2)(C-3)/sum[(C-2)(C-3)].

Table 7.1 is based on a "population" of a deck of ten playing cards for which there are four kings and six queens (Shao 1976, 506). This information is given as ratios in column 2 (C-2), labeled as prior probabilities. There are five black cards and five red cards. Only values for the black cards are shown in table 7.1. Of the five black cards, two are kings and three are queens. These ratios are designated posterior probabilities and are shown in C-5. The

Table 7.1 Black Cards

	(1) Event	*(2) Prior prob.*	*(3) Likelihood*	*(4) Conj. prob. (2)x(3)*	*(5) Post. prob. (4)/P(B)*
(1)	K	P(K) = 4/10	P(B|K) = 2/4	P(K and B) = 2/10	P(K|B) = 2/5
(2)	Q	P(Q) = 6/10	P(B|Q) = 3/6	P(Q and B) =3/10	P(Q|B) = 3/5
(3)	Total	10/10 = 1		P(B) = 5/10	1

Computation of posterior probabilities (column 5) using Bayes' Theorem based on ten cards: kings (K) and queens (Q). (Created by the author)

number of black kings and black queens as a percentage of the total number of kings and queens, respectively, are shown as likelihoods in C-3. C-4 gives the products of the values of C-2 times C-3. (These are labeled "conjoint probabilities." A conjoint probability is "the probability of two things happening together" [Kruschke 2011, 42].) The sum of C-4 is the proportion of black cards out of the total number of cards. This sum is sometimes called the "evidence" (2011, 57–58). The values in C-5 are the posterior probabilities and are equal to the values in C-4 divided by the evidence. The evidence is referred to as a "normalizer" because when used as a denominator for the values in C-4, the results (i.e., the posterior probabilities in C-5) sum to one.

Based on the definition of probability I have suggested, these proportions would not be probabilities unless they were used in prediction. For instance, the proportion of kings, .40, may be used to predict the proportion of kings that might be selected out of repeated random draws from the deck with replacement. The percentage of kings drawn would tend to be closer to 40%, the larger the number of draws. However, predicting the proportion of kings on repeated draws has little to do with Bayes' Theorem. Typically, it is assumed in the application of Bayes' Theorem that the make-up of the underlying population is unknown. Often the prior probabilities are unknown or little is known about them. The likelihoods are based on collected data. The posteriors are a result of the application of Bayes' Rule using hypothetical priors and the likelihoods.

A Bayesian Example: Estimating Posteriors with Weakly Informed Priors

A more typical example of Bayes' Theorem than that given in table 7.1 is shown in table 7.2. Table 7.2 assumes that there is some prior information on the percentages of drug users, P(U), and nonusers, P(F), perhaps based on a previous study, and these estimates are 10% and 90%, respectively, as shown in C-2. A drug usage testing study now finds that 95%, P(Y | U), of

Table 7.2 Drug Testing Positive

	(1) Event	*(2) Prior prob.*	*(3) Likelihood*	*(4) Conj. prob. (2) × (3)*	*(5) Post. prob. (4)/P(B)*
(1)	Drug user (U)	P(U) = .10	P(Y|U) = .95	P(U and Y) = .095	P(U|Y) = .601
(2)	Drug free (F)	P(F) = .90	P(Y|F) = .07	P(F and Y) = .063	P(F|Y) = .399
(3)	Total	1.00		P(Y) = .158	1.00

Computation of posterior probabilities (column 5) using Bayes' Theorem based a hypothetical drug-testing experiment for participants testing positive who where drug users (U) and drug free (F). (Created by the author)

its participants who were drug users tested positive for the presence of drugs, and 7%, P(Y | F), of those who were drug free tested positive for drugs; which are presented in C-3. (The percentages for those that tested negative are not shown in table 7.2.) Of course, it would be preferable for a drug testing procedure to find that the respective figures where 100% and 0%, but that would rarely be the case.

Typically, one of the things a drug tester would like to know is the percentage of participants who had a "false positive"—that is, the percentage who tested positive for the presence of drugs, but were in fact not drug users, that is, P(F | Y). In order to calculate that percentage, the prior probability, P(F) = 0.90, or 90%, as shown in C-2, row 2 (R-2), is multiplied by the likelihood, P(Y | F) = 0.07 (C-3, R-2), which equals P(F and Y) = 0.063 (C-4, R-2), and this is divided by the percentage that tested positive P(Y) = 0.158 (the total shown in C-4), which gives P(F | Y) = 0.399 (C-5, R-2). That is, the estimated proportion of those testing positive while being drug free was 39.9% (Winston and Albright 1997, 435). That is, almost 40% would be falsely accused of drug use. Also, of interest to the study is the proportion of those testing positive that were drug users, which is P(U | Y) = 60.1% (C-5, R-1).

Priors make a difference. If no prior information had been available, then uninformed priors would be assumed, which would mean equiprobability for the priors (i.e., P(U) = P(F) = .50). Based on this assumption, of all of those testing positive, an estimated P(F | Y) ≈ 7% would have been drug free and an estimated P(U | Y) ≈ 93% drug users. The posterior proportions would be probabilities (based on the proposed definition) if used for prediction.

Bayesian Analysis: A Binomial Example

Unlike Orthodox analysis, Bayesian analysis does not restrict the investigation to the estimation of a specific point, but is concerned more with distributions. In his tutorial *Doing Bayesian Data Analysis,* Kruschke (2011) devoted the first part of his discussion on Bayesian analysis examining binomial

Table 7.3 A Binomial Problem

	(1) Event	*(2) Prior prob.*	*(3) Likelihood*	*(4) Conj. prob. (2) × (3)*	*(5) Post. prob. (4)/P(D)*
(1)	0.25	0.25	0.001173198	0.000293300	0.705433
(2)	0.50	0.50	0.000244141	0.000122071	0.293600
(3)	0.75	0.25	0.000001609	0.000000402	0.000967
Total		1.00	0.001418948	P(D) = 0.000415773	1.00

Computation of posterior probabilities (column 5) using Bayes' Theorem for a coin-tossing problem in which the "probability of heads" is the event (column 1). (Created by the author)

problems. His primary focus was on flipping a coin and his interest was in the probability distribution for θ, the proportion of heads. An example is given in table 7.3. C-1 gives values for three possible biases for θ: 0.25, 0.50, and 0.75; where θ = 0.50 indicates a balanced coin, other things equal (2011, 61). Note that the "event" is a *value* for the parameter θ, where θ is a probability—the probability of heads. The event is not a label, such as "Kings" or "Queens" (shown as K and Q) in table 7.1. C-2 gives the prior beliefs, p(θ), about the biases, which equal 0.25, 0.50, and 0.25 for the respective values for θ in C-1. The most weight (i.e., 0.50) is given to θ = 0.50, a fair coin. The sum of the prior probabilities in C-2 equals one. C-3 gives the likelihood values that correspond to the biases shown in C-1 based on the actual results of tossing a coin *N* times. The likelihoods are the probabilities of tossing 3 heads ($z = 3$) out of 12 tosses ($N = 12$) for the θ values in C-1. These are based on the Bernoulli likelihood function (2011, 79, 133):

$$p(z, N \mid \theta) = \theta^{z}(1-\theta)^{(N-z)}.$$

For instance, for θ = .5, the likelihood is: $(0.5)^3 \times (0.5)^9 = 0.125 \times 0.001953125 = 0.000244141$, which is shown in C-3, R-2. C-4 gives the conjoint probabilities, equal to C-2 times C-3. The sum of C-4 is the "evidence." The posteriors, shown in C-5, are the respective conjoint probabilities in C-4 divided by the evidence. The sum of the posteriors equals one.

According to Kruschke (2011, 62), Bayesian probabilities reveal how much prior beliefs change. The posterior probability of 0.705433 (C-5, R-1) is the revised believability that the probability of heads is 0.25. The prior believability for θ = 0.25 was 0.25 (C-1, R-1). Considerably more weight is given to the bias of the coin being 0.25 after the introduction of new information (based on the actual sample data) than initially was thought.

Binomial Examples Using Beta Prior Distributions

Typically, likelihood functions are associated with conjugate prior distributions, which results in a posterior distribution having a functional form that is the same as the prior (2011, 67). For binomial problems, such as coin tosses, the beta distribution is a conjugate prior for a Bernoulli likelihood (2011, 159). For a coin toss for which the probability of heads is θ, a beta($\theta \mid a, b$) prior is one for which a and b are the number of heads and tails, respectively; $n = (a + b)$ is the hypothetical sample size for the prior; and the prior mean is the percentage of heads for the prior sample and is equal to: $m = a/(a + b)$. The posterior distribution is beta($\theta \mid a + z, N - b + z$), and the mean of the posterior is $(z + a)/(N + a + b)$, where z is the number of the heads in the actual sample of size N (2011, 81–84). (Note that n and N ordinarily denote the sample and population sizes, respectively. In the Bayesian discussion, n and N represent the prior sample size and the actual sample size, respectively. Note also, one of the alternative notations for beta($\theta | a, b$) is beta($\theta; a, b$).)

A major criticism of Bayesian probabilities is that they are based on priors that are often "subjective," in the sense that they are not "known frequencies" based on previous research (Jaynes 2003, 419–20). The priors are said to represent the degree of knowledge about the value of the parameter θ. For a binomial problem, complete ignorance would be represented by a uniform distribution, beta($\theta | 1, 1$). This is referred to as an uninformed prior. The values for a and b increase with knowledge, which translates into a more informed prior distribution. Whether uninformed or informed, priors have less influence on the results (i.e., the posteriors) the larger the sample size N. That is, in Bayesian analysis, "knowledge" enters in two ways: through information regarding the prior distribution and through the amount of empirical data.

In *Bayesian Basics*, Clark (2015) discussed three possible binomial problems. The first had a prior of beta($\theta | 10, 10$)—that is, the prior was centered at $\theta = 0.5$. He assumed an actual sample size of $N = 10$ observations. The second problem had a vague prior of beta($\theta | 2, 2$) with $N = 10$. The third had the same prior as that for the first example, beta($\theta | 10, 10$), but had a larger actual sample size than $N = 10$. These examples were designed to illustrate the effect of priors and of sample size on the posterior. All three problems assumed that the value for θ based on the actual sample data was .6. For the likelihood, Clark (2015, 10) used the binomial = $\binom{N}{z}\theta^{z}(1 - \theta)^{N-z}$. The factor $\binom{N}{z} = N!/[z!(N - z)!]$ was not used in the calculation of the likelihood entries given in column 3 in table 7.3 using the Bernoulli likelihood function. The $\binom{N}{z}$ factor is not necessary. It was used by Clark to normalize the likelihood. (Note also that in the binomial distribution discussed in the subsection "Example Using the Binomial Distribution" under the section "The Proposed Definition of the Concept of Probability," both θ and N were constant, and z varied. In Clark's examples and in the Bernoulli likelihood function used for table 7.3, θ varied and both N and z were constant.)

In Clark's first problem with the more informed priors (i.e., beta[$\theta | 10, 10$]), for which $N = 10$, the maximum-likelihood (ML) estimate of θ for the sample was the actual sample proportion, .6. As expected, the posterior mean for θ, equal to .56, fell between the prior of .5 and the ML estimate of .6. In the second problem, with the vague prior of beta($\theta | 2, 2$) and $N = 10$, the likelihood had a greater influence on the posterior than did the prior. (If a uniform distribution of beta($\theta | 1, 1$) had been chosen, the posterior results would have been equivalent to ML estimation (MLE). Clark stated that the majority of the methodologies that employ MLE can be viewed as special cases of Bayesian analysis.) A third example that used the original prior of beta($\theta | 10, 10$) and a larger sample size illustrated that more data outweighs a more informed prior. That is, more weight is given to the likelihood relative to the prior in the posterior distribution as the sample size increases (2015, 11).

In general, an uninformed prior is equivalent to MLE (2015, 11). The stronger the prior, the more influence the prior has on the posterior. However, when there is sufficient data, the prior is essentially irrelevant (2015, 30). When there is little data, the Bayesian approach is more useful because it will provide an answer when Orthodox methods break down (Jaynes 2003, 192–93). If the prior information is clear and available, then informed priors are recommended. Clark makes the point that almost any prior can be seen as weakly informative (Clark 2015, 30).

A Comment on Priors and Epistemology

When dealing with a familiar structure—such as a coin, it is known at the outset that there are two sides, that is, two categories. What is unknown are all of the initial conditions when a coin is thrown (Boydstun 1995, 114, 1996, 187). Typically, this information cannot be known. What may also be unknown is whether the coin is fair. Fairness is an attribute that may be discovered through tossing the coin a number of times. Initially, however, it may be assumed that the coin is fair. One way of expressing this assumption in Bayesian analysis is that, for a given prior distribution, more weight is placed on the prior probability value for $\theta = .5$.

Kruschke pointed out that Bayesian analysis shows how the posterior distribution changes relative to the prior distribution with knowledge (2011, 62). In this sense, Bayesian analysis is consistent with Objectivist epistemology, which regards concepts (as well as knowledge) to be open ended. It is also consistent with the way in which people learn. For instance, in concept formation, the essential characteristics on which a concept is based may change as more is learned (Gotthelf 2013, 33, 38; Lennox 2013, 121; cf. Griffiths 2013, 140). A chair may be thought of as a structure used for sitting. Later, the definition of the concept may be refined to include another essential characteristic, such as a back support. The lexicon for a specific scientific discipline is more complex, but the trajectory of discovery is similar to that for a single concept. For instance, the categories that represent species must be discovered. Unlike a die, for which the number of categories is known, the number of species is unknown at the outset. The number of categories may change over time, as well as the essential characteristics that define the categories. Also, unknown or inestimable at any given time may be the relative number of units that comprise each category. The categories as well as their relative sizes change over time not only due to advances in human knowledge but also due to births, deaths, extinction, etc. Whether it is the number of categories or their relative sizes, initially, judgments are made with very little information. As more information is available, it is incorporated into existing knowledge concerning the categories and their relative sizes. This is not unlike the way in which prior information is dealt with in Bayesian analysis.

Bayesian Analysis and the Proposed Definition of the Concept of Probability

As has can be seen, much of the focus of Bayesian analysis is on distributions; one of the main interests being the change that occurs between the prior and the posterior distributions (Kruschke 2011, 62). As has been discussed, the change in the posterior relative to the prior is dependent upon the vagueness of the prior and the amount of data available. These will also affect how close the posterior mean for the parameter θ is with respect to the prior mean or with respect to the mean for the data. Other things equal, the more informed the prior is, the closer the expected value of the posterior is to the prior mean than it is to the mean for the data, and conversely. The greater the number of observations, the closer the posterior mean is to the mean of the data than it is to the prior mean, and conversely. With sufficient data, the prior is rendered irrelevant.

According to Kruschke (2011, 87), the expected value of the posterior distribution is used for prediction. The use of the posterior mean for prediction is consistent with the definition of probability that I have proposed. The prior, likelihood, and the posterior "probabilities" are percentages. Whether they would be regarded as "probabilities" according to the proposed definition would depend upon whether they are used for prediction. A question arises as to whether the prior distribution is a predictor of the posterior distribution and therefore a "probability distribution" according to the proposed definition. If a distribution is used to predict another distribution, then the former distribution would be considered a probability distribution.

In most instances, referring to prior and posterior distributions as "probability" distributions does not result in confusion. With the proposed definition, what can be avoided are the inconsistencies that exist with the current definitions of probability, and the confusion that can result when discussing them. One problem with the relative frequency definition based on the RFT is that it requires the concept of infinity to be applied to actual calculations of relative frequencies, which is a metaphysical impossibility. It also leads to ambiguity in the use of the term "long run" when applied to relative frequencies or proportions when the context is not specified. A second problem arises when referring to a proportion as an "estimate of a probability." Probabilities are not estimated; proportions are or can be.

Although Jaynes does not define the concept of probability in the way in which I have proposed, the distinctions he makes between probability and frequency in the following quote are consistent with the proposed definition:

> [A] *probability* is something that we assign, in order to represent a state of knowledge, or that we calculate from previously assigned probabilities according to the rules of probability theory. A *frequency* is a factual property of the real world that we measure or estimate. (2003, 292; italics in original)

According to Jaynes, the phrases "estimating a probability" and "assigning a frequency" are logically inconsistent. (I would add that according to the proposed definition, as I have stated previously, a frequency can become a probability—not an estimate of a probability—if and when it is used to predict a future proportion.)

In the following, I reference three quotes from Kruschke (2011) and examine some of the inconsistencies in them. I use these quotes to analyze the problems inherent in the current definitions of probability, not as a criticism of Kruschke's treatment of them in these quotations per se. For example, Kruschke refers to "approximating a probability" by a long-run relative frequency. He states that one method for arriving at a long-run relative frequency is by repetitive sampling N times, then counting the number of times H (the event) occurs, and calculating the relative frequency as an estimate of $\theta = \hat{\theta} = \#H/N$. He *assumes* that the probability is .5 based on the assumption of tossing a fair coin (2011, 26). Based on $N = 500$ tosses, he finds the proportion of heads to be 0.494. Quote 1 is his statement in this regard.

Quote 1:

> [A]t the end of the long sequence, the proportion of heads is *near* 0.5 but not necessarily exactly equal to 0.5. This discrepancy reminds us that even this long run is still just a finite random sample, and there is no guarantee that the relative frequency of an event will match the true underlying probability of the event. That's why we say we are *approximating* the probability by the long-run relative frequency. (2011, 27; italics in original)

In Quote 1, by long run, he means a large but finite sample. The last sentence would be the reverse of the definition I have proposed. There is no "approximating a probability," because a probability is used to approximate (that is, predict) a proportion. That probability may be a proportion (equal to .494), which is based on a large (finite) sample ($N = 500$), that is to be used to predict another proportion in a subsequent experiment. However, note that Kruschke initially makes the assumption that the probability is .5. If before the sample is taken, it is assumed that the coin is fair, then the probability would be .5, based on the proportion of heads for a two-sided coin—which would be used to predict the proportion of heads that would be expected in an experiment of 500 tosses of a coin. The result of that experiment, 0.494, would be a relative frequency, not a probability, unless, as stated above, it in turn is used to predict another proportion.

Kruschke gives a second method of arriving at the long-run relative frequency as follows.

Quote 2:

> Sometimes, when the situation is simple enough mathematically, we can derive the exact long-run relative frequency. The case of the fair coin is one such simple situation.
>
> The sample space of the coin consists of two possible outcomes: head and tail. By the assumption of fairness, we know that each outcome is equally likely. Therefore the long-run relative frequency of heads should be *exactly* one out of two (i.e., 1/2), and the long-run relative frequency of tails should also be *exactly* 1/2. (2011, 27; italics added)

Quote 2 seemingly contradicts Kruschke's following statement.

Quote 3:

> [I]f I say that for a fair coin the probability of heads is 0.5, what I mean is that if we flipped the coin many times, about 50% of the flips would come up heads. In the long run, after flipping the coin many, many times, the relative frequency of heads would be *nearly* 0.5. (2011, 25; italics added)

In Quote 2, Kruschke states that the long-run relative frequency is known to be *exactly* 1/2, and in Quote 3 it is *nearly* 1/2. The reason for this discrepancy is that he is using two different definitions of long run in the quotes as well as different contexts for those definitions. Initially, in Quote 1, he refers to a large, finite sample of 500 tosses. In Quote 2, the long-run means infinity; that is, this is a theoretical long-run relative frequency, not one based in reality. Theoretically, based on a hypothetical probability distribution, in the long run (infinity), the proportion of heads would be exactly 1/2 based on the assumption of fairness. However, it cannot be said that the long-run relative frequency for a (finite, but large) sample would be *exactly* 1/2. In Quote 3, as in Quote 1, the long run is finite, indicating that the proportion of heads based on an experiment involving a large number of tosses would be close to 1/2. These quotes seem contradictory in part because the definition of long run and its context have not always been sufficiently clarified. This is largely a result of the second source of confusion, which is the use of the word "probability." This can be avoided if a proportion—whether theoretical or actual—is only regarded as a probability when it is used to predict another proportion.

If the long run is infinity, then that concept cannot be applied to a relative frequency in the real world. The infinite can be applied to theoretical proportions, such as those that comprise the binomial distribution. The expected value (long-run proportion, long-run meaning infinity in this context) of the theoretical binomial distribution can be viewed as a probability when it is used to predict a real-world proportion. The probability is used to predict a proportion, the latter of which is based on empirical data. The real-world proportion is what it is. It is an actual proportion, not a probability—unless in turn it is used to predict another proportion. Then it becomes a probability, not an "estimate" of a probability. An interval of probabilities may be used to predict a proportion. The values within this interval are not "estimates" of probabilities. They are all probabilities that estimate or predict a real-world proportion.

Bayesian Highest Density Interval (HDI) and Orthodox Hypothesis Testing

Similar to the Orthodox notion of a confidence interval (CI) is the Bayesian concept of the highest density interval (HDI), which is a range of values of θ over the posterior distribution, typically 95%. One interpretation of the posterior distribution over θ is that it measures the degree of belief in each possible value of θ. Values of θ within an HDI are interpreted as being more credible than any value of θ that lies outside the interval (Kruschke 2011, 85). Kruschke (2011, 297) gave as an example, an HDI that was used to test whether respondents answered randomly to a yes/no question; that is, the "null" was $\theta = .50$, where θ was the proportion of yeses (which would be a probability based on the proposed definition). Given that thirty-five out of fifty answered yes, and given a uniform beta prior, the posterior distribution was beta(θ|36, 16). The range for the 95% HDI was given as 0.567 to 0.813. Because the null of $\theta = 0.5$ was outside the HDI, a random response was not credible. It was concluded that the respondents did not answer by "guessing." The actual percentage of yeses for the sample was 0.7. The mean value of θ based on the posterior, beta(θ|36, 16), was 0.69, which according to Kruschke (2011, 87) would be the predictor (and when used for future prediction, 69% would be the probability based on the proposed definition).

One difference between Bayesian HDI testing and Orthodox tests using CIs is that the results of the latter can depend on the "intent of the experimenter," and the former does not. As an example of how a test using CIs can depend on the researcher's intent, Kruschke (2011) considered an experiment for $N = 26$ tosses of a coin for which there were $z = 8$ heads. The null hypothesis was that $\theta = .5$. Two alternative 95% confidence intervals (CIs) were presented. For the first CI, equal to [.144, .517], the intent was to continue to toss the coin until $N = 26$ was reached. For the second CI, of [.144, .493], the intent was to continue until $z = 8$ was reached (2011, 280). The actual proportion for the experiment was 0.308 (8 heads in 26 tosses), yet the conclusions for the two tests differed. In the first, the null hypothesis of a fair coin, $\theta = 0.5$, was not rejected. In the second, $\theta = 0.5$ was rejected. For the first, it could be said that .5 was a good predictor of outcome in the sense that 0.5 fell within the CI; however, for second, 0.5 was not a good predictor of the outcome. (Because $\theta = 0.5$ was used in prediction, 0.5 would be the probability according to the proposed definition. Once the actual proportion is available, it may be used as a probability to predict a future proportion. Although only one actual proportion exists, there are two different CI. For a given CI, all of the values within that CI may be regarded as probabilities when used for future prediction.)

Two different conclusions were possible using the Orthodox approach because the two CI tests used different sampling distributions. (The first used the binomial and the second used the "negative binomial," which is equal to $(z/N)\binom{N}{z}\theta^z(1-\theta)^{N-z}$ [Kruschke 2011, 271].) This ambiguity in conclusions does not occur with the Bayesian HDI because it relies exclusively on the posterior distribution (which, for instance, in the previous Bayesian problem was beta$(\theta|36, 16)$ and equaled the prior beta distribution multiplied by a Bernoulli likelihood). There is only a single posterior which is not governed by the experimenter's intent (2011, 281).

Sampling distributions, per se, do not enter into Bayesian inferences about parameters, which are made based on a given data set (Kruschke 2011, 286). (Clark [2015, 28, 37] refers to the likelihood as incorporating the assumptions with respect to the sampling distribution for the data.) That is, the posterior distribution, and, therefore, the HDI are not assumed to be based on repetitive sampling. Consequently, the HDI does not have the same interpretation as the CI. A 95% CI is interpreted to mean that if the experiment was repeated an infinite number of times, and a CI was calculated every time, 95% of the CIs would include the true parameter. The interpretation of the HDI is more in keeping with the way the ordinary person thinks about the problem; that is, based on this experiment, there is a 95% probability that the "true value" will fall within the interval (Clark 2015, 6, 17–18).

A Note on Bayesian Analysis and Linear Regression

Because regression analysis is the foundation for most courses in statistics, linear regression is the focus of Clark's Bayesian analysis (2015, 5).

Kruschke (2011) provides a fairly detailed treatment of a large number of statistical problems using the Bayesian approach, including linear regression. Again, Bayesian parameter fitting results in a distribution of estimated values for a given parameter, not simply a single point. This applies to every parameter for a given problem.

For a binomial problem, such as tossing a coin, the Bernoulli likelihood function is typically used. The likelihood function that is employed for a given parameter depends upon the scale type for the data. For a metric scale, a normal distribution may be the appropriate likelihood function (2011, 361). Normal priors are conjugate to normal likelihoods. Linear regression models that use metric data often use normal likelihood distributions. The data for the dependent variable, y_i, is assumed to be normally distributed with parameters μ and σ, where $\mu_i = \beta_0 + \beta_1 X$ (2011, 420). Often, instead of σ, the precision $\tau = 1/\sigma^2$ is used. The prior for the precision may be a gamma distribution (with shape parameters, *S* and *R*) (Kruschke 2011, 423, 408; cf. Clark 2015, 15). The priors for intercept and slope (or slopes, if it is a multiple regression equation) are assumed to be normal (with means and precisions of M_0 and T_0 and M_1 and T_1, respectively) (2011, 423).

When there are a number of independent variables for which it is suspected that "false alarms" may be an issue (i.e., estimated slopes may be deemed non-zero, when they are actually zero), then all the regression slopes may be described by an over-arching prior t-distribution with parameters $\mu\beta$ and $\tau\beta$ and degrees of freedom, df. An example by Kruschke depicts the parameter $\mu\beta$ with a normal hyper-prior (with parameters, $M\beta$ and $T\beta$) and $\tau\beta$ with a hyper-prior gamma distribution (with parameters $S\beta$ and $R\beta$) (2011, 463). The hyper-prior for the df parameter assumes sampling from a uniform distribution; the sampled value is then transformed so that it falls between one and infinity (2011, 432). A hyper-parameter is one upon which other parameters depend (2011, 192). Instead of being assigned fixed values by the researcher, the hyper-parameters, in this case for the t-distribution, vary. Associated with each hyper-parameter is a hyper-prior distribution. It is worth noting that, the number of priors and hyper-priors can be quite large when estimating a number of parameters (2011, 458) and when there are repeated measures (2011, 436).

When the parameter space is large—as it tends to be with multiple regression, sampling procedures such as Markov Chain Monte Carlo (MCMC) are often used (Clark 2015, 16). (Clark [2015, 34] mentioned alternative methods to MCMC. See, for example, Beal [2003].) Until relatively recently, Bayesian estimation using MCMC and similar sampling techniques was impossible because the computation time was prohibitive. Because of advancements in computer technology, this is no longer an issue. Of primary interest in regression estimation is the slope (or slopes). For a multiple regression problem, Clark presented the mean values for several slopes. Clark noted that because the sample size was large, the likelihood carried more weight than the prior in the posterior. Therefore, the mean estimates of the posterior distributions for the slopes were essentially the same as standard regression coefficients (Clark 2015, 17–18). Again, in Bayesian estimation, the aim is in the distributions for slopes, not simply a single slope estimate. The posterior distribution for a slope is a weighted combination of the prior and the likelihood (2015, 7). Posterior probability distributions for slopes for four subjects involving repeated measures were depicted by Kruschke based on a study by Feldman (1988). Also shown was the posterior slope distribution at the group level (Kruschke 2011, 435; also see the results of an exercise in [2011, 448]).

COMPUTER LEARNING AND PROBABILITIES

The discussion that follows focuses on computer learning models. It begins with principal components analysis (PCA), which is followed by facial recognition using PCA. It concludes with an overview of neural networks, focusing specifically on adaptive resonance theory (ART).

Principal Components Analysis (PCA)

PCA takes a cloudy data base in which there is redundancy and noise and transforms it in a way that more clearly and efficiently captures the underlying distribution of the data. Redundancy is reduced by transforming a correlated data set into uncorrelated variables. Noise is lessened by eliminating data that does not capture most of the variation in the data (Shlens 2003). In facial recognition, relatively few "faces" (eigenfaces) can be used to adequately reconstruct the faces in the data base. To find whether a "new" face is already in the data base, the new face image is also recreated using these few eigenfaces. To reconstruct a face, eigenfaces are factored by "weights." The weights that represent the new face can be compared against the weights for the reconstructed faces in the data base to test whether there is a match or if the new input indeed represents a new face; which if it is new, may be added to the data base (Cendrillon and Lovell 2000).

PCA Overview

PCA is a nonparametric technique that extracts pertinent information from cloudy data (Shlens 2003, 4). Nonparametric statistics, unlike parametric, are methods based on few assumptions about the underlying distribution of the population from which data are drawn. However, as is typical of many non-parametric applications, in PCA the individual observations are assumed to be drawn from a normal distribution (2003, 7; Hollander and Wolfe 1973, 1).

PCA transforms a cloudy or unclear data set into a system that "best represents" the data. For a linear system, such as PCA, an unclear data set has two possible sources of cloudiness: noise and redundancy. The objective of PCA is to filter out noise and eliminate redundancy in data. Noise can be measured by a ratio of variances of "signal" to "noise." For instance, a signal-to-noise ratio (SNR) equal to one or greater reflects high data precision, whereas a low ratio indicates data contamination (Shlens 2003, 4). Redundancy exists when variables are correlated. PCA orthogonally transforms data to a new coordinate system. Original data for correlated variables are transformed into values for linearly uncorrelated variables called principal components (PCs). The number of PCs will be less than or equal to the number of original variables. This is the essence of dimension reduction (2003, 5).

Each transformed data point associated with a given PC is a linear combination of the original variables' data (which is either mean adjusted or transformed into *Z*-scores) with a unit vector, called an eigenvector. The transformed data associated with the PCs reflect the underlying patterns within the original data (2003, 11). The first PC, which also corresponds to the first coordinate (eigenvector) in the new system, accounts for the largest variance in the data. Subsequent components, which are respectively orthogonal to the previous PCs, account for the next greatest variability. (For example, if there are only two variables, the first eigenvector will give the best fit when the original (mean-adjusted) data is plotted against both eigenvectors [Leskovec et al. 2014, 413, 415; cf. Delac et al. 2005, 152]. The second eigenvector will be orthogonal to the first and will not fit the data as well.)

In effect PCA rotates the original data points around their mean, aligning them with the eigenvectors. As a result, much of the total variance ("signal") is moved into the first few PCs. That is, there is a higher SNR associated with the first few PCs. The latter PCs will be dominated by "noise" and therefore can be eliminated with little sacrifice of information. Thus dimensionality reduction is achieved. (If there are two variables, elimination of the second PC and the eigenvector associated with it will result in only one dimension; that is, one eigenvector will remain [Smith 2002, 17–19; also see Leskovec et al. 2014, 416]. The transformed data associated with the second PC will be eliminated. The remaining transformed data will only be in terms of the values associated with the first PC.)

It is possible to restore the original mean-adjusted data (by multiplying a matrix of the PCs by the transpose of the matrix of eigenvectors). The means of the respective original variables must be added back in order to return to the original data. With dimensionality reduction, there will be data reduction; therefore not all of the original data will be recaptured. The data associated with those PCs that are chosen are thought to more "truly" reflect the underlying probability distribution (Shlens 2003, 11). (Thus, in the two-variable case, once the original values have been restored, a plot of that data onto the new axes will only show variation associated with the first eigenvector. The data associated with the second PC will have been eliminated [2003, 12; Smith 2002, 20]. PCA is typically applied to very large data sets and/or a large number of variables, not two variables as the example parenthetically discussed in this section.)

Eigenfaces Using PCA

Computer facial recognition was once regarded as intractable because of the computational complexity involved in pictures stored in pixel form (Turk and Pentland, "Eigenfaces for Recognition," 1991, 71; Navarrete and Ruiz-del-Solar 2002, 1). This can result in a very high dimension, say N^2 per image. For instance, if each facial image has $N = 100$ pixels then the dimension associated with one facial image would be 100 by 100, or 10,000. Using PCA in the ordinary way (via an N^2 by N^2, or 10,000 by 10,000, covariance matrix, C) would result in inordinate number of eigenvectors (10,000), many of which would be zero. Using facial images rather than pixels to form matrices to perform eigen-decomposition greatly reduces the number of eigenvectors to be calculated, from N^2 to M, where M is the number of pictures, say 300 (Turk and Pentland, "Face Recognition Using Eigenfaces," 1991, 587).

Facial images are used to statistically extract those features that account for the variation among the images. Those features are represented by eigenfaces, analogous to eigenvectors. (Calculation of the eigenfaces is "training" and is performed offline [Turk and Pentland, "Eigenfaces for Recognition," 1991, 76].) Eigenfaces, in turn, are associated with PCs. (Recall that a PC is a variable that is a linear combination of the associated eigenvector with the mean-adjusted data.) Only those eigenfaces associated with PCs that account for the greatest variation in the images are selected to form the basis of "face ingredients" (Navarrete and Ruiz-del-Solar 2002, 2–3; Cendrillon and Lovell 2000, 2).

Eigenvalues (λs), which are associated with the M eigenfaces, are used to rank them, where M is also the number of face images in the data base. The sum of all of the eigenvalues is proportional to the total variation in the data. Larger eigenvalues are associated with eigenvectors that capture more of the variation in the data. The eigenface with the largest eigenvalue accounts for most of the variation in the data, the eigenface with the second largest eigenvalue explains most of the variation after accounting for the first eigenface, and so on (Dutta 1975, 238; Johnston 1972, 327). The number of eigenfaces (M' in this example) is chosen based on the ratio E, equal to the sum of the first M' eigenvalues divided by the sum of all eigenvalues, exceeding a predesignated percentage—typically 90%. (Alternative criteria for selection also are given in Delac et al. [2005, 153].) The deletion of eigenfaces associated with small eigenvalues eliminates noise from the data (2005, 153). Thus, the relevant number of "facial images" is reduced from M to M', where M' may be few, say 40. (See Turk and Pentland, "Eigenfaces for Recognition," [1991] for actual values for N, M, and M' used in their research.) These two factors—PCA using the images rather than pixels in eigen-decomposition and choosing only those eigenfaces that account for the greatest variation—significantly improve computational efficiency.

The covariance matrix is $C = SS^T$, where the matrix $S = [X_1\ X_2\ \ldots\ X_M]$, and X_i are vectors that are formed by taking the original data images, Γ_i, and subtracting the mean face, Ψ. (The eigenfaces, u_g, can be expressed as: $u_g = \sum_{k=1,\,M} v_{gk}X_k\ g = 1, \ldots, M$, where v_g are the eigenvectors for $G = S^TS$ [Turk and Pentland, "Eigenfaces for Recognition," 1991, 74–75]. Note also, in the above, I have changed the notation given in [1991, 75] from A to S, from L to G, and from to Φ to X.)

Any face image vector, Γ, whether in the data base or a new face inputted into the system, can be transformed into its components or weights, given by a weight vector $\Omega = [\omega_1\ \omega_2\ \ldots\ \omega_M']$ (Turk and Pentland, "Face Recognition Using Eigenfaces" 1991, 588). The weights, ω_i, represents "the proportions of each eigenface needed to construct that face" (Cendrillon and Lovell 2000, 2). Each weight is the dot product of an eigenface with the input face data less the mean and has the form of a PC; that is,

$$\omega_k = u_k^T(\Gamma - \Psi) \cdot k = 1, \ldots, M',$$

where Ψ is the average face in the data base and u_i are eigenfaces, which form the basis for the face images.

Recognition of a new face, Γ, can be based on a comparison between ε and φ; where ε represents the difference, or more accurately the Euclidean distance, between the vector of weights that represent the new face and the vector of weights that represent a face (or face class if there is more than one image for a given face) in the data base, and φ is a predetermined value (Delac et al. 2005, 154; Cendrillon and Lovell 2000, 2; Turk and Pentland, "Face Recognition Using Eigenfaces," 1991, 589). That is, Euclidean distance may be used for facial recognition:

$$\varepsilon_k = \sqrt{\|\Omega - \Omega_k\|^2}$$

A match exists between a new input weight vector (Ω) and the weight vector for the kth face in the data base (Ω_k) if ε is below or equal to the threshold φ; otherwise the input is classified as unknown and is considered a new face. If there is no "match," that is, there is no ε that is less than or equal to φ—then the face is categorized as a new face and may be added to the data base.

In the equation for ε_k, the vector $\Omega = [\text{ɯ}_1\ \text{ɯ}_2\ \ldots\ \text{ɯ}_M']$ is the representation of the input face. It describes "the contribution of each eigenface in representing the input face image, treating the eigenfaces as the basis set for face images" (Turk and Pentland, "Eigenfaces for Recognition," 1991, 75). The transformed data associated with eigenfaces can be regarded as more "truly" reflecting the underlying probability distribution (Shlens 2003, 11). Any new face or any face in the data base, Γ, can be reconstructed as the mean face, ψ, plus the sum of the weights, ɯ_i, multiplied by the respective eigenfaces, u_i; that is:

$$\Gamma\hat{} = \Psi + \text{ɯ}_1 u_1 + \text{ɯ}_2 u_2 + \text{ɯ}_{M'} u_{M'}$$

(Turk and Pentland, "Face Recognition Using Eigenfaces," 1991, 589). Each of the set of weights, Ω, associated with a face image are viewed as representing the probabilities, or likelihoods, associated with what that face might look like because the vector of weights is assumed to capture most of the variation. That which is left out eliminates "noise" from the image. Insofar as how this interpretation of the weights as probabilities fits in with the definition of the proposed concept of probability is concerned, the question is which of the vectors of weights is used for prediction—the vector associated with the new face input or the vectors associated with the faces (or face classes) that are in the data base? In this context, the weights associated with the new face would be considered "proportions," and the weights associated with those that are in the data base would be the proportions used to predict—that is, the "probabilities."

ART: Match-Based Learning

Adaptive resonance theory (ART) is a set of neural networks created by Stephen Grossberg along with Gail Carpenter. Neural networks are computer methodologies that attempt to replicate how the brain learns. According to Grossberg: "There is an intimate connection between learning and predictive dynamics in the brain" (Grossberg 2013, 4). The developers of neural networks and related computer learning techniques have attempted to devise systems or models that reflect the link between learning and prediction. To Grossberg: "Humans are *intentional* beings who learn expectations about the world and make predictions about what is about to happen" (Grossberg 2013,

6; italics in original). Grossberg divided neural network learning into two broad categories: error based and match based. It appears that the "what" processes (i.e., perceptual/cognitive) and the "where" processes (spatial/motor) employ different predictive methods (2013, 4).

In a "where" process, the objective is error reduction. The end or target is known, and it is possible to know when the target has been achieved (or not). Error-based learning (EBL) is spatial-motor learning that is related to the "where" processing of data. An example of EBL is an arm movement, which involves two "where" vectors. One is a representation of the current position, *C*, and the other is the target, *T*, or desired position. *C* is subtracted from *T* giving the difference or "error," *E*. The objective is to reduce *E*. Once the arm has moved to the T position, the difference between the two vectors equals zero. EBL is therefore inhibitory (Grossberg 2013, 5). Repetitive EBL can be thought of as "practice makes perfect."

An example of error-based "machine" learning is back propagation (Back Prop). One problem with using Back Prop for certain kinds of learning—in particular, "what" learning—is that it can result in catastrophic forgetting. Forgetting may not be a problem for "where" learning; for example, it would be counter-productive for adult bodies to remember movements learned as infants (Carpenter and Grossberg 2002, 3). (See Grossberg [2013, 2, 4, 11] on advantages of ART over Back Prop and other models; also see Carpenter and Grossberg [1990, 131] and Grossberg [2016, 12]; see Carpenter et al. [1992] for comparisons between ART and Back Prop based on simulations; see Grossberg [1987, 47–48, 50–53] for a detailed comparison of ART with Back Prop and other models; cf. Anderson [1995, 249–52] on Widrow-Hoff.)

ART is primarily a "what" network. It is "a cognitive and neural theory of how the brain autonomously learns to categorize, recognize, and predict objects and events in a changing world" (2013, 2). According to Grossberg (2013, 4): "The world is filled with uncertainty, so probability concepts seem relevant to understanding how brains learn about uncertain data." Because of this, many computer-learning investigators thought that the brain would conform to Bayesian laws. Grossberg (2013) pointed out, however, that the generality of Bayes' Rule allows it to accommodate any system whatsoever. This permits the rule to be a worthwhile statistical tool; however, reliance on it alone is insufficient in uncovering learning principles involving the brain. Also, in Bayesian and other probabilistic models, it is necessary to calculate an entire probability distribution, often relying upon nonlocal computations (2013, 2; Anderson 1995, 438). These models perform best with stationary data. They are also subject to catastrophic forgetting, especially in a fast-learning mode.

In contrast, ART can take in enormous quantities of input and learn quickly and stably in real time, while simultaneously being flexible enough to respond to the unexpected without catastrophic forgetting that which it has already been learned. According to Grossberg (2013, 2), even though ART models "may exhibit Bayesian properties, these properties emerge from organization principles and mechanisms that do not invoke Bayesian ideas." He continued:

> ART uses only local computations to model how the brain may embody a novel kind of real-time probability theory, hypothesis testing, prediction, and decision-making whose local computations enable fast autonomous adaptation to a non-stationary world whose rules can change through time, and in unexpected ways. (2013, 4)

ART networks are match based. Matched-based learning involves "what" processing. Perceptual data (bottom-up input) is matched against (top-down) categories. The categories represent entities that are independent of spatial position and size (2013, 5). When there is a good enough match, learning commences; that is, connective weights are refined (2013, 7). ART match-learning results in learning stability. In addition to stability, ART also resolves the problem of plasticity; that is, it is capable of handling novel information without forgetting that which has been previously learned. Thus, ART is capable of learning both the expected or familiar and the unexpected or unfamiliar. When sufficiently novel inputs are presented, ART engages in memory search, or hypothesis testing. If there is no category that is a sufficiently good match, a new category is formed whose top-down weights learn the input (2013, 8).

The ART search process can be regarded as a type of probabilistic hypothesis testing, error correction, and decision-making (2013, 9–10). For those ART models in which input varies with time, such as LAMINART, hypothesis testing operates "in response to non-stationary time series of input patterns" (2013, 10). Also, the category network's ability to "self-normalize its total activity enables the activities of these categories to be interpreted as a kind of real-time probability distribution" (2013, 10). LAMINART'S self-normalizing circuits conduct a form of probability theory in real time in which input amplitude covaries with the certainty of the network's choice of a grouping. Its circuits perform as quickly as possible. Acting like real-time probabilistic decision circuits, they operate "in a fast feedforward mode when there is little uncertainty, and automatically [switch] to a slower feedback mode when there is uncertainty" (2013, 18).

ART Hypothesis Testing

It was once thought that neural networks could process distributed patterns, but not symbolic categories. ART is capable of connecting critical feature patterns to categories (Grossberg 2013, 9). Distributed data is compressed into categories, or, as in the case of maximal compression as with winner take all (WTA), a single category is chosen. This is the single category that receives the largest total input, thereby surviving a competition among established categories (Grossberg 2016, 3, 9).

The focus in this subsection is primarily on ART1, which is WTA. In ART1, the winning category node, say *J*, is the one associated with the largest input, which is given by the maximum value of the vector T_j:

$$T_j = \sum_{i = 1, M} x_i z_{ij},$$

where x_i is defined in Carpenter et al. (1993, 10–11) in equations (1) and (5), and z_{ij} are the bottom-up weights. It is assumed that input vector *I* is fixed (i.e., it does not change with time) (Carpenter et al. 1992, 4). When vector *I* is first presented, $X = I$, therefore I_i replaces x_i in the equation for T_j (Carpenter et al. 1993, 10–11, 13).

The match may not be a good one. A criterion for testing whether the match is adequate is to compare a recognition match ratio, *R*, with a vigilance criterion, ρ; where ρ is a function of how general the category is (the closer to zero the more general the category). In ART1, the recognition match ratio, *R*, is one for which the numerator and denominator are both counts of binary bits. The numerator is the number of features that the input shares with the prototype (top-down weights for a winning category, *J*). That is, the numerator is obtained by counting matched bits between the input vector, *I*, and Z_J, where Z_J is the top-down vector of weights z_{ji} associated with category *J* (Carpenter and Grossberg, "ART-2: Self-organization of Stable Recognition Category Codes," 1987, 4926). $X^* = I \cap Z_J$ represents a matched critical features vector. (The analog equivalent is $X^* = (I \wedge Z_j)$, where $(a \wedge b)_i = \min(a_i, b_i)$ (Carpenter et al. 1992, 4).) The denominator of *R* is a count of the total features for input.

The adequacy of the match is based on the following matching criterion:

$$|X^*| / |I| = |I \cap Z_J| / |I| \geq \rho,$$

where the norm $|\bullet|$ is defined as $|a| = \sum a_i$ (i.e., $|X^*|$ is the sum of matched features and $|I|$ is the sum of positive inputs) (Carpenter and Grossberg, "A Massively Parallel Architecture," 1987, 69; Carpenter et al. 1993, 11; Grossberg 2013, 10). $|X^*|/|I|$ is equivalent to R discussed above, and ρ is the vigilance parameter. Smaller ρ values result in broad categories, for example, the category "face." Larger ρ values result in narrow categories, such as a specific face.

For binary input, which is the only kind of input in ART1, *R* (the ratio of critical features to the features of an input pattern) is a proportion in a hypothesis test in which it is compared to ρ, the proportion used to predict.

In that sense, ρ can be thought of as a probability. If the ratio *R* exceeds ρ—that is, the expected category is a match for the input—then either there is no change to the weights (if the category is stable) or learning commences (i.e., the weights change). If the matching criterion fails—that is, there is a predictive error caused by a category mismatch—there is a reset and the orienting system is engaged, which results in a memory search for a better category match.

Reset involves self-normalization of the categories and consists of suppressing the mismatched category (code *J*) from further search for this input cycle, and re-activating those categories that were formerly suppressed and restoring their features so that another category match can be found (Grossberg 2013, 10). A search commences in which, for each recognition category, the vigilance parameter, ρ, is compared with *R*. Reset-search continues until a there is a category match. If there is no established category for which *R* exceeds ρ, a new category is created (if the system is not at capacity) that learns the current input (Carpenter and Grossberg 2002, 2).

ART Learning

When a new category is formed for a given input vector, the weights simply learn the input. As new input is matched and assigned to a category, the weights are refined or pruned. Learning involves adjusting the weights (the *z*'s) associated with the winning category toward the features of the input pattern. Learning in ART1 is based on gated steepest descent (Carpenter et al. 1993, 12; Carpenter and Grossberg 2002, 8).

Once a category becomes predictively accurate and consistent, the weights no longer change; that is, learning is complete and the critical features are invariant. When a category is stabilized, the search process is disengaged; that is, an input that shares invariant features with a category will be confirmed as belonging to the category and automatically assigned to it without triggering a search process (Grossberg 2013, 11; Carpenter et al. 1993, 2; Carpenter and Grossberg, "A Massively Parallel Architecture," 1987, 55, 59, "ART-2: Self-organization of Stable Recognition Category Codes," 1987, 4921, 4923, 4928).

Once the weights no longer change, the ratio of critical features to input, *R*, is established. The proportion is permanent (and in turn is used as a "predictor," or a probability, against which new input is compared), in that sense.

ART: A Note on Search

T_j is the dot product of two vectors which, when input vector *I* is first presented, is equal to:

$$T_j = \sum_{i=1,M} I_i z_{ij} = \|I\| \|Z_{ij}\| \cos(I, Z_{ij})$$

(Carpenter et al. 1991, 495–96), and, if $z_{ij} = z_{ji} = z_j$, T_j is equal to vector length I times vector length Z_j times $\cos(I, Z_j)$:

$$T_j = \|I\| \|Z_j\| \cos(I, Z_j).$$

For instance, $z_{ij} = z_{ji}$ is the case for ART2 (1991, 497–98). When a choice among categories is to be made, a specific node J becomes active if T_j is maximum (1991, 496). Note that when the vectors, I and Z_j, are normalized, $T_j = \cos(I, Z_j)$. When the angle between the two vectors is zero, the cosine equals one and there is a perfect match. When the angle equals one, the cosine equals zero and the vectors are orthogonal. T_j therefore falls between zero and one when the vectors are normalized (Carpenter and Grossberg 1990, 142–43; cf. Anderson 1995, 76–77, 179–80).

In the fast learning case, the weights are normalized by the completion of an input presentation; therefore, search order depends on $\cos(I, Z_j)$ alone. Also, convergence of the long-term memory vectors (the Z's) is complete on each input presentation. If the first committed category node that is chosen resets, then all other nodes will also reset. Therefore, once the first reset occurs, an uncommitted node will be selected. A problem with fast learning is that it can result in a proliferation of categories if the data is noisy. Slow learning in ART2 is better at handling noise than fast learning, but is not capable of rapid computation. ART2-A rectifies the problem of computation speed for slow/intermediate learning.

The truncated search process for fast learning is not sufficient in many instances. A search of committed nodes with slow learning may be required (Carpenter et al. 1991, 497–98). With slow learning, learning time may be insufficient to allow weights to become very large. Also, with slow learning, weight vectors are not normalized. If for slow learning (or any other situation when weights are not normalized), maximum $\|I\| \|Z_j\| \cos(I, Z_j)$ is used as the search criterion, a weight vector (say, associated with category J) may be chosen simply because it has become large due to prior learning even though a better match (say, J^*) based on $\cos(I, Z_j)$ exists but was not chosen because of its smaller weight due to insufficient learning time. In such a situation, search order based on the inner product would not necessarily result in the best category match. For this reason, a search of committed codes is needed in order to find the better category match (i.e., J^*). In ART3, this was based on the match criterion of the cosine of the angle between the input function and the signal vector. A trade-off between pattern match and weight size was illustrated (see Carpenter and Grossberg 1990, 142–43; cf. Anderson 1995, 199; see Carpenter and Grossberg [1990, 139–40] for a discussion of the search process for ART2.)

ART: A Varying Vigilance Parameter ρ

In the above discussion, ρ was assumed to be fixed. The vigilance parameter can be fixed for a given input presentation cycle, or it can iteratively change by becoming increasingly large on a "trial by trial" basis, thereby tightening up the level of specificity for the category (Carpenter et al. 1993, 4). In the case in which ρ changes, it is, in a sense, "discovered" rather than imposed.

For those ART systems for which ρ varies, the degree of match between an input and a category is tracked. (For example, see Fuzzy ARTMAP, a supervised learning system in Carpenter et al. [1992].) In "match tracking," the value of ρ changes so as to maximize category generalization while also minimizing predictive error (Grossberg 1999, 30). Prior to the presentation of each new input, ρ returns to a baseline value—the lowest figure to have resulted previously in predictive success. ART attempts to learn the broadest category consistent with the input data (Grossberg 2013, 10). A baseline of $\rho = 0$ would maximize category generalization (Carpenter et al. 1993, 8). On a trial-by-trial basis, ρ increases by the least amount necessary to result in a predictive error, thereby triggering reset and a new search (Grossberg 2013, 10). When ρ is allowed to vary, a single ART network can incorporate a wide range of category abstractions (Grossberg 2013, 11). A single network can include the category "faces" as well as categories for individual faces.

Comparison of ART Categories to Objectivist Concepts

In Objectivism, a concept *means* the existents in reality that are subsumed by the concept. Concepts are defined based on essential characteristics. The essences are not metaphysical, but epistemological. However, they are reality based—they are learned based on experience. Concepts are open ended, as is all knowledge. They are also context sensitive (Rand 1990, 102).

In ART, categories are based on essential characteristics that are learned based on experience. That is, in ART the LTM (long-term memory) traces (the *Z*'s) learn to correlate the activation of the category nodes with the critical feature vectors based on all input that has been experienced (cf. Lennox [2013, 127] on a concept's *pattern* of development, discussed in Rand [1990, 45]). In ART, there is a point at which categories become "closed" in the sense that critical features are no longer learned or refined. After that point, the network continues to experience input and to assign the input to categories based on the invariant critical features the input shares with those categories (Grossberg 2016, 3). Although concepts in Objectivism are open ended, they share this feature with ART—that is, their definitions tend to become stable over time (see Griffiths [2013, 140] on Rand's view of a definition as a "resting place" in the continuing quest for knowledge).

Also, ART networks embody a feature central to Objectivism, and that is "context." In ART, a feature pattern is converted into a "context-sensitive state that is linked to its category" (Grossberg 2013, 9). For instance, in "A Massively Parallel Architecture" in Carpenter and Grossberg (1987, 58, 67), an example is given that demonstrates that a key feature in one input pattern may be regarded as noise in another (depending upon the vigilance parameter). Similarly, in Objectivist Epistemology, a concept's "essential characteristics are determined contextually" (Rand 1990, 102). This is why the same concept can have different definitions in different cognitive contexts (1990, 102).

Computer-Learning Probabilities

The objective of reviewing ART as well as other computer-learning models has been to briefly touch upon some of the ways they are related to probability. In PCA, data that is redundant and noisy is eliminated which results in a probability distribution that more clearly reflects the underlying data pattern. For facial recognition using PCA, a vector of weights ("probabilities") is associated with a given face image or face class.

In ART, the critical features associated with a category depends on context—specifically the vigilance parameter. The vigilance parameter is related to the level of generalization for a category and operates like a proportion used in prediction (a probability) in hypothesis testing. Categories can be created or refined based on input. Probabilities and probability distributions are dynamic. They are responsive to change. ART relies exclusively on local computations to model how the brain performs a type of real-time theory of probability that tests hypotheses, predicts, and makes decisions. The computations adapt autonomously and quickly in a dynamic world in which rules may change unexpectedly over time (Grossberg 2013, 4).

The probabilities related to PCA and ART were shown to be consistent with the proposed definition of the concept of probability. They are proportions used to predict other proportions. More importantly, the calculation of probabilities in these learning systems can update with changes in input. Also, with ART, they change with context. If ART models do replicate human thought processes to some degree and probabilities are inherently a part of these processes, then probability is much more local and dynamic than the philosophy of probability has allowed for. If the philosophy of probability is to encompass the ways in which probabilities appear to be utilized by the human mind, it would seem to follow that examining what these networks have to offer in advancing that understanding would be an important first step. An overarching definition of the concept of probability that allows for contextual flexibility with respect to definitions of probability could facilitate that investigation. This chapter has proposed a definition of the concept of probability which permits that flexibility.

Chapter 8

Risk-taking

INTRODUCTION

This chapter considers the question: Why would a person willingly risk his life if life is the ultimate value? To do so would seem to be a contradiction. It also would seem unethical. Yet, in some professions, individuals do this on a continual basis for years. And societies depend on them to do so, and in a free society—to do so voluntarily—be they firefighters, combat soldiers, or police officers. It is considered rational to undertake an action if the expected return exceeds the expected risk (loss). Yet in some professions, such as firefighting, the pay received is relatively modest. One reason why a person might willingly and rationally undertake such a risk is that he makes efforts to reduce that risk prior to taking it. The risk is lowered through training. The person's aim is the achievement of excellence to reduce the risk of danger in order to achieve a worthy objective.

The chapter begins with a discussion of excellence, specifically the relationship between practice and excellence. In *Talent is Overrated*, Colvin (2008) argued that to excel, a person must engage in practice—deliberate practice. To become a world-class achiever, "experience" is inadequate. According to Colvin, deliberate practice must be undertaken and it must be pursued over a number of years.

A discussion of risk management follows. One of the primary objectives of risk management is organizational safety (Duffey and Saull 2008, 134–36, 278). In *Managing Risk*, Duffey and Saull (2008, 52–53, 508) presented the universal learning curve (ULC), which was based on 200 years of world data and showed error reduction as an exponential function of experience (Duffey and Saull 2009, 4). They equated risk reduction to learning, and viewed exposure to risk as synonymous with experience. More in keeping with the interest in this chapter is that Duffey and Saull also found the same exponential relationship at the individual learning level, which they labeled the universal law of practice—ULP (2008, 508). That is, they concluded that experience at the systems level is equivalent to practice at the individual level. The so-called power curve used by cognitive psychologists and others to empirically estimate the relationship between success and practice at the individual level fails to take into account the minimum error rate. This is not the case for the ULP. A minimum error always exists—whether at the systems level or the individual level, because of the human factor. As Fiondella and Duffey said, practice doesn't make perfect; it makes "nearly perfect" (2015, 2).

According to Duffey and Saull, the "learning paradox" is that in order to learn, humans must take on risks they would prefer to avoid. Risk is a fact of human life, and if humans do not learn, they face even more risk. The highest risk is at the beginning of an experience—estimated at a 63% chance of failure (2008, 60, 404). This probability is particularly disturbing when the risk one faces is the loss of his life. Why would a person ethically undertake such a risk (if he has an alternative)? Russian roulette offers better odds. Russian roulette would not be ethical because it is a game of pure chance. There is no opportunity to reduce the odds through learning. A person would rationally undertake a risk if he can reduce the risk of danger through training (formal training, if available)—that is, by achieving excellence through deliberate practice.

The balance of the chapter deals with measuring difficulty (of a task) and risk. It does so by examining the "expected life" of a "training module"—specifically a piece of music—that has a positive "fatal error" rate (force of mortality) and a potential maximum length of life. The expected life span relative to the maximum length of life is an "index of difficulty." One minus the "difficulty index" is a measure of risk. It is true that in most instances, the force of mortality would not be zero—that is, the "fatal error rate" based on a group would be positive; thus the "difficulty index" typically would be less than one. The "risk index" would give an idea of the degree of risk to overcome in order to achieve "perfection." Perfection may be possible for an individual, whether playing a given musical piece or undertaking a training module for a dangerous occupation. "Perfection" depends upon how an error is defined. The defining characteristic of a dangerous occupation is the risk of death or serious injury to oneself and/or others. If an error is defined as serious enough to be regarded as fatal (i.e., to cause death or serious "injury"), then perfection in the performance of a task is possible.

PRACTICE IS UNDER-RATED

In *Talent Is Overrated*, Geoff Colvin's interest was in addressing the mystery of what determines excellence; that is, what makes some people world-class performers. First he ruled out those things that don't (necessarily) make people excel. He ruled out experience. There are people with years of experience, who are not at the top of their fields. He also ruled out particular inborn abilities or traits. He cited evidence that casts doubt on their existence and added that even if they do exist they are not determining factors. Finally, he eliminated I.Q. and innate memory from consideration. A high I.Q. is no guarantee of success, and there is ample evidence of those without high I.Q.s who have made outstanding contributions (2008, 50–51). Yet, when music professionals were surveyed, 75% (a higher percentage than for any other field) said that talent was a requisite for musicianship (2008, 17).

Colvin challenged this belief. He pointed out that in 1878, famed violinist Leopold Auer said of Tchaikovsky's Violin Concerto that it was too difficult to be performed. Today, however, the piece is performed by virtually every Juilliard graduate (2008, 10). Humans are no more "talented" now than 140 years ago. One difference is that people have amassed more knowledge. Another is that they have learned how to improve their performance. Colvin's focus was on the value of practice in performance excellence.

A national study of music students reported that those students, age twelve, who went to elite music schools, practiced on average two hours per day; eight times more than those at the lowest level, who practiced fifteen minutes a day (2008, 19). A study of violinists at the acclaimed post-secondary school, the Music Academy of West Berlin, found that of three groups of experimental subjects (good, better, and best), all expended the same number of hours per week in music-related activities—about fifty-one (2008, 58). However, by age eighteen, the "good" group had accumulated about 3,200 hours of practice on average, the "better" group about 2,000 more hours than the "good" group, and the "best" about 4,000 more than the "good" group (2008, 60).

Practice is not simply experience. Working hard at a job for many years does not necessarily make a person great at what he does. As Aristotle (1976, 92) pointed out, a person becomes a good builder by building well and a poor builder by building poorly. Most people improve for a while and then plateau (Colvin 2008, 64). Those who excel at what they do, work at continuing to improve. They never stop practicing. For instance, in addition to performance work, professional violin virtuosos continue to practice an average of thirty hours per week, or an accumulated 1,500 hours per year (2008, 172).

It's not just practice; however, it is *deliberate* practice. With deliberate practice, a person's aim is to avoid performing unconsciously. The objective is to strive for those things that are uncomfortable, which means they cannot be performed automatically. Great performance is always conscious and controlled. Deliberate practice requires advancing oneself beyond one's current capabilities (2008, 83–84). It is most effective when it is repetitive and can be done at a high volume. It involves the person seeking to improve what he is not good at (2008, 70–71). Excellent performers typically do not blame errors on bad luck, but see themselves as responsible (2008, 119). They specify that aspect of their performance that is related to the error, and work on that. Error is inherent in achieving excellence. Colvin estimated that Olympic skater Shizuka Arakawa fell a minimum of 20,000 times over the nearly twenty years it took her to win the gold medal. Metaphorically, landing on one's backside thousands of times is what makes an exceptional performance achievable, according to Colvin (2008, 187–88).

Deliberate practice tends to be designed and systematic. A challenge is identifying the steps involved. Some fields have been in existence for some time, which has allowed them to become more structured—such as for playing a piano (2008, 109). Practice must also be cumulative. To reach the top ranks in any domain demands thousands of hours of sustained study and practice. The Berlin study found that by age twenty, top violinists had accumulated approximately 10,000 hours of practice (2008, 171). William Chase and Nobel Prize winner Herbert Simon put forth the "ten-year rule" based on their research on chess players. They found that top-tier chess players had spent at least ten years in concentrated study (2008, 61). The ten-year rule has been found by researchers in the achievement of excellence for any field of endeavor—whether it involved invention, performance, creativity, or discovery (2008, 152).

As Aristotle (1976, 92) acknowledged, those who have an opportunity to start early can have an advantage. The human brain and the rest of the body are more adaptable when young. The cerebral cortex has more plasticity at early ages (Colvin 2008, 103). Relatively more space in a violinist's brain is devoted to the left hand than in the brains of others, and this is more evident for those who begin musical training as children. Another effect of sustained practice is the slow build-up of myelin around neurons. Myelin build-up is more pronounced with practice in childhood than in adulthood (2008, 171).

As Colvin pointed out, ongoing deliberate practice for an adult who has family and career responsibilities is taxing. The inclination is to maintain a course that is doable and relatively comfortable (2008, 173). An adult who is considering a new endeavor with the commitment to the practice, study, and expense it entails, faces the challenge (a possibly hopeless one, according to Colvin) of trying to catch up to professionals who already have accumulated years of intensive practice and continue to amass hundreds of hours of practice each year. As Colvin said, "get out a calculator and face the music" (2008, 172).

To demonstrate the effect of sustained, intensive practice starting at an early age in a particular field on eventual success, Hungarian educational psychologist, Laszlo Polgar conducted an experiment with his three daughters, who all received instruction in chess. Polgar and his wife devoted themselves full time to homeschooling their daughters, primarily in chess—several hours a day. At the outset, Polgar was an average chess player, and his wife had no ability. The eldest daughter, at age seventeen, was the first female to qualify for what was later to become the World Chess Federation; however, she was not allowed to compete because of her sex. Four years later, she became the first female grand master. At fifteen, the youngest daughter became the youngest person to be named a grand master (2008, 76–77). She ranked number one in the world among women players in 1989 and continued to do so with few exceptions until February 2015 (World Chess Federation 2019). As a team, all three daughters along with another woman won against the Soviets in the women's Olympiad in 1988. Colvin noted that none of the daughters made it to world champion. In his view, what may have contributed to this is that in their twenties, they chose to have families, which gave them less time to devote to the game. Colvin quoted the oldest daughter as saying: "It's not that chess was too much for me; it was too little" (2008, 78).

Howard Gardner, who studied several high achievers, said that the great performer sacrifices normal personal relationships. They are "committed obsessively to their work. Social life or hobbies are almost immaterial" (2008, 205). The price for excellence in a chosen field can be extremely high. However, as Colvin said, "by understanding how a few become great, anyone can become better" (2008, 206).

RISK MANAGEMENT

Understanding the relationship between risk reduction and experience has been an interest to those in risk management. Using 200 years of world data, Romney B. Duffey and John W. Saull estimated a relationship between error reduction and experience at the systems level they referred to as the universal learning curve (ULC) (2008, 52–53, 506, 2009, 4). The focus in risk management is at the "macro" level—technological systems at the organizational and/or industry level. More relevant for the discussion in this chapter is the "micro" or individual level, which has been the interest of cognitive psychologists as well as those in the study of learning behavior. Interestingly, and surprisingly, Duffey and Saull have found a common predictive basis for their work at the macro level and the empirical work at the micro level conducted by cognitive psychologists and others. Specifically, whether at the systems level or the individual level, the relationship between error reduction and experience can be represented by a single exponential equation, the universal law of practice (ULP) (2008, 508; Fiondella and Duffey 2015, 5–6).

The following subsections will briefly overview the ULC and the ULP. Of the equations that are presented, those that are most significant to this discussion are those for ULC, ULP, and RT*. Other equations are presented to provide the background for the linkages between these equations to the extent they apply. All derivational steps are not included and can be found in the references provided. Definitions that are particularly relevant are those for $E^* = A^*/A_0^*$, $N^* = \varepsilon_i/\varepsilon_T$ (where N^* may stand for a nondimensional measure for either accumulated experience or depth of experience, depending upon context), $t^* = t/t_T$, and $p_i = n_i/N_j$. The notation used here is from Duffey and Saull (2008). It can be a bit confusing. For instance, E^* is a nondimensional measure of *errors*, and ε is used for dimensional measures of *experience*; N^* is a non-dimensional measure of *experience*, and n_i and N_j represent dimensional measures of *errors*.

Universal Learning Curve (ULC)

The ULC is given by:

$$E^* = e^{-3N^*}.$$

E^* is the nondimensional error rate, N^* is a nondimensional measure of accumulated experience, and 3 is the learning rate constant, k. The estimated value for k was based on 200 years of world data that included approximately 800 data points from numerous technological systems (Duffey and Saull 2008, 52–53, 506, 2009, 4).

In the ULC, E^*, the nondimensional error rate, can be expressed as:

$$E^* = A^* / A_0^*, \quad \text{where}$$

$$A^* = \left(1 - A_m / A\right), \quad \text{and}$$

$$A_0^* = \left(1 - A_m / A_0\right).$$

E^* is a normalized error rate where A is the error rate, A_m is the minimum error rate, and A_0 is the initial error rate (2008, 298). A high initial event rate tends to often decrease rapidly with learning. The following equation (2008,

199, 208, 211) can be used to approximate the value for A_0 as well as estimate the values for A_m and trend:

$$A \approx A_{\mathrm{m}} + A_0 \mathrm{e}^{-\varepsilon i/K},$$

where ε_i is accumulated experience (2008, 298). As an example, Duffey and Saull (2008) provided worksheet data for U.S. tanker oil spills over 1,000 gallons (1973–2000) for which the following equation was estimated:

$$\mathrm{IR}(\text{Spills per Mtoe}) = 0.018 + 0.4\mathrm{e}^{-(\mathrm{accMtoe}/21{,}600)}.$$

In this case, IR, the spill rate, was used as the dependent variable instead of the number of spills because the latter concealed the learning trend. IR is the number of oil spills that exceed 1,000 gallons per year divided by ε_i—the accumulated oil shipped per year (measured in million tons shipped, Mtoe). The predicted minimum is 0.018 spills per Mtoe, which had not yet been reached during the observation interval (1973–2000) (2008, 358–59). A plot of the oil spill data against the ULC equation: $E^* = \mathrm{e}^{-3N^*}$ revealed a close fit (2008, 363–64). (Duffey [2011, 16] noted that for the learning "constant," *k*, in the E^* equation: "progressively lower values mean less and less learning.") The measure for N^* (nondimensional accumulated experience) is $\varepsilon_i/\varepsilon_T$; that is, accumulated oil shipped per year divided by the total oil shipped over the observation interval 1973–2000. (See Duffey and Saull [2008, 320] step (c) for further clarification on N^*.)

Universal Law of Practice (ULP)

In addition to the systems level, the relationship between learning and error reduction has also been of interest at the individual level among cognitive psychologists and those in the study of learning behavior. Specifically, this is represented by the "law of practice" based on an empirically observed nonlinear relationship between practice and the number of successes:

$$S_N = \alpha t^{\mathrm{m}}$$

where S_N is the number of successes, and *t* is a count of practice trials. (In order to avoid confusion with N^* and N_j, I have replaced N_s, which is shown in [2008, 507, 2009, 4; Fiondella and Duffey 2015, 2], with S_N to represent number of successes.) J. C. Stevens and H. B. Savin estimated this equation using data for stylized tasks that included, among other things, running a maze, writing upside down, memorizing a series of words, and throwing a ball at a target. As shown in Duffey and Saull (2008, 507–508, 2009, 4), when the number of successes was transformed into failure rates, the individual practice curve conformed almost identically with the ULC. The ULC was thus transformed into the universal law of practice (ULP):

$$E^* = e^{-3t^*},$$

where t^* is nondimensional practice equal to t/t_T, where t is the number of practice trials or the amount of practice, and t_T is the maximum number of practice trials or the maximum amount of practice.

In Fiondella and Duffey (2015), the following relationship between k in the ULC and m in the S_N equation was presented:

$$k = (1/t^*)\left[\ln(t_0)^{m-1} - 1\right] / \left[\ln(t^*)^{m-1} - 1\right]$$

Fiondella and Duffey used this equation to plug in a range values for the m estimated by Stevens and Savin as well as others of $0.2 < m < 1$, and a range of values for the estimated t^* of $0.1 < t^* < 1$. They found that on average k equaled 2.92, which is very close to $k = 3$ found at the systems level. They concluded: "*Systems behave, reflect and exhibit externally the same learning trends as the humans within them. The collective of individuals reflects precisely the individuals within the collective*" (2015, 4; italics in original).

Response Time Reduction (RT)

(This subsection discusses response time reduction, a second category of learning. It provides background into this second category of learning for those interested; otherwise, it may be omitted without loss of continuity.)

Duffey and Saull categorized learning involving human subjects into two types: error rate reduction and response time reduction. The former is related primarily to the learning of repetitive skills and depends on accumulated experience. It was discussed in the previous subsection in relation to the ULC and resulted in the ULP. The second, response time reduction in the instantaneous recognition of patterns, is postulated to be related to depth of experience (2008, 506, 2009, 3).

Unlike "accumulated experience," "depth of experience" requires experience data specific to the individual "type" under investigation. To illustrate, in an examination of pilot fatalities and experience, depth of experience required data on the amount of flying time (in hours) the pilot had clocked in the type of aircraft in which the fatal accident had happened (2008, 212). To clarify:

> The number of pilots killed, n_i, were binned into 100-flying-hour experience intervals, where the intervals were up to 100 flying hours, then to 200 flying

> hours, 300 flying hours, etc. all the way up to 1,000 flying hours. These experience 100-hour "bins" represents the levels of the depth of experience in the chosen 15-year observation interval, with mean experience levels of 50, 150, 250, etc., flying hours, up to the maximum of 1,000 flying hours.
>
> This prior flying experience in flying hours is called "time on type," and is *exactly* a relevant measure of the depth of experience from learning, risk exposure and skill acquisition. (2008, 212; italics and ellipses in original)

Experience was measured at $\varepsilon_1 = 50$ flying hours for the 100th interval, $\varepsilon_2 = 150$ for 200th, and so on. The number, n_1, were those who were killed who had clocked up to 100 hours, n_2 for those with up to 200, etc. The depth of experience for the 100th interval was $(\varepsilon_1 \text{n}_1)$; for the 200th, it was $(\varepsilon_1 n_1 + \varepsilon_2 n_2)$; etc. $N_1^* = (\varepsilon_1 n_1)/\varepsilon_T$, $N_2^* = (\varepsilon_1 n_1 + \varepsilon_2 n_2)/\varepsilon_T$, etc. were the nondimensional depths of experience for the *i*th levels, where $\varepsilon_T = \sum \varepsilon_i n_i = 43{,}600$ total pilot flying hours is the total experience for the 15-year period under investigation (2008, 213–14). (Recall that N^* is nondimensional and represents accumulated experience or depth of experience depending upon context.)

Like error reduction, response time as a function of practice can be shown to conform to the exponential form; specifically, in Duffey (2017, 112) and Fiondella and Duffey (2015, 6), a response reduction time ratio, RT*, is presented as an exponential function of non-dimensional practice, t^*. To arrive at this equation for RT*, response time (RT) can be represented first as a linear function of information entropy, H. This is the Hick-Hyman law, which can be expressed as follows:

$$\text{RT} = \text{c} + \text{d}H.$$

Information entropy is given as (2015, 5; Duffey and Saull 2008, 339; Duffey 2008, 3):

$$H = -\sum p_\text{i} \ln p_\text{i}.$$

In Duffey (2011, 39), entropy is defined as "an objective measure of what we know about what we do not know, which is the risk." The (prior) probability is: $p_\text{i} = n_\text{i}/N_\text{j}$, where n_i is the number of errors per time period, and N_j is the total number of errors for the observation interval (the entire range of the data under investigation) (see Duffey and Saull [2008, 320] step (d)). As an example, Duffey and Saull (2008, 321) depicted the estimated equation for "entropy," $E = 0.28 - 1.11N^*$, where E (which denotes "entropy" rather than "error") is the absolute value of ΔH, the change in H for a given experience increment. ΔH was calculated as $p_i \ln p_i$, where $p_i = n_\text{i}/N_\text{j}$ was based on well drilling injuries. In this case, N^* was based on accumulated experience of well drilling hours for 1996–2005.

To derive an equation for the "H-factor," p_i is given as

$$p_i = p_0 e^{-\alpha N^*}$$

where α is a learning constant and N^* is nondimensional "depth of experience" (Duffey and Saull 2009, 7). For simplification, p_0 is normalized "to the initial probability at the initial or lowest experience, where we take $p_0 = 1$, by definition" (2008, 320). The "best" value for α is approximately 3.5, which is based on data for automobile deaths and aircraft near-misses (2008, 345, 2009, 7; Duffey 2011, 42).

When $p_0 e^{-\alpha N^*}$ is substituted for p_i in the solution for the integral form of H (Duffey and Saull 2008, 317, 2009, 7), this gives the "H-factor":

$$H_j = 1/2\left\{p_0 e^{-\alpha N^*}\right\}^2 \left\{\alpha N^* + 1/2\right\}.$$

The H-factor is a measure of uncertainty (or order); thus, it quantifies risk for any system. Uncertainty is determined by probability. As seen in the p_i equation above, probability is a function of the learning exponent, α, and depth of experience. Given $p_0 = 1$, then as $N^* \rightarrow 0$ (experience decreases), $H_j \rightarrow 0.25$. As α (the learning rate) or N^* (depth of experience) increases, H_j decreases, which is accompanied by a more uniform distribution and more order (Duffey 2008, 3–4, 2011, 41; Duffey and Saull 2008, 317).

Substituting an expression for H_j (2008, 339–42, 509–10) into the RT equation shown above results in the ABC Law of Practice:

$$RT_j = A_j + B_j e^{-\alpha t} + C_j e^{-2\alpha t}$$

where t is the numbers of trials or practice time.

The ABC response time reduction ratio equation is:

$$RT^* = RT(t)/RT_0,$$

where RT_0 is response time at $t = 0$. Fiondella and Duffey (2015, 5) showed that RT* has a nondimensional form similar to that for error rate reduction, $E^* = A^*/A_0^*$, shown above. Thus, RT* can be expressed in an exponential form written as a function of $t^* = t/t_T$. This equation is presented in Duffy (2017) and Fiondella and Duffey (2015) as:

$$RT^* = 0.4e^{-4t^*},$$

which is comparable to the error rate reduction equation: $E^* = e^{-3t^*}$. Fiondella and Duffey pointed out: "Here the response times decrease slightly faster then [*sic*] error correction by or with repetition, by about approximately 30% since the slope ratio is 4/3" (2015, 6). Or, equivalently: "From the slope ratio of 4/3 …, recall of semi-automatic learned reactions or responses are quicker than recall from memory with subsequent physical and mental error correction" (Duffey 2017, 112).

Overall the conclusion is that in comparisons between the ULC based on systems data and empirical learning curves with human subjects for both error reduction (the S_N equation) and response time reduction (RT), a common predictive basis was found for time frames involving multiple years for macro-technological systems to those that occur within a tenth of a second at the individual learning level (Duffey and Saull 2008, 506, 2009, 3).

Minimum Failure Rate

Risk reduction (i.e., learning) is, according to Duffey and Saull (2008, 216), proportional to the error rate, which is described by the ULC. The ULC shows the error rate as an exponential function of experience (risk exposure). The trend represented by the ULC has been observed for railroad injuries, automobile deaths, oil spills, nuclear power plant incidents, and many others. Duffey and Saull examined a myriad of error and experience data in systems with dramatically diverse technologies and all of it conformed to their Learning Hypothesis.

They also observed that there has been no apparent change in the minimum failure rate for over 200 years (Duffey 2011, 7–8, 12, 27). A minimum failure rate is consistent with their learning theory and has been observed throughout the world. Zero errors do not occur in any technological system because of human involvement (2011, 15; Duffey and Saull 2008, 216). A nonzero minimum failure rate is also found in testing of learning by human subjects. The so-called power law prediction of zero asymptotic failures is not found in reality. Although the power law (S_N equation above) might suggest that "practice makes perfect," in reality it only makes "nearly perfect" (Fiondella and Duffey 2015, 2). Power curves can greatly under-predict the chance of failure at high levels of experience, because they do not take into consideration the minimum failure rate, which is largely the result of the human factor (Duffey 2010, 4). Even though the power curve may give a better fit in the early learning stage, it does not provide as good a fit as the exponential curve (ULP) in the later learning stages (Fiondella and Duffey 2015, 7).

As Fiondella and Duffey (2015, 4) pointed out, there is a mathematical relationship between the power curve and the ULC (as shown by the *k* equation above) that reveals an equivalence of their exponents. Also, as they noted, both for purposes of comparison and for prediction, it is best to normalize data thereby transforming it into non-dimensional values. Duffey and Saull's learning theory suggests how data on error rates should be adjusted to achieve nondimensional equivalents using values for initial and minimum error rates (analogous to $E^* = A^*/A_0^*$ above). For tests involving human learning, the minimum failure rate takes place at the maximum practice, t_T.

"Practice" or number of trials was shown to be equivalent to "experience" in the ULC. This equivalence is represented by the more general (in terms of application) ULP. To reiterate, a key finding is that learning behavior at the individual level as a function of practice has the identical form and predictive basis as learning at the systems level as a function of experience (Duffey and Saull 2008, 506, 508, 509).

Error Reduction and Excellence

Duffey (2011) expressed the learning paradox, which indicates that in order to learn, it is necessary to take on the very risks that humans strive to avoid. Errors or accidents are random in occurrence, and thus cannot be predicted with certainty. Yet, it is through randomness that learning emerges. Order is created from disorder. The essence of the Learning Hypothesis is that humans learn from mistakes. Learning is synonymous with risk (or error) reduction. It is through experience that humans expose themselves to risk—in fact, Duffey equates experience with risk exposure. Risks increase by driving a car, making an investment, flying an airplane, and so on. "The rate at which we make errors … reduces both as we gain experience and if and as we learn" (2011, 20). It is through experience that individuals learn (or can learn), and by learning, the risk of making an error is reduced. However, the risk of a future error is never zero, primarily because humans make errors. A point that Duffey appears to be making is an existential one—that risks are inherent in human life. Individuals take risks because risks are a fact of reality for humans. And it is only by exposure to risk—that is, experience—that humans can discover how to reduce the risk of error; that is, learn. Nevertheless, risk is never eliminated.

If humans do not learn, then they face more risk (2011, 13). Duffey and Saull stated: "*[L]ack of experience represents the greatest risk!*" (2008, 215; italics in original) They pointed out that risk is greatest at the onset of an experience (2008, 161). They set the probability of a beginner making a mistake at about 63%; that is, (1 – 1/e) (2008, 60, 404). That probability is high, and is particularly disturbing if the error involved is a potentially fatal one. There are different approaches to learning. A person can learn through trial and error—that is, experience. At times, this is necessary. A person must venture outside the cave. Of course, experience needn't be without design;

for instance, on-the-job training (OJT) can be highly structured. However, for occupations that are particularly hazardous, more systematic training is typically in order.

This kind of formal training is highly organized and rigorous and is typically undertaken in a controlled environment. In dangerous occupations, the risk to the person's life and to those around him are jeopardized beyond that which is necessary if a novice has not engaged in prior training. During training, errors are expected. However, because training is supervised, the risks are typically of the "incidental" variety. Errors are reduced by repetition, followed by testing. Training of this kind is synonymous with Colvin's deliberate practice.

Deliberate practice also involves "upping one's game"—that is, mastering one thing, then proceeding to the next level. Continually challenging oneself can result in more cumulative errors than if one is maintaining a status quo. The focus here is on a given level of training—a single "training module," so to speak, not on several levels of training of increasing difficulty. (Depending upon the context, a "given level of training" could apply to a single module composed of a number of steps or to a given training course comprising a number of modules. For simplicity, I will usually refer to a single module or task.)

The purpose of training is to prepare the trainee for the real world. For purposes here, training can be thought of as falling into two categories: those that allow for variability and those that conform to a fixed structure. The former prepares the trainee for situations in which an action allows for more than one (correct) response. The environment is controlled; however, by necessity it allows for variability. This would involve training for combat—such as field training, as well as team sports and games—such as baseball and chess. The second type of training deals with training for specific tasks that follow a fairly rigid pattern. For example, in deep sea diving, assent follows a rigid procedure (*U.S. Navy Diving Manual* 1978, 7.9–7.15). Learning a particular piece of music would be another example. The focus here will be on this second type of training or practice.

One of Duffey's points was that perfection is not possible. This is true for systems over time. It is also true for training a group of novices for a given task (learning module). It applies as well for specific individuals who are continuingly trying to improve. However, for a given person pursuing a specific task (training module), perfection is possible. Of course, to assess whether a performance is perfect, it is necessary to define what an error is. For dangerous occupations, the primary objective is to avoid a fatal error—that is to avoid an error that could lead to death (or serious injury) involving oneself and/or others. (I should clarify that by "others" I mean other co-workers and those who are being rescued or treated. To achieve particular military objectives in certain combat situations, for instance, the expectation is that the enemy will be injured or killed.) "Fatal errors" are a defining feature of dangerous occupations. If avoidance of a fatal error is the objective, then perfection in the performance of a task (training module) is achievable. A "fatal error rate" (force of mortality) may be positive for a task under certain specified assumptions; however, an individual may achieve perfection in his performance if the objective is the avoidance of a fatal error for a given task.

This is where epistemology intersects with ethics. A person may pursue training that is designed to sufficiently learn a task that results in risk reduction. However, he may also learn with the goal of achieving *excellence* in the performance of a task thereby avoiding a fatal error.

Training

As mentioned, voluntarily undertaking a risk is considered rational if the expected return is greater than the expected loss. However, many people undertake significant risks (including death) which appear to exceed the return. For instance, professional firefighters take significant risks for relatively modest pay. One reason they may be willing to undertake the dangers involved in an occupation of this kind is that they engage in training that is designed to lower the risks. Training involves learning in modules in which activities are broken down into steps. These learning modules are undertaken by trainees under controlled settings. For a given module, the steps are repeated and then testing takes place before a trainee proceeds to the next module. Colvin would call this "deliberate practice."

My husband was a firefighter and one of the more demanding physical aspects of the training was to carry a body (200-pound dummy) up a flight of stairs and return it to the first floor while wearing fire fighting gear, including (SCBA) air tank. The "turn-out" gear can weigh forty-five to seventy-five pounds. The inner layers of the coat can protect the skin for temperatures up to 212 degrees. Of course, this exercise only simulates an actual experience because in a real firefight the firefighter not only has to fight a fire in order to rescue the person, but the person may not be cooperative. During training, the trainees also spend a good deal of time on the more mundane (but necessary and life preserving) aspects of firefighting such as learning how to carry a ladder. In *Essentials of Fire Fighting* (1983), Chapter 5, every aspect of dealing with ladders—of carrying, raising, securing, climbing, etc.—is broken down into numbered steps with notes and cautionary warnings.

The entire firefighting course was almost six months in duration. (Now it is longer because it also has incorporated emergency medical technician, EMT, training.) Length of training depends in part on the circumstances. For instance, in the military during wartime, training time may be curtailed from what would exist under "ordinary" circumstances. According to the *American Air Museum in Britain* (2018), Colonel Donald Blakeslee, 4th Fighter Group Commanding Officer during World War II "told his pilots that they could learn to fly the Mustang on the way to the target. And that's just what they did on 28 February [1944] when they flew their first mission in the beloved and esteemed P-51 Mustang." Of course, technically this "time on type" training would qualify as OJT.

When time is a critical factor in the length of training, attrition takes on a larger role. To varying degrees, all training relies not only on teaching but also attrition. This can be particularly the case in a wartime setting. For instance, when my husband, who was in Marine Corps reconnaissance, went to dive school during his tour in Vietnam the length of training was four weeks. Those who started training had been carefully selected and each man had every incentive to perform well, since he otherwise was returned to his Marine Corps or Army combat unit. Even so, of the eighty who began training, only twelve completed it.

Years later, my husband returned to the military as a Navy diving and salvage officer. Unlike his earlier training that focused primarily on SCUBA, this training required divers to learn virtually every diving apparatus. U.S. Navy dive training is quite technical as well as physical. The standard Mark V was still being used at that time (*U.S. Navy Diving Manual* 1978, 6.1–6.20). The rig in its entirety weighs approximately 200 pounds (United States Undersea Museum 2016). The belt weighs about eighty-four pounds, the shoes weigh about thirty-five pounds (*U.S. Navy Diving Manual* 1978, 6.6–6.7), and the helmet and breast plate weigh a little over fifty-five pounds (Divers Institute of Technology 2019). One of the more challenging physical aspects of the Mark V was, after training under-water, climbing a ladder to board the ship with the outfit filled with water and the oxygen shut off. In diving and dive training, timing related to a particular task can be critical. When a diver has to go into a decompression chamber, the timing for removing his gear cannot exceed 3.5 minutes (*U.S. Navy Diving Manual* 1978, 6.94). Some gear, such as the Mark V, is more challenging than others (1978, 6.12).

In training environments, danger is controlled, but it is not eliminated. The point here is that the person is willing to undertake a risk, because he anticipates that through learning, the risk of death or other dangers will be reduced. And this can be achieved initially by learning in structured "chunks," that are further broken down into steps in a controlled environment. These steps are typically repeated (at least once), and ultimately, the trainee is tested on what he has learned (or on some variation or combination of what he has learned).

The question of why a person would undertake such risks is not merely about learning—that is, it is not confined to epistemology. The question is primarily an ethical one. Why would a person choose to engage in activities that risk his life, if life is his ultimate value? I think the answer lies in a person's strive for excellence. It would be foolhardy and unethical to play Russian roulette. This "game" is based solely on chance. There is no skill involved. There is no opportunity available for a person to learn a skill that could change the odds in his favor. However, this is not the case for, say, firefighting. Here a trainee can strive to learn to be excellent in order to reduce the risks associated with dangers thereby ultimately achieving a worthy outcome—in this case saving lives and/or property. Excellence and striving for it are virtues. Excellence also has an aesthetic dimension—although the emphasis here is on the ethical aspect.

Dangerous Occupations are Dominated by Men

A free society not only depends on the risk-taking of entrepreneurs, it relies upon the voluntary risk-taking of combat soldiers, firefighters, and police officers as well as those in other high-risk occupations. Physically dangerous occupations are more often employed by men. In the United States over 90% of work-related deaths are men (Bureau of Labor Statistics 1998; "Men Dominate in Workplace Deaths," 1995). This is not only true in the United States, but also in other countries. At least one source put the comparable U.K. figure at 97% (*Inside Man* 2015).

Certainly, sex differences in strength and size have some bearing on occupational choice. There are no female NFL players, for instance. Strength is undoubtedly more important than size—my husband is 5'4," and weighed 117 pounds when in Vietnam. For many of these occupations, personal preferences are also a factor. This leads to the question of what the bases for preferences are. Gerianne M. Alexander presented evidence that at least some preferences have a biological basis and indicated further that they have evolutionary roots. As reported by Connellan et al. (2000), in a test with infants, one-day-old boys were found to have a visual preference for movement of mechanical objects over faces; the opposite was found for girls. Boys tend to have an object movement visual bias and girls tend to have a form/color visual bias.

Alexander presented experimental evidence that the hormone androgen may play a role in visual pathway specialization that leads to visual biases either in form/color or in object movement. Based on studies by evolutionary theorists and researchers, Alexander also suggested that hunting may have provided an evolutionary basis for spatial pathway bias for males. Foraging may have been the evolutionary basis for form/color bias for females. In the latter case, foraging requires red on green color detection. The X-chromosome transmits red/green sensitivity, and males, who have only one X-chromosome, are more apt to be red/green color deficient (Alexander 2003, 9–11).

A visual pathway bias in males for the spatial movement of objects, which is linked to androgen levels, and has a possible evolutionary basis in hunting is only a single contributive factor that could influence preferences for occupations whose risks share similarities with hunting. It is merely suggestive, but it does point to physiological differences that could underlie preferences.

People in dangerous occupations typically have a higher tolerance for and preference for physical risk than other people. This would imply that those who do not choose these professions have less of a tolerance for physical risk. It would seem to follow that women, in general, have less of a tolerance for risk—specifically risk related to occupations in which there is a relatively high probability of death. As mentioned, over 90% of work-related deaths are men. However, 100% of pregnancy-related deaths are women. I realize that the bases are different for these two percentages. Nevertheless, I mention the latter figure to suggest that one reason women may not have a preference for occupations that have a high risk of death is that women face inherent physical risks that men do not. Therefore they may be less willing to pursue occupations in which there would be additional physical risks.

Women are born with a probability of experiencing discomfort or pain that can range from mild to extreme over the course of their lives (from puberty through menopause) as a natural course of living. There is or can be a good deal of uncertainty—not only related to discomfort, pain, or even death, but also as to when, and/or if these will occur. (See Touchstone [2017] on how uncertainty related to pregnancy may have a bearing on how women view the axiom "A is A." Specifically, it addresses the question: Where does one stop and two begin?) The probability of death from pregnancy complications is relatively low in the United States. In 2015, pregnancy complications (pregnancy, childbirth, and the puerperium) was less than 3% for women 25 through 34 of all causes of death (Heron 2017, 22). Of course, more economically developed countries have a lower probability of pregnancy-related deaths than less developed countries. In 2017, maternal deaths per 100,000 live births ranged from a high of 396,638 in Afghanistan (i.e., approximately four women died for every one live birth) to a low of 2 per 100,000 in Belarus, Italy, Norway, and Poland (Central Intelligence Agency 2017). Historically, pregnancy-related deaths have been a risk for women and remain a high risk in some countries. In 2002, in Afghanistan, pregnancy-related deaths accounted for half of the deaths in females 15 through 49 ("Afghanistan is Among Worst Places on Globe for Women's Health," 2002). Given that life expectancy for women in Afghanistan was reported to be 44 years in 1995 (the only country of 109 to have a lower life expectancy than men) (*SPSS* 1999), this was a high risk they faced for the vast majority of their lives. In economically developed countries, the benefits of modern medicine have significantly reduced this risk; however, a figure of

50% probably reflects the probability faced by women of child-bearing age prior to medical advances. It is likely that, given this built-in physical risk, historically, women (generally speaking) have been averse to accumulating additional risk by voluntarily seeking occupations involving a high probability of physical danger.

As an aside, many women in more economically advanced countries are opting out of this risk. As of 2017, in the United States, the reproduction rate was 16% below that necessary for replacement (Braine 2019). A reproductive rate below replacement has been the trend for most of Western Europe for more than two decades (Touchstone 2006, 30–31). I have made the point that as paid employment opportunities have increased for women in these countries, non-remunerative work (particularly childrearing) has become less attractive. I have also noted an additional factor, and that is the relatively low esteem with which childrearing is held by a culture (2006, 233). Moreover, people are quite willing to do volunteer work and charitable work for no pay, and to engage in time-consuming and sometimes expensive hobbies. I don't think the lack of remuneration (or the risk of death, which is relatively low in economically developed countries) is the only factor that discourages childbearing. I think the lack of esteem with which it is held may be another disincentive.

MEASURING DIFFICULTY AND RISK FOR A "TRAINING MODULE"

The ULP curve shows the decrease in the error rate as training or practice increases. For training involving a given training module, a given level of proficiency specific to that task is expected after a given period of practice. The length of training can vary. When time is of the essence, as in a war time setting, the training period may be shorter than would exist under "normal" circumstances. Consequently, potential trainees may be screened (or screened more rigorously) for certain skills (or levels of ability or proficiency) prior to training. Also, part of the training process involves not only learning, but also attrition. A given training module's difficulty level may be reflected in its rate of attrition.

In what follows, I address estimating a "fatal error" rate for a given "training module" for a given task. In order to do that, I assume that the "trainee" is at a given overall proficiency level as well as a given practice level for the specific "module" or task. In other words, the levels of proficiency and practice for a given "module" are fixed. "Timing" is an important element in training. For some types of tasks, it is vital. This is true, for instance, in diving, where the timing for air decompression at various levels of ascent is very precise (*U.S. Navy Diving Manual* 1978, 7.8). As will be seen, time is also a factor that is fixed in the discussion below.

Many of the elements that are critical to occupational training modules apply to any fixed routine where learning is involved. In the following, I focus on the playing of a musical piece. However, the fundamentals of the discussion could apply to a training module for deep-sea diving, a gymnastics routine for the Olympics, or a choreographed dance. The focus is on the "expected life span" of the piece itself. An expected life span can be calculated for a musical piece just as it can for a human life. In order to do so from a theoretical perspective, a force of mortality (fatal error rate) is needed. The expected life span of a piece can be seen as a measure of difficulty. The value of one minus the ratio of the expected life span relative to the maximum potential life can be viewed as a "risk index," which gives an idea of the degree of risk that must be overcome to achieve "excellence."

Music and the Tyranny of Time

Duffey and Saull (2008) have demonstrated theoretically and empirically that experience is comparable to practice insofar as they relate to the ULC and the ULP. Even so, it would seem to be a stretch to equate risking a serious physical injury or death with that of making an error playing a piece of music. Yet, for George Plimpton, a person for whom this comparison was made concrete, the trepidation he felt about making a mistake playing a musical instrument exceeded the fear of a potentially serious physical injury in professional sports—at least for those sports in which he participated. Plimpton worked for *Sports Illustrated* and wrote books on professional sports in which he actively participated as an amateur. Among other things, he played quarterback with the Detroit Lions, pitched an all-star game at Yankee Stadium, boxed with Archie Moore (the light heavy-weight champion of the world), and was a goal tender for the Boston Bruins. When he discussed these experiences, he said:

> The most terrifying thing to me … The one that terrified me more than any of the other things that I did was playing with the New York Philharmonic. I played the triangle … and some of the other percussion instruments. And, of course, the reason it was so terrifying was that in music you cannot make a mistake. You know, sports is all predicated on the idea that somebody is going to make an error. In fact, you can't have a sport without somebody making an error. But in music if you make an error, you destroy a piece of art. (Plimpton 1997)

In Plimpton's biography, *George Being George*, Bob Johnson of the New York Philharmonic echoed the sentiment above, saying of Plimpton:

> He was terrified. In fact, he said that playing in the orchestra was the hardest thing he ever did, because of the tyranny of time: In sports, you can call time-out or you can mop your brow or whatever, but in music, once your piece starts, it's not over until the measure's been played, and your part will be noted. There's nothing else like that in the world of competition. It was very unnerving. (Aldrich 2008, 217)

Plimpton discussed this further at the 5th Annual Writers Symposium at Point Loma Nazarene University's (Plimpton 2000).

Two Times

When thinking of time with respect to music, two aspects that come to mind are tempo and meter. Instead of tempo or meter, the focus in this subsection is on two other attributes of time in music. One is that music is heard sequentially over time. Another is a musical piece has a limited duration. These two aspects of time are similar to a life of a biological entity (or the existence of a physical asset). A human being, for instance, exists sequentially over time, and also has a finite life. A musical piece can be thought to come to life, so to speak, when it is performed.

The performance of a musical piece is similar to that of a learning module that has a fixed pattern. It is also similar to reciting a monologue or performing a gymnastics routine at an event, such as the Olympics. In each of these cases, the performance occurs in a sequence. It has a known, rigid structure, and it has a known end. This characteristic of having a known, fixed structure is not always the case for the real-world counterparts that learning modules for dangerous occupations aim to replicate; nor is it true of games, such as chess or soccer, or for improvisation in theatre or jazz. Although the discussion will revolve around written music, it might equally apply to a learning module, a written monologue, or a gymnastics routine. For the most part, it would not always apply to real world events that some occupational training modules are designed to approximate, nor will it apply to games or musical improvisation.

As with a biological life, the life of a musical piece is finite. In the case of a musical piece, that end is known. By this I mean that it has a given number of measures. It would also have a fixed clock time for a given tempo. (A life span can be approximated for biological life forms or for capital assets; however, an exact known time of death is generally not the case.) As with biological life and physical assets, there can be accidents that occur over time. These accidents may not be fatal. However, for the purposes considered here, I will focus only on those accidents that are "fatal." That is, I am interested in the "mortality" associated with a musical piece. Like a human life, the objective of the performance of a musical piece is to make it to the end (maximum life span) without an "early death."

For biological life forms, "premature death" has been posited to be related to two broad categories of death; those due to "accidents" and those due to factors related to aging. The former are modeled as being unrelated to time and relatively constant. The latter are assumed to increase with time (i.e., with age) (Kurtz 1930, 110–11). For the performance of musical pieces, the causes of "early death" are more akin to the former. With respect to a musical piece, the concentration will be on two categories of death—early death due to accidents and death that would occur if the performer makes it to the end of the musical piece without a fatal error. An accidental death would be a mistake or error that would occur during the performance of a piece that would either bring it to an early end or would be serious enough to be regarded as "fatal." (Identifying what that might be would require some informed judgment.)

There are a number of accidents that could occur during the performance of a musical piece unrelated to the piece itself that could prematurely end it, such as equipment failure or sudden illness. Separate from these possibilities would be an "accident" or a mistake that relates to the difficulty of the piece. The latter would be a distinguishing factor across musical pieces since they vary in difficulty. These errors will be the focus of the discussion. Generally speaking, one would expect that the more difficult a given piece of music is to perform, the more likely it is to have a higher "early death" rate.

No Early Death

There is the possibility of no early death for a particular musical piece. That is, the piece would be performed until its "natural" end at time $t = T$, without the chance of a "fatal" error. For example, this could apply to an extremely easy piece of music for which it would be virtually impossible for a trained musician to make a significant mistake. There is no possibility of "early death," therefore there are no probabilities involved in this case. One consideration is the units in which time, t, is measured. Time could be measured in musical time, measures (bars), for instance, or it could be measured in clock time, such as minutes or seconds. For instance, if a musical piece was, say, ten measures long, T would equal 10. T is the potential life span. With no early death, T would have the same value as the expected life span (to be discussed next).

Early Death

There are musical pieces for which there is the possibility of performance errors significant enough to be considered "early death" of the piece of music.

These errors are very likely to be correlated with the difficult passages of the musical piece. In order to measure these errors, a number of conditions would need to be in place. For testing purposes, it would be assumed that musicians play the piece at a given tempo. That is, during testing, the tempo for a given piece should be held constant across musicians to the extent possible. It is obvious that the more skilled the musician, the less likely there is for errors, so the skill level would have to be kept constant. Also, the more rehearsed the piece is, the less likely there would be for errors, so there would need to be a given level of practice for the piece. Sight-reading limits the complexity of the piece chosen (Lehmann and Ericsson 1993, 184), so if a relatively complex piece is desired, it would be preferable that there is rehearsal time. At the other end of the spectrum, memorized pieces that require significant practice have fewer errors, particularly serious errors. Also, the piece is assumed to be performed on a particular type of instrument. In addition, it must be decided in advance what constitutes an error and what the threshold is for a "fatal" error. The method of identifying and calculating mistakes must be determined as well. Finally, in order to assess criterion validity, it would be desirable to have an alternative source of measurement with which to compare the degree of difficulty of the musical piece.

The same influences that would be held "constant" in an experimental setting would likewise be assumed constant in a theoretical discussion. As previously mentioned, for biological populations, death due to "chance" (accidents) is assumed to be unrelated to time and to be at a constant rate, say, r. Now, as this applies to the performance of a given musical piece, the survival probability per period would be e^{-rt}. From period zero through T, the survival of "early death" due to mistakes is assumed to be associated with a constant force of mortality, r. Whether this assumption is reasonable or not may be tested empirically (which will be discussed later).

Because of early death, the expected life span at the beginning of the musical piece's "life" would no longer be equal to T as it is when there is no chance of early death. T would still be the maximum potential life span if there were no fatal accidents before T, but now the probability of early death (force of mortality) exists, equal to r. The expected life span would be equal to the integrated sum of the per period survival rates, that is, $\int_0^T e^{-rt}$ dt. For each period, the expected number of periods (that is, life) remaining would be given as $PV_t = \int_0^T e^{-rt}$ dt (where T falls by one each time period). This formula is much the same as the formula for the present value of one dollar per year for an economic asset (with no scrap value), $\$PV = \int_0^T e^{-\rho t}$ dt, where ρ is the discount rate. The integrand can be multiplied by the per year income, Y, to give the $PV for a particular asset that has a constant or permanent income stream. For the expected life span, there is no income to consider and the discount rate is now the force of morality, r, but otherwise the equation is conceptually the same. (For the \$PV of an asset, the interest rate, ρ, corresponds to a return of interest that is a "sure thing." The force of mortality is a probability—which means *if* death does not occur, the "return" is equal to that probability multiplied by the expected life remaining, PV_t. See appendix section "Present Value Equation" for further discussion on some of the differences between PV_t and \$PV. Also see appendix section "Return to Not Dying" for a "summary" indicator that reflects the advantage of not dying early.)

For the purposes here, it is preferable to work with the discrete version of the PV equation, which is $PV_t = \sum_1^T [(1/(1 + r)^t]$, where r in the discrete version does not have the same value as r in the continuous version. Using the discrete version and the assumption that $r = 10\%$ and $T = 10$, the expected life span at $t = 1$ would be 6.1445 periods. A theoretical "difficulty index" for the musical piece could be given as the expected life span at $t = 1$ (using the discrete version) divided by the maximum life span T, or PV_1/T. In this case, this would equal 6.1445/10, or .61445. The closer the theoretical difficulty index is to one, the less difficult the piece of music is for a given skill level, tempo, and rehearsal time.

Literature Review

As mentioned, the theoretical difficulty index is PV_1/T. Later I will address how measurement of an actual difficulty index might proceed for a given piece of music. The difference between one and the difficulty index is a measure of the degree of risk that must be overcome to achieve "perfection." A difficulty index could apply to risks other than those related to a piece of music, such as a choreographed dance or others mentioned above. In conducting a test to measure a "difficulty index," a number of influences would need to be held "constant," and these would vary depending upon the particular risk that was being examined—whether that risk involved a training module for deep-sea diving or a gymnastics routine for the Olympics. As mentioned previously, for a specific musical composition for a given instrument, measuring the difficulty index would require (to the extent possible) keeping tempo, amount of rehearsal time, and level of musicianship constant.

Before presenting the "difficulty index" and its measurement, there will be a brief review of the literature on rating musical performances, judging musical performances, grading musical compositions, and defining musical proficiency. Also addressed are considerations related to instrument, tempo, time, and fatal errors. Following the literature review will be suggestions on how to test for a constant force of mortality based on experimental data, how to estimate a force of mortality given that data, and how to measure a "difficulty index" and a "risk index."

Rating Performances

Performance assessment encompasses a wide range of factors such as the type of musical instrument, the purpose of the performance, the level of musicianship of the performer, and the degree of prior rehearsal of the musical piece. The performance assessment measures that have appeared in the literature have been designed for various musical instruments and levels of musical ability (Gutierrez 2005, 5–9). The venues for the performance assessments have included experiments, contests, examinations, and recitals. Assessments have been made on both solo and group performances. Assessments have been done for sight-reading performances, rehearsed performances, memorized performances, and playing by ear. The media by which the assessments were made included both live and recorded performances. Performances were judged or graded by humans as well as by computers (Zdzinski 1991). In research studies on performance assessment, the selection of the piece or pieces of music was dependent on the purpose of the study (Huron and Berec 2009). In some cases, the music was created for the specific project (Delzell et al. 1999). Interestingly, the difficulty of the musical piece was at times not taken into consideration in the assessment of the performance (Latimer et al. 2010, 171).

According to Gutierrez (2005, 7), research in the development of tools to assess musical performances has been limited. Among those performance assessments that were reviewed by Gutierrez were two grading scales, the only ones of which were published and available: the Watkins-Farnum Performance Scales (WFPS) (Watkins and Farnum 1954, 1962) and the Farnum String Scale (FSS) (Farnum 1969). The WFPS and the FSS provide grades based on a number of errors and have been used for both sight-reading and rehearsed performances (Zdzinski 1991, 48). Although the WFPS and the FSS have been subject to criticism for such things as arbitrariness concerning errors, they are regarded as comparatively objective insofar as guidelines for rating aspects of performances are concerned (Gutierrez 2005, 7).

There has been considerable research on how musical performances are assessed within the educational system (e.g., see Thompson and Williamon 2003, 22). Typically, particularly in the past, single grades have been assigned for exam and audition performances, usually with no criteria provided on how the grade was to be assigned. More recently, there have been developments in the measurement of specific skills associated with performances in which each skillset is scored separately (Gutierrez 2005, 4–9). These skill category guidelines, or "rubrics," have been devised in order to improve the reliability of grading because scores based on vague or unspecified guidance tend to be subjective and biased. "A rubric is a scoring instrument that specifies expectations for a given task by dividing it into its component parts and providing a detailed description of what constitutes various levels of performance for each of those parts" (Latimer et al. 2010, 169–70). In some cases, skill categories have been linked to attitude measurement scales, such as the Likert scale. Early on, the Likert-type scale was criticized for providing limited descriptive information on the skills. More descriptors improve reliability, according to Gordon (2002), so long as they number five or fewer (Latimer et al. 2010, 169–70).

In order to reduce bias and thereby improve consistency, assessment criteria focus on musical elements of the performance rather than extraneous factors (Thompson and Williamon 2003, 23; Zdzinski 1991, 50; McPherson and Thompson 1998, 17). The Music Performance Assessment Tool (MPAT) created for St. Scholastica's College of Music by Gutierrez (2005, 18) was comprised of four criteria (technique, stylistic interpretation, memorization, and stage deportment) with four quality levels (excellent, good, satisfactory, and needs improvement). In addition to the category scores, there was a holistic grade. The holistic measure was not based on a composite of the separate grades. There was some overlap in the MPAT categories. For instance, "technique" included correct pitch and rhythm accuracy. By "memorization" was meant perfect recall of the performer's repertoire (2005, 17–20). If there is exact recall of a musical composition, it follows that there is also note and rhythm accuracy. When there exists an overlap between two or more assessment categories (independent or predictor variables), this can result in multicollinearity.

Thompson and Williamon (2003) statistically analyzed the categories that they used in scoring of musical performances for multicollinearity. The score for overall quality of a performance was estimated as a function of the overall grades for instrument competence, musical understanding, and communicability. Multicollinearity was found among the three predictor variables. If the segmented scores are not independent of one another, a composite score that combines segmented category scores can be problematic. Even if there is no overlap in the definitions of the categories, they may tend to move together. For instance, a performance that is deemed technically inferior would be unlikely to be rated stylistically superior. This latter issue also raises the larger question of whether judges are capable of scoring separate aspects of a musical performance (2003, 31–32, 35).

There has been some research into the agreement among judges on overall scores relative to segmented scores, and the results have been mixed. Fiske (1977) reported greater variability among judges for segmented scores than for overall scores (Thompson and Williamon 2003, 26). Thompson and Williamon's results differed from Fiske's (although the results may not have been comparable due to differences in methodologies) (2003, 29). Mills (1991) cast doubt on "holistic scores" that are based on a compilation of segmented scores (Thompson and Williamon 2003, 25). She argued that when listeners evaluate a musical performance they do not use a bottom-up approach; that is, an evaluator does not start by parsing a performance based on a set of factors and then arrive at a total assessment. Instead, Mills said, listeners arrive at an overall evaluation and then justify their assessment based on various aspects of the performance, a top-down approach (McPherson and Thompson 1998, 19).

When there is a divergence between a holistic score that is not based on a compilation of segmented scores and a composite grade that is based on segmented marks, this is not necessarily a strike against the composite approach, per se. It could be that the weighting system assigned to the individual marks that comprised the composite score was wrong. Devising a mathematical equation for overall quality as a function of segmented scores introduces the problem of what weights to apply to the categories as well as whether the categories are additive or not.

In a sight-reading study for piano accompaniment, Lehmann and Ericsson (1993) proposed a single overall score that accounted for separate skills without having to deal with the weighting issue. They pointed out that the single measure of "correctly timed notes" has the advantage of circumventing the problem of assigning weights to categories to arrive at a composite score (1993, 192). The total number of correctly timed notes as a percentage of total notes for a composition includes two skill dimensions, pitch accuracy and rhythm accuracy. The measurement used by Lehmann and Ericsson (1993, 198) counted only the notes that were correctly played within a composition. Timing was based on correct onset, which was judged as being a note initiated within the range of (i.e., plus and minus) a sixteenth note of the notated time. In order to test the criterion validity of their measure, it was compared with the assessment of two judges whose scores were based on overall performance. Because of the close agreement between their measure and the grades of the judges, it was concluded that "correctly timed notes" captures performance qualities other than simply pitch and timing, and that it is a valid measurement of performance quality (in this case for sight-reading) (1993, 190–91).

There needn't be a one-size-fits-all performance assessment instrument. The assessment should fit the objective. One advantage of using segmented scores or rubrics is that by parsing a performance, feedback can be provided to musicians that might be useful in improving their performance (McPherson and Thompson 1998, 21; Thompson and Williamon 2003, 23). An overall score may be desirable in some contexts, but if one of the objectives is skill improvement, segmented scores may be preferred.

Judging Performances

Ideally, measurements should be objective, consistent, and repeatable. If bias is present, then measurements may not meet these criteria. The word "bias" does not mean that judges intentionally are influenced by factors other than quality when assessing a performance. Many times judges are unaware of their biases. For instance, in Thompson and Williamon (2003, 30–31) a judge appeared to have stricter standards for musical performances using his own instrument. Williamon (1999) found that the presence of a music stand (without music on it) lowered the scores of performers relative to scores when no stand was present. There also tends to be an order of performance bias to assessment in that later performances are scored higher than early performances. Other factors that could influence the bias of judges are personal characteristics of performers, such as nervousness, gender, or race (Thompson and Williamon 2003, 27). Judges may be influenced by knowing the performer either personally or by reputation. Evaluators may also be influenced by their familiarity with a piece of music. Time of day and level of evaluator fatigue could be factors (McPherson and Thompson 1998, 14–16). Judges may be affected by the purpose of the performance; that is, whether it is for a competition, a festival, an exam, an audition, etc. They may be swayed by the type of performance; that is, whether it is for sight-reading, a rehearsed repertoire, a memorized piece, playing by ear, or improvisation (1998, 12).

Not all of these possible influences have been subjected to testing. In some cases, procedures have been put into place to lessen some suspected sources of bias. For example, a method employed to reduce bias that may be due to the personal characteristics of the musician has been to place a screen in front of the performer. Another method of dealing with human bias is to sound record a performance for later evaluation rather than watching it live or on video. Of course, in some cases assessment is not limited to measuring the accuracy of the mechanical aspects of a performance. For those times in which it is desirable to take into account that ineffable quality that makes a performer a performer rather than merely a musician, visual observation becomes necessary (McPherson and Thompson 1998, 16–17). As Schumann pointed out: "'If Liszt played behind a screen, a great deal of poetry would be lost'" (cited in Davidson [1993]; quoted in McPherson and Thompson [1998, 21]).

The notion that a musical performance is subject to assessment implies that it is a similar listening experience for knowledgeable judges for a given musical style (independent of composition quality). It is also assumes that experienced listeners are capable of making consistent judgments of the quality of a musical performance. For instance, if a given performance is recorded, then it would follow that a judge would assign it the same grade with each listening experience. (This is not always the case, as was evident in Fiske [1978] [McPherson and Thompson 1998, 17].) Additionally, it is assumed that the experienced listener can analyze separate aspects of a musical performance. A corollary to the concept of the quality of a musical performance is that some aspects of it are separable from the realm of human perceptual experience and can be measured independently (by computers, for instance) (Thompson and Williamon 2003, 23–24). R. E. Radocy took issue with the idea of nonhuman judgment, maintaining that only human observers are capable of successfully evaluating the musical worth of a sound or a sequence of sounds (Radocy 1986). At the same time, Radocy recognized that humans are biased, writing: "'Any measure that involves human judgment is inherently subjective because it involves human impressions'" (Radocy [1989, 30]; quoted in Latimer et al. [2010, 169]).

If judgment is limited to the mechanical aspects of a performance, then acoustic equipment and computers can be useful (Zdzinski 1991, 52–55). The research by Lehmann and Ericsson (1993, 189) on sight-reading accuracy for piano was based on manual computations using notated printouts derived from recorded performances. In measuring beat and rhythm accuracy, Gutierrez (2005, 6) reported the computer to be precise to the millisecond. A study by Campbell (1970) found computer-generated scores for solo vocal accuracy to be as reliable as those for human evaluators if not more so (Zdzinski 1991, 54). Utilization of computers does not eliminate human judgment. Humans still must decide what to measure, how much tolerance to allow for errors, and how to arrive at a total score, to name a few considerations.

The focus thus far has been on the judgment of performances and sources of biases as well as methods of reducing bias; however, the musician's performance may also be affected by the presence of judges. A judge's attitude or demeanor may affect the musician. The musician's familiarity with the venue may also affect his performance as well as such things as equipment failure (McPherson and Thompson 1998, 14–15). Not all of these influences can be eliminated or controlled.

Grading Musical Compositions for Level of Difficulty

Ratings for the difficulty level of musical compositions are compiled in repertoire lists for various instruments and for voice. Many listings provide a single grade for the entire piece—for instance, *Solo Vocal Repertoire for Young Singers: An Annotated Bibliography* by Boytim (1982) (Ralston, 1999, 164) and *Guide to the Pianist's Repertoire* by Hinson and Roberts (2014). Although some listings provide descriptors for ratings such as 1, 2, or 3 or expressions such as "easy," "moderate," "difficult," in some instances the descriptors are vague. Ralston (1999, 165) noted that Boytim's *Bibliography* lacks a methodology for rating the level of difficulty.

Instead of providing grades or ratings, some researchers have ranked musical pieces by difficulty; for instance, Klein (1989, 67–68) rank ordered a list of Chopin Etudes in his doctoral dissertation. Rasmussen (1962) devised an approach to rating difficulty using a coding scheme for technical aspects for trumpet compositions. According to Rasmussen, the coding scheme is useful because, unlike repertoire guidelines that give an overall grade such as "E" for easy or "D" for difficult, the symbolic system she constructed reveals why the piece is easy or difficult; for instance, whether the piece is written in a high register or is rhythmically difficult (1962, 78). Descriptors designed to indicate the difficulty of a musical piece are typically related to skills required to perform the piece. This is helpful to both musicians and instructors to aid in the development of skills that may be lacking or in avoiding certain pieces that require a skill or skills beyond the capability of the musician. For instance, in *Guide to the Pianist's Repertoire*, Maurice Hinson and Wesley Roberts warn that for Chopin's Etude No. 9 in G flat: "Small hands should forget this one!" (2014, 243)

Criteria for repertoire difficulty can be divided into two broad categories: technical and interpretative (Huron and Berec 2009, 106). One approach to assessing or scoring the difficulty of a musical piece involves describing technical and interpretive aspects of a composition that depend on skills, which at times are measurable. The technical aspects of a musical piece are more readily subject to quantification than are the interpretive. This is generally true in a relative sense, and does not mean that the technical aspects of a composition are easily measured. The technical aspects of a piece differ depending on the type of instrument or voice. For instance, for voice, the technical criteria would include factors such as "phrase length" which is related to the skill of "breath control" (Ralston 1999, 167). For the trumpet, breath endurance would be a consideration as it is for voice, but so would tonguing speeds and embouchure (Huron and Berec 2009, 109–11). For piano, the number of hand displacements would be a factor (Sébastien et al. 2012, 574).

To overcome limitations observed above for Botim's *Bibliography*, Ralston (1999) developed and tested the Ralston Repertoire Difficulty Index (RRDI). The RRDI is a scoring system that rates the difficulty of a solo voice repertoire using seven aspects of technical difficulty with three grades for each: easy, moderate, and difficult. Descriptors are provided for each grade. To establish criterion validity, Ralston compared the score for each technical aspect with Botim's scores. Each of her criteria correlated well with Botim's overall scores. Some of the descriptors that were provided for the three grades were more quantifiable than others. For instance, for the criterion "phrases," the "easy" rate applied to phrases that were two to three measures. Other technical criteria were less quantifiable; for example, the "difficult" rate for "tessitura" was described as "high or low and may be difficult to sustain" (1999, 167). According to Ralston, by rating a piece of music utilizing a set of technical criteria, her indexes allow vocal instructors to focus on technique rather than spending time on trying to build skills that are beyond the capability of the student (1999, 172).

Rather than relying on "human" grading as was done for the RRDI, Huron and Berec (2009) developed a computer model designed to measure the technical difficulty of a musical piece, in this case, a trumpet. Nine average difficulty measures were calculated for each factor chosen for the study (2009, 109). For example, the technical measures included "average fingering difficulty" and "average range difficulty" for a given piece of music. An overall measure of difficulty for the piece was also calculated based on a weighted sum of the scores for the nine technical factors. Since only mechanical aspects were rated and interpretive aspects were not, grading was limited to Etudes. The individual grades for the nine technical dimensions were compared with holistic grades given for curricula for the Royal Conservatory of Music of Toronto (RMCT). In all but one case, the correlations were positive (2009, 111–12). In addition, the composite grade based on a weighted average of the nine technical aspects was found to correlate well with the RCMT scores for the Etudes (2009, 114).

In another attempt to use computer scoring, this time for piano pieces, Sébastien et al. (2012) devised a computer-assisted Score Analyzer (SA) designed to automatically compute overall difficulty as well as difficulty levels based on seven technical aspects of a piano piece. Methods were proposed to extract these criteria from fifty musical scores. In the SA, a ratio was calculated for each of nine numerical variables (based on the seven criteria), using as the denominator, either the number of notes or the number of hand positions (2012, 573–74). Ratio intervals were assigned to allow for correlation with four difficulty grades, ranging from 1 (beginner) to 4 (virtuoso). A global mean based on segmented grades was calculated to give an overall level of difficulty for a piano piece (2012, 575).

The fifty pieces of music were assigned to three classifications. A "subjective" evaluation (based on marks of 1 through 3) by three piano teachers was compared with the SA classification scores for the fifty musical pieces. The SA grades tended to be lower than those given by the teachers for advanced compositions. This was attributed in part to the fact that the automated analyzer only accounted for technical factors.

In order to further improve the SA, Sébastien et al. suggested adjusting the grades to the level of musicianship of the student. They stated: "Indeed, the sense of difficulty within a musical work is mostly dependent from the musician's background" (2012, 576).

Musical Sophistication

If the difficulty of a piece of music is based on the musical ability of the musician who can master it, and if the musical ability of a musician is based on the ability to master a difficult piece of music, there can be a circularity of definitions. This leads to the question of how musicianship has been defined in the literature. One study that examined factors related to musical sophistication was conducted by Ollen (2006). In surveying the literature,

Ollen found that of almost 750 studies performed between 1928 and 2004, musical sophistication was used as a covariate almost 60% of the time and over half of the time musical sophistication was defined as years of "formal musical training" (2006, 690). The results of Ollen's study are not directly applicable to musical ability because it defined musical sophistication rather broadly to include not only vocal or instrumental ability, but also musical knowledge as well as the creation of music. In a self-administered questionnaire, Ollen found that the two indicators, "sight-reading ability" and "self-described title," outperformed all of the other twenty-seven indicators of sophistication included in the study (2006, 691–92). Out of the twenty-nine indicators that were examined in the study, "years of private lessons" ranked tenth (2006, 694) for the survey. Although it was outranked by many of the other variables in Ollen's study, the appeal of an indicator like "number of years of training" is that it is easily quantified. (This is also the case for education in general. Although "years of schooling" is not an ideal measure of education, it has the advantage of being readily quantifiable. Also, because it can be quantified, data on "years of schooling" is more likely to be published and/or available than other less quantifiable measures.)

Classification of musicians by proficiency level may be more easily achieved with students than with professional musicians. This is due partly because research often takes place in academic settings where researchers have access to students as willing participants. A study by Salzberg and Wang (1989) on sight-reading involved students, who initially were placed in five groups based on years of musical training. After a pre-test, they were re-assigned into the five levels based on preliminary test results. Interestingly, there were only minor changes in the groupings. Curiously, identical twins with the same musical history ended up in different groups (1989, 124).

Oftentimes the research that is undertaken is directly applicable to student participants. However, for studies in which a broader sample of musicians would be preferred, it may be difficult to achieve. Ollen's study on musical sophistication found virtuosos reluctant to participate. Although the study involved responses to a self-administered questionnaire (2006, 691) rather than the playing of a musical instrument, the lack of participation by virtuosos in the survey could signal that participation in a proficiency study may be limited to certain levels of musical ability.

Instrument

The instrument or instruments that is/are chosen for a study can be dictated by the availability of musicians. Repp (1997, 427) discovered that pianists are not very forthcoming when experimental testing is involved. The playing of a musical instrument was not required for the study by Sébastien et al. (2012).

It involved analyzing the scores themselves. They chose to use piano music in the development of the SA, partly because of their backgrounds, but also because of the extent of piano repertoire availability demanded for their study (2012, 571). For the study by Huron and Berec (2009, 106), which required trumpet players to perform musical pieces/passages, the trumpet was chosen because the mechanical elements of achieving a given pitch were few relative to other instruments.

Tempo

If the objective is either to assess musical pieces for difficulty or to grade performances for mastery, it would seem that tempo would be a factor. That is, tempo should be held constant for a given piece of music. As a result, the total time to play a piece would also tend to be standardized. In order to measure sight-reading ability, Lehmann and Ericsson (1993) kept tempo constant for pianists by having them accompany a recorded flute soloist. They chose accompaniment because it standardizes tempo as well as delimits the skills required for sight-reading (1993, 182). To test sight-reading, musical pieces are chosen that are below the technical ability of the performer so that they can be learned with relative speed. Testing that involves a broader range of musical compositions may require a different method than "accompaniment" to maintain a constant tempo. Metronomes can be used, but they also can have drawbacks. For instance if a performer slows down at some point, he may try to compensate by subsequently picking up the pace (1993, 184).

Timing is an encompassing concept that may include tempo (Repp 1997, 422); however, in Repp's experiments, timing was analyzed separately from tempo (1997, 430, 432). Timing is related to expressiveness—an aesthetic quality (1997, 429). (Repp investigated quality and individuality of piano performances based on the average performance. One of the experiments isolated tempo and timing, so that averages only varied in these two aspects of the performances.) When examining only technical aspects of a piece, timing related to expressiveness would not be investigated.

Time

Music has its own conception of time. Zdzinski (1991, 48) pointed out that the WFPS (Watkins and Farnum 1954, 1962) takes the measure as the unit in the calculation of a performance score. Although the measure may be used, clock time may also be employed. The latter may be preferred to preserve consistency across musical pieces of varying lengths and within and across scores with varying tempos and time signatures.

Fatal Errors

Since it has been suggested that a serious performance error is to be regarded as "early death" in the calculation of the expected life span of a musical piece, and if research is to be pursued in this regard, there must be a decision as to what qualifies as an error as well as at what point an error becomes "fatal." As has been seen in the cursory literature review, there are a number of errors that qualify depending on the instrument or voice. The number of correctly timed notes as a percentage of total notes, as put forth by Lehmann and Ericsson (1993, 192), has the advantage of being a single figure that does not require a composite score (based on component parts) to be computed, should an overall score be desired. Thus, an "incorrectly timed note" would appear to be a good candidate to be used as the error. In any case, it is necessary to decide before the fact what qualifies as an error. Although the aesthetic aspect of a performance is a factor in achieving excellence, aesthetic "errors" would not be considered in the estimation of a "difficulty index"—partly because of the difficulty of measuring them. In the context considered here, it is also unlikely that they would be "fatal."

Once mistakes that qualify as errors have been identified, then it is necessary to define what comprises a fatal error. Gutierrez (2005, 7) mentioned that the WFPS and the FSS require the musician continue to play a piece for as long as he can "without making excessive errors." Although, she noted these scoring measures have been criticized as being arbitrary in their application of what constitutes an "error," they still may be helpful in determining what is meant by "excessive" in a global sense and may be useful in refining the definition for a "fatal" error. (The WFPS assigns a single score. Errors are deducted on a measure-by-measure basis. A single point is deducted for an error of any type, regardless of the number of errors for a given measure [Zdzinski 1991, 48]. Note that in an experimental test, if a "fatal error" is defined based on a threshold of errors, then it would be preferable to count *all* such errors within every measure until the threshold is reached.) If the performances are scored electronically, then it may be possible (even preferable) for statistical techniques to be employed in arriving at the point at which errors become significant enough to qualify as "fatal." A threshold may exist for a specific error. It is also possible that cumulative errors may reach a threshold and be counted as fatal at the point in time at which the threshold is reached.

A Constant Force of Mortality

The difficulty level throughout a musical piece, and therefore the potential for error, may not be uniform. A mortality pattern based on a constant force of mortality, *r*, is unrelated to time in the sense that the mortality rate does not change with time (either increasing or decreasing). Even though for particular musical pieces, the difficult passages are unrelated to time in this way, they are not necessarily random. At the conclusion of the article by Sébastien et al. (2012, 576), who designed a Score Analyzer for piano music, it was stated that one of their objectives for further research was to specify the difficult parts of musical pieces. Thompson and Williamon (2003, 26) noted that in a study by Thompson et al. (1998), judges of recorded piano performances of a Chopin etude tended to focus on bar 27 as critical to their overall measure of quality. The overarching question is, if there are particular tricky points within a piece of music, to what extent is the assumption of a constant force of mortality justified? How is one to know if the constant force of mortality postulate applies in a specific case?

A study that tested the appropriateness of the exponential and Poisson distributions of soccer goals by Chu (2003) used the Chi Square (χ^2) test as well as other measures. To illustrate how the χ^2 test might apply to an experiment with musicians playing a piece of music, the "actual" results of a hypothetical trial will be presented and compared with "expected" values. Tables 8.1 and 8.2 give "dummy" data for a hypothetical experiment involving 100 musicians playing 10 measures of the same piece of music for a given type of instrument. It is assumed that the level of musical proficiency is the same for the musicians, that they all have had the same rehearsal time, and that they play the musical piece at the same tempo under the same conditions. The hypothetical "actual" fatal error values based on the experimental results can be compared with those that would be "expected," the latter of which are based on the assumption of a discrete survival function $[(1/(1 + r)^t]$ and a per

Table 8.1 Data for a Hypothetical Experiment

	(1) *Survs. (Expected)*	*(2)* *Deaths (Expected)*	*(3)* *Survs. (Observed)*	*(4)* *Deaths (Observed)*
(1)	90.91	9.091	82.65	17.35
(2)	82.64	8.264	82.65	0
(3)	75.13	7.513	66.12	16.53
(4)	68.30	6.830	66.12	0
(5)	62.09	6.209	60.11	6.01
(6)	56.45	5.645	60.11	0
(7)	51.32	5.132	50.09	10.02
(8)	46.65	4.665	50.09	0
(9)	42.41	4.241	47.71	2.38
(10)	38.55	3.855	47.71	0
Total		61.445		52.29

Dummy data on expected and actual "survivals" and "deaths" for a hypothetical experiment in which 100 musicians attempt to play 10 measures of a musical piece. (Created by author)

Table 8.2 Hypothetical χ^2 Test

	(1) Time	(2) Observed	(3) Expected	(4) (O – E)	(5) $(O - E)^2$	(6) $(O - E)^2/E$
(1)	1&2	17.35	17.355	-0.005	0.000025	0.000001
(2)	3&4	16.53	14.343	2.187	4.782969	0.333471
(3)	5&6	6.01	11.854	-5.844	34.152336	2.881081
(4)	7&8	10.02	9.797	0.223	0.049729	0.005076
(5)	9&10	2.38	8.096	-5.716	32.672656	4.035654
Total		52.29	61.445			7.255283

Calculations for a χ^2 using "dummy" data given in Table 8.1. (Created by the author)

period death/fatal error rate $r[1/(1 + r)^t]$. This comparison can be achieved using the χ^2 goodness of fit test.

The entries in table 8.1 are based on the hypothetical experiment. The table provides "actual" data (i.e., dummy data) and "expected" data to illustrate how a χ^2 test might proceed. The "expected" data are shown in column 1 (C-1) and in column 2 (C-2). Entries in C-1 are "expected" survival values based on the equation $100[1/(1.10)^t]$, for t equal to 1 through 10, where $[1/(1 + r)^t]$ is the survival equation on the assumption of a force of mortality, r, of .10, and $T = 10$, and where 100 is the number of musicians. (Time t may be measured in clock time or in measures. It is assumed in this hypothetical experiment that t is in terms of measures. Of importance is that once t is chosen, it is used consistently across musical pieces.) The "expected" death/fatal error values are given in C-2 and are equal to $r = 0.10$ multiplied by the C-1 values. Thus, for example, in period 1, it is expected that there would be 9.091 fatal errors (shown in table 8.1 C-2); therefore, 90.91 musicians (shown in table 8.1 C-1) would continue playing the piece after the first measure. The sum of the survival rates, $\sum_{t=1,10} 1/(1.10)^t$, is equal to the expected life span of 6.1445 (which equals the sum of C-1 divided by 100). The sum of the per period death rates, $\sum_{t=1,10} (.10)[1/(1.10)^t]$, is approximately equal to .6145. The latter value multiplied by 100 is equal to 61.445 (the sum shown for table 8.1 C-2), which is the expected number of total fatal errors for the musical piece.

In table 8.1, entries for C-3 are the "actual" survival values based on the results of the hypothetical experiment, and C-4 gives the "actual" death values. Thus, for period one, the "actual" number of fatal errors would be about seventeen (shown in table 8.1 C-4), leaving approximately eighty-three musicians (given in table 8.1 C-3) to continue playing after the first measure. The "actual" number of deaths for the piece would be 52.29 (the total given in table 8.1 C-4). The "actual" survival rates are not shown in table 8.1, but they would be equal to the entries in C-3 divided by 100. Summing these survival rates for the "actual" data would give 6.134—the "actual" average life span (average age at death).

Although there is greater variation among the "actual" fatal errors (table 8.1 C-4) than for the "expected" fatal errors (table 8.1 C-2), the average age at death (6.134) based on the "actual" data is very close to the expected age at death (6.145), the latter of which is based on the assumption of a constant force of mortality of 10%. It might be concluded that the average force of mortality underlying the "actual" data is about 10% since the "actual" and the expected data result in approximately the same age at death and both have the same potential life span ($T = 10$). This conclusion assumes, of course, that r is constant over time, which is not the case for the "actual" data. However, a constant average force of mortality can be regarded as underlying the actual data even if the period-to-period force of mortality rate appears to vary, as long as the difference between the actual and expected death rates is not significant. This can be investigated with the χ^2 test.

Table 8.2 gives the results of the hypothetical χ^2 test. The "fatal error" data given in table 8.2 C-2 and C-3 are the same as presented in table 8.1 C-4 and C-2, respectively, with the qualification that instead of ten time periods, five periods are shown. Every two consecutive time periods have been summed (time periods 1 plus 2, 3 plus 4, etc.) as indicated in table 8.2 C-1. This time period compression was done because the number of fatal errors for every other period for the "actual" data (table 8.1 C-4) was zero. The calculated χ^2 of 7.255 (shown as the sum of C-6 in table 8.2) is less than the critical value of 7.779 for the 10% significance level (see for instance the Chi Square Distribution table in Zikmund [1997, A-5]), indicating no significant difference between the observed and expected distributions at that level. The results of this test would tend to suggest that an assumption of a constant average force of mortality of 10% for the "actual" fatal error data would not be unrealistic (at the 10% significance level).

A fair criticism of table 8.1 is that the dummy values in C-3 and C-4 should not be expressed in fractions of musicians/fatal errors. (This criticism does not apply to the expected numbers shown in C-1 and C-2 because they are theoretically based.) If the numbers in C-4 are rounded, then the calculated χ^2 would be 7.985, which is greater than the critical value (7.779). Therefore, there would be a significant difference between the expected and "actual" fatal errors at the 10% level. Of course, an average force of mortality of 10% may still apply to the "actual" data, but there could be too much variation to support a constant rate (at least based on the results of this test). The "actual" data in this case was devised to result in an average rate close to 10%. (Note that if instead of one musical measure being the unit of measurement for T, two measures had been used, the force of mortality would have been about 21% given the same death and survival rates compressed into 5 periods rather than 10. This potential variability in r with the units of T is why a standard unit of measurement for T is desirable.)

In an actual experiment, all that would be available would be the actual data. The estimated value of r using the "actual" data can be based on the average of the percentage changes for the "Observed" deaths in C-4 of Table 8.1—which is approximately equal to [the sum of C-4/C-3]/10, or 8.1%. A better figure would be based on the geometric mean; which is equal to the product of 1 plus the percentage change for each of the ten periods raised to the 1/10 power. That value less one equals approximately 7.7%. (Alternative statistical methodologies could be used along with other goodness of fit tests.)

As an aside, even when there is a good deal of variation from one period to the next, as there appears to be in this case, a constant rate may be assumed for some purposes. Whether it applies or not depends upon the decision at hand. As seen with the Milton Friedman's concept of "permanent income," which resulted in transforming lifetime income into a constant amount per year, the concept was relevant for those cases in which decisions were made on that basis (Friedman 1957; Touchstone, "Reproductivity, Capital Theory, and Objectivist Ethics," 2010, 231, 237n9). (Specifically, according to the theory, a consumer's decisions are based on the person's lifetime income.) Typically, summary statistics, such as averages, are useful for global decisions. For instance, an average "fatality" rate may be of use in comparing pieces of music. Similarly, average attrition rates may be of interest in decisions involving training courses comprised of a number of modules.

The "Risk Index"

The "actual" life span value of 6.134 is a measure of the difficulty level of the musical piece in the hypothetical experiment in which it was assumed that a group of 100 musicians, with the same musical proficiency level and rehearsal time, played a given instrument at a given tempo. The actual life span divided by the potential life span, 6.134/10, could be considered a "difficulty index" for the piece. A "risk index" could be given as (1 – .6134). That is, if a musician mastered the piece perfectly, he could be said to have overcome that degree of risk.

In order to check the difficulty index's criterion validity, there would need to be a basis for comparison with the proposed "difficulty index." For instance, the Score Analyzer (SA) assigned overall scores for fifty pieces of piano music (Sébastien et al. 2012, 576). Of course, comparing a "difficulty index" with an overall SA score for a given piece of piano music would not be particularly helpful. In order to discover how well the two methods of measurement compare, it would be necessary to have "difficulty indexes" for several of the musical pieces that were scored by the SA.

Difficulty indexes can be calculated for different rehearsal times for a given musical piece (keeping everything else constant) and/or for different levels of musicianship (keeping everything else constant). In the former case, the primary interest would be in measuring how practicing a particular piece of music improves performance (reduces risk). In the latter case, the primary interest would be in measuring how the mastery of an instrument improves performance (reduces risk).

One objective of the review of the literature on music assessment and the discussion of the hypothetical experiment is to illustrate some of the challenges involved in attempting to actualize a hypothetical equation such as PV/*T* (as it relates to measuring the difficulty of a piece of music). The equation seems simple enough in the context of abstract discussions, but when the objective is to measure it in a particular real-world setting, there are numerous factors to consider—some of which have been addressed above. The foregoing offered a generic sketch. An actual research design would be more elaborate, and, of course, no matter how well a test is designed, many more considerations typically emerge when it is undertaken that were not anticipated.

Chapter 9

Final Thoughts

This chapter recaps some points made in previous chapters as they relate to the equation PV/*T*. Further clarifications involving present value, the "death rate," and measures of the "return to not dying" can be found in the appendix. The appendix examines some of the relationships between the present value equation that has been used for life span, PV_1, and the present value for an asset, $\$PV_t$. The former discounts a year by the force of mortality, *r*, and the latter discounts by an "interest rate," ρ. Time preference is regarded as one of the determinants of the interest rate, and one of the determinants of time preference is mortality; however, as the appendix points out, from the borrower's perspective, the interest rate is separate from the mortality rate. Also addressed in the appendix is the relationship between depreciation and the death rate. From the perspective of an individual "asset," the asset depreciates over time; however, from the perspective of a group of assets (even though individual assets depreciate), the depreciation rate can become part of the replacement or "death" rate. In addition, there is a comparison between present value and expected value as they relate to the age of an asset at death. Finally, an equation based on PV_t/PV_1 is utilized as a "summary" indicator of a "return to not dying."

Measures for a "return to not dying" have been discussed primarily from the individual's perspective. In general, when a single individual pursues a less risky course of action or improves his skills related to a risky endeavor, this reduces the death or failure rate, *r*, for that individual. That single individual's actions have an imperceptible effect on the overall failure rate. However, the failure rate overall is lowered as more individuals pursue less risky behaviors or improve their skills. For instance, if a single firefighter wears protective equipment (that has been proven effective), this may reduce his chance of dying or of suffering a serious injury if he is involved in an accident, but it will not significantly change the overall death (or injury) rate. However, if most firefighters wear protective gear, this may reduce the overall rate.

The assumption of a constant rate of early death, *r*, is a simplistic one (cf. Carnes et al. 1996; Pitacco 2003). The assumption simplifies the mathematics in the examples presented, but does little to alter the conclusions that have been drawn. Early death is regarded as being a result of "accidents." There are accidents or mistakes over which individuals have control that may be avoided or lessened, and there are those over which individuals have little, if any, control. The former have ethical implications.

In the appendix, (subsection "Bounds for PV_1"), it is pointed out that the PV_1 range is: $0 \leq PV_1 \leq T$, and the range for PV_1/T is: $0 \leq PV_1/T \leq 1$. The latter limits are not surprising given the discussion of the ratio, PV/*T*, in chapters 3 and 8. PV/*T* has been discussed within two different but related contexts. One context involved improving one's longevity by reducing the risk of early death, *r*, by pursuing a more ethical course of action, or, more generally, by living a more virtuous life. Virtues are those actions by which a person attains or maintains his values—his ultimate value being his life. It would follow that if a person chose ethical actions rather than those that are unethical, this would (other things equal) enhance his life—both its quality and quantity; although only its quantity is reflected in the PV equation. The ratio, PV/*T*, was also discussed in the context of lowering the risk of early death of a task, *r*, through the pursuit of excellence through deliberate practice associated with the task. Specifically addressed was the expected life span of a musical piece, PV, and how it is increased relative to *T*, by lowering the fatal error rate, *r*, through practice. The same relationship applies to occupational tasks for which the risk of death is high. The pursuit of excellence is a virtue that is achieved by lowering the risk of death or failure by engaging in training in preparation for the eventuality of real-world dangers.

Both of the contexts in which PV/*T* was used dealt with virtues. Aristotle (1976, 91) categorized these virtues as moral and intellectual. To be virtuous in either category requires a kind of excellence that is achieved through practice. Virtues involving "morality" are acquired or perfected through repetition; that is, habit. Of course, there are always situations for which a person cannot prepare himself—such as having the courage to speak up for one's principles when it may damage one's livelihood, or risking one's life to save a person one loves. These actions may threaten one's ability to sustain oneself or may directly result in one's death. They can be difficult to justify if one's life is the ultimate value. Yet there are arguments (as presented in chapter 6) that support taking these kinds of actions. What may seem less difficult to explain is undertaking a profession for which the risk of death is or can be persistently high. Occupational choice and actions associated with it are categorized under the intellectual virtues to which Aristotle referred. Intellectual virtues are related to the arts and the professions.

Why pursue a risky occupation? An answer is supplied by reality—and that is, risk is unavoidable. Life is not riskless. Someone must risk her life for each of us to be born. Childbirth may be less risky today (in developed countries), but historically, it has been risky and to a large extent unavoidable. A person may avoid a risky occupation, but risk, in general, is unavoidable. That does not mean that a person should be foolhardy; however, there are rational risks. Humans rely on their minds to survive, and the pursuit of knowledge is a risky venture. Failure is part of the learning process. Insofar as dangerous professions are concerned, risk can be lessened though deliberate practice in controlled environments designed to minimize or reduce dangers. Practice and training result in the acquisition of skills that can be transferred to real-world settings. Those who master the skills acquire confidence, and those who cannot master them are eliminated through an attrition process that is relatively benign. Virtues may be actions that serve to preserve or maintain our lives, but they are not methods designed to avoid risks. They are tools we can utilize to handle them.

Appendix

Some Clarifications on Present Value, the "Death Rate," and the "Return to not Dying"

INTRODUCTION

The appendix offers some clarifying remarks on present value, the "death rate," and the "return to not dying." The first section of the appendix considers some of the differences between the application of the present value equation to life span, PV_l, relative to the present value of an asset, $\$PV_t$. To arrive at the expected life span of an asset, PV_l, each year is discounted by the force of mortality, *r*. To calculate the PV of an asset in monetary terms, yearly income is discounted by the "interest rate," ρ. One determinant of the interest rate is time preference, and one of the determinants of time preference is the probability of early death. To the extent that early death is a factor in the determination of the interest rate, it is not from the borrower's perspective—at least insofar as being tied to "interest" covering a life insurance premium (which is based on the death rate) is concerned.

The appendix also addresses the relationship between depreciation and the death rate. It discusses views of economists who have either based the death rate (life insurance premium) on depreciation, specifically Irving Fisher, or based depreciation (i.e., the renewal rate approach to depreciation) on the death rate, in particular, Gabriel Preinreich. In the process of looking at an adaptation of one of the depreciation methods discussed by Preinreich, the appendix also examines some of the differences between present value, PV, and expected value, EV, as they are defined herein. Finally, a summary indicator of the "return to not dying" that utilizes PV_t/PV_l is employed in a discussion of PV, the force of mortality, and the depreciation rate.

PRESENT VALUE EQUATION

For the expected age at death, I have been using the same equation as that for the present value of an asset. For each period, the expected number of periods of life remaining would be given as $PV_t = \int_0^T e^{-rt}\,dt$ (where T falls by one for each time period). Unlike the present value for an asset (that yields an income of one dollar per year, $\$PV_t = \int_0^T e^{-\rho t}\,dt$), for the expected remaining life, there is no income to consider, and r is the force of mortality instead of the discount rate, ρ; otherwise the equations are conceptually similar. One difference is that for the present value of an asset, $\$PV_t$, the interest rate, ρ, corresponds to a return that is a "sure thing." The force of mortality is a probability—which means *if* death does not occur, the "return" is equal to that probability, r, multiplied by the expected remaining life, PV_t. The "return" is the gain that corresponds to that portion of one's life that was "unexpected." As seen below, the return to escaping death for period t is not confined to the expected loss for the single year t, but also includes the expected losses for all subsequent years, because if one dies, it is not simply the current year that is lost, but one's whole life.

Time Preference and Mortality

The present value of an asset, $\$PV_t = \int_0^T e^{-\rho t}\,dt$, is discounted by ρ, which is often set equal to the "interest rate." (For purposes of illustration, it is assumed that there is a single rate of interest.) The idea underlying discount, which is referred to as time preference, is that a dollar today is preferred to a dollar a year from now (or ten years from now, or fifty, etc.). One of the reasons that a person prefers a dollar now to one later is that he may not be alive later to receive it. Thus, when a person lends money, and therefore forgoes having it today, he expects a return on the money from the borrower. Death is not the only risk the lender faces, of course (nor is risk the only reason that a return is expected), but it is a factor (Fisher 1930, 62, 65, 71).

If the risk of death figures into the value for ρ, whose death is it—the lender's or the borrower's? Based on the above reasoning, intuitively, it would seem to be related to the lender. To the extent that the probability of death of the lender is a factor in the value of ρ, it would not be the risk of death for a particular lender, but would be determined by market forces that would include the risk for lenders in general. From the borrower's perspective, is his probability of dying a factor influencing ρ? When a person borrows, the expectation is that he will earn enough to pay off the loan. A typical economic example envisions the borrower as, say, purchasing a piece of equipment that is projected to earn enough revenue to pay off the loan (Valentine and Ellis

1991, 227); for example, he may buy a washing machine for a coin laundry business. The return (income) generated from the purchase must be enough to cover the interest and depreciation.

"Interest" is a tricky concept. From an economic perspective, interest is equal to the interest rate multiplied by $\$PV_t$ of the machine. For purposes of illustration, it is assumed that $\$PV_1$ has the same value as the loan (as well as the same value as the machine's price), where $\$PV_t = Y\int_0^T e^{-\rho t}\,dt$, assuming Y is constant, or in discrete terms, $\$PV_t = Y\sum_{t=1}^{T}(1/(1+\rho))^t$, (where the ρ's in the two formulas are not equal). In the discrete equation, the $\$PV_t$ is recomputed each year so that the lower bound in the summation is reset to $t = 1$. Thus, for a piece of equipment that yields $Y = \$1{,}000$ a year for $T = 10$ years at $\rho = 10\%$, $\$PV_1 = \$1{,}000\ \sum_{t=1}^{10}(1/(1.10))^t = \$6{,}144.45$. $\$PV_2$ would equal $\$1{,}000\ \sum_{t=1}^{9} = \$5{,}758.90$, etc. The difference between $\$PV_t$ for two consecutive years is equal to depreciation (Fisher [1906] 1965, 235), which for $t = 1$ (i.e., between $t = 1$ and $t = 2$) is equal to income multiplied by the depreciation rate (expressed as a percentage of one dollar of income); that is, $1,000 × .3855, or $385.55. The interest in $t = 1$ is $\rho(\$PV_1) = (.10)$ ($6,144.45). In $t = 2$, depreciation would be ($1,000 × .4241), and interest would be $\rho(\$PV_2) = (.10)(\$5{,}758.90)$. Thus, with each additional year, depreciation would increase and interest would decrease. Also, for each year, the sum of depreciation plus interest equals income of $1,000; for example, for $t = 1$: ($385.55 + $614.45), and for $t = 2$: ($424.11 + $575.89), etc.

The per year interest of $(\rho)(\$PV_t)$ is not the amount that is paid to the lender per year. That amount can depend on any number of factors. For instance, the amount paid in "interest" each year to the lender could be $614.45 = (.10) ($6,144.45). If so, the borrower would need to set aside a yearly sinking fund (SF) amount, in discrete terms equal to $SF = [\$PV_1](\rho)/[(1+\rho)^T - 1]$ (Allen 1967, 240). The SF is a constant yearly amount that equals depreciation in $t = 1$, in this case $385.55, and would collect interest (based on $\rho = 10\%$) so that by the end of $T = 10$ years, the total accumulated SF amounts would equal the sum of per year depreciation over the 10 years, which in turn would equal $\$PV_1$. In other words, the SF would accumulate to equal the value of the loan in year 10, which would be used to pay off the loan. Thus, the sum of the SF amount per year plus the "interest" paid to the lender per year would equal income: $385.55 + $614.45 = $1,000.

Alternatively, the borrower could pay "interest" of $1,000 per year for 10 years to the lender; in which case the borrower would not pay the value of $6,144.45 at the end of 10 years and a SF would be unnecessary. In either case, the borrower would be paying $1,000 per year. If the vending machine earned $1,000 per year, it would just pay for itself (and would have to be replaced after 10 years.) Now, where does the risk of death enter the picture? Another way of expressing this is: where does insurance enter the picture—since insurance is a payment to cover the risk of death? From the borrower's perspective, the machine would not have generated enough money to pay for insurance (to cover risk of death) for the machine and/or for himself. (The insurance that would be relevant in this example would be to cover the machine. The focus in the following will be on life insurance to cover the borrower's life, which is assumed for simplicity to extend from $t = 1$ through 10.)

The dollar payment necessary to cover the life insurance premium would have to be separate from the interest payment to the lender. Since the income ($1,000 per year) would only be sufficient to cover the loan, there would not be sufficient funds to pay for life insurance. To the extent that an "interest rate" reflects "time preference," it does not include the probability of dying of the borrower—at least, not in this example. To earn enough to cover the probability of the borrower's death would require more than $1,000 so as to pay the sinking fund amount of $385.55, an "interest payment" of $614.44 to the lender, plus a life insurance premium. (If a life insurance policy only covers "early death," a SF would be necessary; however, as will be seen below, if the insured has "full coverage" (i.e., coverage includes not only the risk of early death but also death at T), it is unnecessary to have a SF—although the "asset" would still depreciate in value.)

Life Insurance Premiums

A very simple net level premium rate (NLPR) per dollar of life insurance per time period can be given as: $NLPR_1 = \sum_1^T \Pi d_t / \sum_1^T \Pi a_t$, where Πd_t and Πa_t are the probabilities at time t of dying and being alive, respectively. For a nonconstant rate of mortality, r_t, the numerator of the $NLPR_1$ becomes $\sum_1^T r_t \Pi a_t$. If r_t is constant, r can be factored out, and the numerator becomes $(r\sum_1^T \Pi a_t)$; thus, the $NLPR_1$ becomes simply r. Actual actuarial tables are based on historical death rates for which the payout of death benefits is assumed to be delayed one period, and interest is assumed to be received on (unpaid) premiums by the insurance company (Huebner and Black 1976, 271–72). Also, actual premiums are "loaded" (i.e., they are not actuarially fair) as well as discounted. For simplification, these are not taken into account in the NLPRs considered here. Also, unlike the previous example, here it is assumed that for $\$PV_1$, $\rho = 0$; however, because of the possibility of early death, the force of mortality, r, is positive and assumed to be equal to 10%. The purpose for this is that in the former example, the focus was on the interest rate. Here the objective is to isolate the effect of the mortality rate on the insurance premium.

Based on these assumptions, a net level premium payment of $614.45 per year would be sufficient for a policy with a face value of $6,144.45 (equal to $\$PV_1$ of the insured, based on $\rho = 0$, $r = 10\%$, and $Y = \$1,000$). If it is assumed that \$614.45 is paid each year until death at $T = 10$, then enough would be paid to the insurance company to cover the possibility of early death for years 1 through 10; however, the premiums would not be sufficient to cover death at the end of year 10. This conclusion can be seen by constructing a "reserves" table (e.g., see Huebner and Black, 280–81) in which, from the insurer's perspective, yearly receipts are based on a premium of \$614.45 multiplied by Πa_t, the probability of being alive for year *t*, and claim payments are based on \$6144.45 multiplied by Πd_t, the probability of dying for year *t*. (For example, if it is assumed that $\Pi a_t = 1/(1 + r)^t$ and $\Pi d_t = r[1/(1 + r)^t]$, the ending reserve at $T = 10$ would be zero.) For $T = 10$, the probability of survival is 38.55%, 100% of whom will die by the end of that year. This eventuality would not be covered by the policy. (Of course, the assumption that death at $T = 10$ is *certain* is a simplistic one.)

$NLPR_1$ only covers early death (based on the force of mortality, *r*); it does not cover death at the end of life at time *T*. If the NLPR covers death from both sources (i.e., from early death as well as death at time *T*), then $r = 10\%$ would apply for periods 1 through *T*; however, for the percentage remaining alive at the end of year *T*, the "probability" of dying would be one, or 100%. For the example considered here, $NLPR_2$ would be: $NLPR_2 = [.10\sum_{t=1}^{10} 1/(1.10)^t + 1.00(.3855)]/[\sum_{t=1}^{10} 1/(1.10)^t] = 1/6.1445$. Because the numerator is the sum of the death rates (i.e., $\sum_1^T r_t\ \Pi a_t$) over the course of the life, the numerator is equal to one. The denominator is simply the sum of the survival rates ($\sum_1^T \Pi a_t) = \sum_1^T \left[1/(1+r)^t\right]$—which is to equal PV_1 (the expected age at death). Therefore $NLPR_2$ in this case is simply one divided by the expected age at death = $1/\sum$survival rates = 1/6.1445.

To arrive at how much is to be paid in insurance per dollar of income per period (i.e., the net level premium, NLP_2), the $NLPR_2$ is multiplied by the expected life span of the insured. That is, for $r = 10\%$ and $T = 10$, $PV_1 = 6.1445$, the $NLP_2 = (1/6.1445)(6.1445) = 1$. In general terms: $NLP_2 = (1/\sum$survival rates$)(\sum$survival rates$) = 1$ (see "alternative net level rate 3" in Touchstone [2006, 396]).

NLP_2 can be multiplied by the yearly income (assuming that either actual income is constant, or that it is transformed into permanent income) to arrive at the premium. (Permanent income may be given by the equation: $Y_p = \rho(\$PV_1)/(1 - e^{-\rho T})$, see Yaari [1964, 312]; Touchstone, "Reproductivity, Capital Theory, and Objectivist Ethics" [2010, 237n9]. In discrete terms: $Y_p = \rho(\$PV_1)/[1 - 1/(1+\rho)^T]$, where the ρ's are not equal in the continuous and discrete versions.) In this example, the yearly income is \$1,000.00; therefore the yearly premium would be: (NLP_2)(\$,1000.00) = (1)(\$1,000) = \$1,000.00. The same result can be obtained by multiplying $NLPR_2$ by $\$PV_1$, (1/6.1445)(\$6,144.50) = \$1,000.00. (Recall in this example that $\$PV_1$ is discounted by the force of mortality not the interest rate.)

In the construction of a reserves table, a premium of \$1,000.00 per year would provide sufficient reserves to cover the expected death claims. (Based on my calculations, given the same probability assumptions associated with $NLPR_1$, except for a negligible amount due to rounding error, there were no reserves at the end of $T = 10$.) The assumption of whether or not interest is earned is important since, in most cases, insurance companies do earn interest on unpaid premiums, or "reserves." However, in order to facilitate ease of calculation, it has been assumed that the interest rate is zero. As stated earlier, when insurance covers both "early death" as well as death at *T*, it is not necessary to have a SF because the face value of the policy is paid regardless of when death occurs. Of course, *T* is rarely known, and insurance companies typically cover risks, not certainties. (Also, a policyholder typically would not pay all of his yearly income on an insurance premium.)

DEATH AND DEPRECIATION

According to Fisher (1965, 111–12), the life insurance premium paid by the policyholder should be equal in value to a yearly SF payment (cf. Touchstone 2006, 392–95). This assumes that the SF earns interest. If it did not, the premium would be equal to depreciation, which (unlike the SF, which is a constant yearly amount) increases in amount over time to equal the yearly SF amount plus interest—or, expressed in terms of rates, $Dep_t/\$PV_1 = DR_t = \delta[(1 + \rho)^{t-1}]$. There are a couple of conceptual problems with the yearly SF being equivalent to the yearly premium. One is that a SF is relevant even if there is no threat of early death. It is the amount set aside to collect interest so as to equal PV_1 in year *T*, regardless of whether or not there is a probability of early death. Second is that the SF reflects depreciation, and, in some contexts, depreciation is related to survival rather than death in the sense that depreciation can be roughly thought of as "aging."

For example, if ten machines were all purchased at the same time, and there were no possibility of early death, $r = 0$ (and the interest rate were zero—which is assumed throughout the following), each piece of equipment would depreciate (age) by one year per year, $1/T$. (When $r = 0$, for a single machine, a per year sinking fund amount, which would equal depreciation when $r = 0$, would accumulate to equal the value of a machine at the end of ten years.) All machines would have to be replaced at $T = 10$ to maintain a constant stock. The early death rate, *r*, is based on a given population all of which begin "life" at the same time (as is assumed in this example). The change per year due to death for this population over the ten-year period would be zero.

Depreciation can be envisioned as a death rate if the focus is on the replacement of a large number of identical physical assets. For instance, if it is still assumed that there is no early death (and, again, no interest rate), and ten new pieces of equipment have been staggered in purchase at a rate of one per year over ten years, all of which have the same life span of $T = 10$ years, then, the replacement rate would be one per year ($1/T$) if the ultimate objective were to keep the number of machines constant at ten machines. It appears as if the death rate (not the "early" death rate) is one (machine) per year ($1/T$). However, for a given machine, this is not a death rate, but a depreciation rate. (Each machine will depreciate, or age, by one year per year, $1/T$.)

For a single machine that has a potential life of $T = 10$ years, but there is an early death rate—say, a force of mortality equal to 10%, then the expected life of a machine would be 6.1445 years. The replacement rate would be $1/PV_1 = .1627$, which when multiplied by 6.1445 gives a replacement of one year per year; or in general terms: $(1/PV_1)PV_1 = 1$. That is, a replacement of one year per year would replace a machine valued at 6.1445 years by the end of 10 years.

Note that because of early death at 6.1445 years, a single machine is being used up at a rate of $T/PV_1 = T(r + \delta)$ per year, or 1.627 years per year. (One way of viewing this is that 1.627 years is "valued" at one year = $1.627 \times .6145$). To maintain a machine value of 6.1445 years would require replacing 1.627 years ("valued" at $.61445 \times 1.627 = 1$ year) per year for 6.1445 years. To maintain a machine value of 10 years would require replacing 1.627 years (valued at $.61445 \times 1.627 = 1$ year) per year for 10 years. To maintain a machine value of 6.1445 years would require replacing 1 year (valued at $.61445 \times 1 = .61445$ year) per year for 10 years. If 10 machines were purchased at the same time then on average all would have to be replaced in 6.1445 years to maintain 10 machines, or a replacement rate of 1.627 machines per year would keep the stock constant at 10 machines. A rate of one machine per year would keep the stock constant at 6.1445 machines.

In this example, $PV_1/T = .6145$. As an aside, using the continuous versions of PV, the value of PV_1/T will approximately equal .6321 whenever $r = 1/T$. The value of $(1 - e^{-rt})$ is referred to as the cumulative probability of dying (in the sense that Sachko [1975, 31] used the term "cumulative"). In physics, the time $t = T$ when $T = 1/r$ is referred to as tau (τ), the lifetime of the excited state for a population of atoms, when approximately 63.21% will have decayed, based on the equation $(1 - e^{-1})$ (Knight 2004, 1339–1342). For the continuous equation: $PV_1 = (1/r)(1 - e^{-rT})$. Therefore, in the special case in which $r = 1/T$, $PV_1 = T(1 - e^{-1}) = T(.6321)$. Thus, $PV_1/T = .6321$, and $T/PV_1 = 1.5820 = T(r + \delta)$. As seen above, using the discrete forms of the equations, the *approximate* values of $PV_1/T = .6$ and $T(r + \delta) = 1.6$ hold for $T = 10$ and $r = .10$ (i.e., $r = 10\%$). These approximate values also hold for $T = 5$ and $r = .20$, $T = 20$ and $r = .05$, and so on.

The renewal rate, $1/PV_1$, is the same as the $NLPR_2$, the latter of which may be viewed as an "average death rate" when taken over the course of a person's whole life (i.e., the $NLPR_2$ includes death at T). As a renewal rate, $1/PV_1$ appears to correspond to an average death rate, rather than to include both early death and "depreciation." (By that I mean that, for a single machine, depreciation roughly reflects "aging" rather than death.) A renewal rate equivalent to $1/PV_1$ is consistent with (under certain simplifying assumptions) a rate of renewal presented in an article on the theory of depreciation by Preinreich (1938). Preinreich (1938) examined four methods of depreciation that applied to a group of machines (several pieces of equipment) under expanding and static conditions. He found that under static conditions, the depreciation rate would be the same as the rate of renewal; which, if there is no scrap value, is the same as straight-line depreciation, $1/a$, where a is the average life of the machine (1938, 232, 223, 227). Although Preinreich's equations are presented in general terms, $1/a$ could be expressed as $1/PV_1$ under the assumption that the survival function is $SR_t = [1/(1 + r)^t]$. (See [1938, 220] for Preinreich's description of the mortality curve he put forth.)

Preinreich defined $R(t)$ = the "remaining services per centum" for a group of machines in general terms (1938, 221). Translating his general equation into one consistent with the SR_t equation (given above) would give $R(t) = EV_t/PV_1$, where EV_t is the expected value at time t. In Preinreich's static example of depreciation, the "book value" of a group of machines purchased at the same time is given as $c_s(t)$ (1938, 225). Under the simplifying conditions mentioned above (i.e., under static conditions with no scrap value), $c_s(t) = R(t)$ (1938, 221). That is, the book value, $c_s(t)$, is "normalized" in the sense that EV_t is divided by PV_1.

Under the assumption that book value is kept constant, then C_t can be defined as $c_s(t) = 1$ for all t. That is, machines are assumed to be renewed so as to maintain a constant value, $C_t = 1$; thus, the renewal rate would be $1/PV_1$. However, for any particular machine with book value of, say, c_t, the depreciation rate would be the change in "value" from one period to the next, Δc. To be in keeping with the "usual" definition of the depreciation rate, this change in value, Δc, would be $DR_t = \{(r)/[(1+r)^T - 1)]\}[(1+r)^{t-1}]$. (As discussed below, in order to arrive at the "usual" depreciation rate, DR_t, book value would have to be PV_t/PV_1.) However, because book value is defined as EV_t/PV_1, the change in value is equal to SR_t/PV_1.

EV_t is the expected value at time t. Given the survival function $SR_t = [1/(1 + r)^t]$, $EV_t = \sum_t^T \left[1/(1+r)^t\right]$, and $PV_t = \sum_t^T \left[1/(1+r)^t\right]$. EV_t differs from PV_t in that EV_t sums from $t = t$ through T, where t increases by one each period and T is fixed; whereas PV_t sums from $t = 1$ through T, where t resets to equal one each time period and T falls by one each time period. (The relationship between the two can be expressed as $EV_t = [PV_t]\ [1/(1+r)^{t-1}]$.)

At $t=1$, $EV_t=PV_t$; thus, for a given machine, $c_1=EV_1/PV_1=1$. For $r=10\%$ and $T=10$, both EV_t and PV_t equal 6.1445 in $t=1$. In $t=2$, $EV_2=[.8264 + .7513 + \ldots + .3855] \approx 5.2354$ (whereas, by comparison, $PV_2=[.9091 + .8264 + \ldots + .4241] \approx 5.7590$). For a given machine, EV_2/PV_1 would equal 5.2354/6.1445 $\approx$ .8521. The difference in asset value from $t=1$ to $t=2$ would equal [(6.1445 – 5.2354)/6.1445] $\approx$ .1479. This equals the renewal rate for a given piece of equipment (for its expected value at $t=2$), which is equal to the constant renewal rate multiplied by the survival rate for year one $=[1/PV_1][1/(1 + r)^t]$; that is, [.1627][.9091] = .1479. And, as stated above, this equals the survival rate in year one divided by PV_1; that is, $SR_1/PV_1=.9091/6.1445$. Thus, when book value is defined as EV_t/PV_1, the depreciation rate is SR_t/PV_1, and depreciation would be equal to the survival rate, $(SR_t/PV_1)(PV_1)$, or .9091 for year one.

Present Value and Expected Value

In applying (or adapting) Preinreich's methodology, the reason that the depreciation rate for a single machine equals SR_t/PV_1 for a given year is that the value of the machine has as its numerator EV_t. SR_t/PV_1 is multiplied by PV_1 to give $SR_t = 1/(1 + r)^t$. The "survival rate" is not the definition for depreciation commonly used. To arrive at the "typical" depreciation rate would require PV_t to be in the numerator rather than EV_t; that is, if PV_t/PV_1 were used, then, for $t=1$, $[(PV_1 - PV_2)/PV_1] = [(6.1445 - 5.7590)/6.1445] = .0627$—this is the "typical" depreciation rate value for year one based on the equation for DR_t given in the previous subsection, which when multiplied by PV_1 gives depreciation of .3855.

One difference between the two value concepts—that is, EV and PV—is that (given r and T), with the exception of year one, EV gives shorter remaining life expectancies than PV. If the individual survives the first year, his average remaining life based on PV_2 is 5.7590 years rather than the EV_2 of 5.2354. Since the PV_2 calculation assumes that the individual has survived the first year, the summation for PV_2 starts with the probability of survival for year one ($[1/(1.10)^1]=.9091$). This is higher than the cumulative probability of survival for year two ($[1/(1.10)^2]=.8264$) on which the first year of EV_2 is based. From the *perspective of the present*, because the probability of survival is not reset to equal $[1/(1 + r)^1]$ for the first year in the calculation of EV_t, the mortality rates increase at a faster rate than is assumed by a constant force of mortality; that is, in effect for EV, the "force of mortality" increases over time—which is contrary to the assumption that the force of mortality is constant for "accidents." (This assumption is discussed in chapter 8, subsection "Constant Force of Mortality.")

The differences in EV and PV affect not only the definition for the depreciation rate and the "effective" force of mortality rate, but also the interpretations for the "return to not dying as a result of early death." The question regarding the EV approach is: if the asset survives a given year, how is the "return to not dying due to early death" measured? Using the EV approach, the "return to not dying due to early death" for year one would be equal to the force of mortality (.10) multiplied by the survival rate for year one (.9091); which equals .09091 or 9.091%. That is, it is equal to the death rate for year one only (or, for any given year, $r[1/(1 + r)^t]$).

The PV approach to the "return to not dying" takes into account that when the first year is survived, the asset has survived not only the risk of early death for the first year but also the other risks of early death throughout its lifetime. That is, using the PV approach, in year one the "return to not dying" is valued at 10% of the sum of the survival rates for the lifetime; which is 10% of PV_1 equal to .6145, or 61.45% (or, for any given t, rPV_t). If the asset dies during year one, it does not simply lose the first year of its life, but the entirety of its life.

THE "RETURN TO NOT DYING"

In an approach to depreciation attributed to Preinreich, machine value was normalized by dividing EV_t by PV_1. (This is an adaptation of one of Preinreich's approaches to depreciation based on a general equation—the latter of which, of course, was appropriate for Preinreich's purposes.) It was pointed out above that PV_t/PV_1 would result in the usual depreciation value (based on the change in PV_t/PV_1 from one period to the next multiplied by PV_1); whereas dividing EV_t by PV_1 results in the survival rate per period as the depreciation value. PV_t/PV_1 can also be used in an application unrelated to the discussion above.

The ratio PV_t/PV_1, which I will label B (where PV_t, the expected remaining life of an asset at time t, is divided by PV_1, the expected length of life of the asset), can be compared against the survival rate $[1/(1 + r)^t]$. For instance, B_t is equal to one minus the sum of *depreciation rates* up to time t, which equals $[1 - \sum_1^t(Dep_t/PV_1)]$; whereas the survival rate is equal to one minus the sum of the *death rates* up to time t, which equals $(1 - \sum_1^t \Pi d_t)$, where $\Pi d_t = r[1/(1 + r)^t]$ is the death rate for a given year. Also, the change in B_t from one period to the next is the *depreciation rate* (DR_t, as defined in the previous two subsections) $= (Dep_t/PV_1)$; whereas the change in the survival rate, $[1/(1 + r)^t]$, from one period to the next is the *death rate* $= r[1/(1 + r)^t]$. As has been noted earlier, the sum of the survival rates over the life of an asset is PV_t; which equals $\sum(1 - \sum\Pi d)$. The sum of B_t values over the life of an asset is $(\sum B)_t = \sum_1^T PV_t/PV_1 = \sum[1 - \sum(Dep_t/PV_1)]$. It is $(\sum B)$ that is utilized in the following discussion.

The value of $B_t = [1 - \sum(\text{Dep}_{t1}/\text{PV}_1)]$ is the percentage of the life of an asset that remains at time t after deducting the sum of the depreciation rates up to that point. $(\sum B)_1$ is the sum of the values for $[1 - \sum(\text{Dep}_t/\text{PV}_1)]$ over the life of the asset. $(\sum B)_1$ gives a rough indicator that summarily reflects the return to not dying due to early death. When r is high, the depreciation rate (in year one) is low—which means PV_1 is relatively low, and, therefore, the asset does not have a high expectation of surviving for any given year. Thus, if the asset does survive a year, there is a large "return to not dying." This is reflected in a relatively large $(\sum B)_1$. If r is low, the depreciation rate (in year one) is high—which means PV_1 is relatively high, and in relative terms the asset has a high expectation of surviving any given year (i.e., T is a bigger factor in determining death's occurrence). Thus, if the asset survives a year, the "return to not dying" is not high in a relative sense. This is reflected in a comparatively low $(\sum B)_1$. $(\sum B)_1$ moves in the opposite direction of PV_1.

Bounds for PV_1

This section examines the upper and lower bounds for PV_1. The limits to PV_1 are based on the values for r and the depreciation rate (in year one) for a given value of T. The force of mortality multiplied by PV_t plus depreciation in year t equals one; that is: $(r\text{PV}_t + \text{Dep}_t) = 1$. The force of mortality plus the SF rate, $(r + \delta)$, is equal to $1/\text{PV}_1$ (where δ is depreciation in year one as a percentage of PV_1). Therefore, the lower the SF rate, the greater is r, and vice versa. (Although a sinking fund per se is irrelevant in this discussion, I will refer to the depreciation rate in year one as the SF rate, since they are equivalent in value.)

In general, for an asset for which there is no early death, $(r=0)$, PV_1 will be equal to T. That is, for $r=0$: $\text{PV}_1 = \sum_1^T 1/(1+r)^t = T$. T is the upper bound for PV_1. In other words, the maximum value for the expected life span, PV_1, is equal to the maximum potential life of T. When r equals zero, this also corresponds to the maximum SF amount of one per year, that is: $(1/T)(T)$.

The maximum value of $r = 100\%$ presents a problem in the calculation of PV. In continuous terms:

$$\text{PV} = \int_0^\infty e^{-rt}\text{dt} = \lim_{T\to\infty}\int_0^T e^{-rt}\text{dt} = \lim_{T\to\infty}(1/r)\left(1 - e^{-rT}\right)$$

$$= 1/r\ (\text{Chiang 1974, 459}).$$

For $r = 100\%$, $\text{PV} = 1$. This is a problem, to which Jaynes (2003, 485) referred, for functions that are "everywhere zero," but which integrate to equal one.

Intuitively, it would seem that if the force of mortality was 100%, then the expected life span would be zero, but this is not the result *unless* $T=0$, for which $PV=(1/1)(1 - e^0)=0$. Of course, if $r=100\%$, it would follow that $T=0$—which is the lower limit for PV_1. Thus, the limits for PV_1 will be given as: $0 \le PV_1 \le T$. To "normalize" or standardize the limits would require dividing the upper and lower boundaries for PV_1 by T. That is, $0 \le PV_1/T \le 1$.

Bounds for $(\sum B)_1$

As was the case for PV_1, the upper and lower bounds for $(\sum B)_1$ are dictated by the limits for r and the SF rate for a given T. The upper bound for $(\sum B)_1$ would seem to occur if depreciation is equal to zero. If depreciation is zero then it would seem to follow that the depreciation rate (Dep/PV_1) would always equal zero; thus, $B_t=[1 - \sum(Dep/PV_1)]$ would equal one for each year. Furthermore, since for each year, $B_t=1$ for any value of t, then $(\sum B)_1=T$ for any value of T. The problem is that when depreciation equals zero, PV_1 (which is the sum of depreciation) would equal zero as well. Because division by zero is undefined, technically, the upper bound for $(\sum B)_1$ would be given as $< T$.

For the lower limit for $(\sum B)_1$, $r=0$, $PV_1=T$, and depreciation $=1$ per period. With no early death, then there would be straight-line depreciation per year; that is, the rate of depreciation would be equal to one divided by T years, $1/T$. Since $B_t=[1 - \sum(Dep/PV_1)]$, then in this case B_t would equal to $(1 - t/T)$. (That is, $[\sum Dep/PV_1]=t/T$. This is because in the numerator, $\sum Dep$ equals t for any year t since $Dep=1$ each year; and in the denominator, $PV_1=T$.) The continuous version of $(\sum B)$ is $\int(1 - t/T)\,dt$. This results in a lower bound of $T/2$:

$$\int (1-t/T)\,dt = t - t^2/(2T) + C$$

$$= t(1-t/2T) + C$$

$$t(1-t/2T)\Big|_0^T = T - T^2/2T = T - T/2 = T/2$$

In general terms, the lower and upper bounds for $(\sum B)_1$ would be: $T/2 \le (\sum B)_1 < T$.

"Normalizing" or standardizing the limits requires dividing the upper and lower boundaries for $(\sum B)_1$ by T. That is, $1/2 \le (\sum B)_1/T < 1$.

Relationship between PV, $(\sum B)_1$, r, and δ

$(\sum B)_1$ and PV_1 are inversely related. The lower r is, the higher PV_1 is and the lower $(\sum B)_1$ is for a given T. In the "low r" case, T (old age) prevails insofar as determining death's timing. There is a low risk of cutting life short. The opposite is the case when r is high. In other words, when $(\sum B)_1$ is close to T, r "rules" as being a factor related to death; when PV_1 is close to T, T "rules" as being the factor accounting for death. In terms of the "life of a piece of music," roughly speaking, if $PV_1 > (\sum B)_1$, r is relatively low, and the piece is more likely to end without a fatal error. If $(\sum B)_1 > PV_1$, then the risk of a fatal error is greater; however, there is a relatively large return if the piece is finished (i.e., *if* T is reached without a fatal error).

The effect of r for a given T on the values for PV_1 and $(\sum B)_1$ can be illustrated by considering three values for r equal to 3%, 10%, and 32% for a given $T=10$. For a relatively low force of mortality of $r=3\%$ (and $T=10$), the SF rate is 8.72% and PV_1 is 8.530, which is close to the upper limit of 10. The $(\sum B)_1$ value is 5.744, which is close to the lower limit of $T/2=5$ (based on the continuous equation shown above) for $T=10$ at $r=0\%$. That is, when the risk of death is relatively low, there is not a big return from "cheating death." An asset with a low r and a relatively high depreciation rate per year is more likely to die due to T. A calculation of the B values that make up $(\sum B)_1=5.744$ compared with the survival rates which comprise $PV_1=8.530$ would reveal that, except for $t=1$, the yearly survival rates exceed the yearly B values.

When $r=10\%$ and $T=10$, $(\sum B)_1$ (equal to 6.275) slightly exceeds PV_1 (equal to 6.145), indicating r is a somewhat more important factor affecting death than T. An examination of the pattern of the B values that make up $(\sum B)_1=6.275$ compared with the survival rates which comprise $PV_1=6.145$ would show that until $t=8$, the yearly B values exceed the yearly survival rates, then the pattern reverses.

B values are large when r values are relatively large, which reflect a large payoff to surviving an early death. For instance, this is apparent when $r=32\%$ and $T=10$. In this case, the SF=2.13%, $(\sum B)_1=7.538$, and $PV_1=2.930$. Calculation of the B values and survival rate values would reveal that all of the yearly B values that comprise $(\sum B)_1$ exceed the yearly survival rates that comprise PV_1. There is a high risk of early death, thus a relatively large return if the asset survives. Depreciation is relatively low; therefore $(\sum B)_1$ is close to the upper limit (which is close to 10 when r is close to 100 percent). PV_1 is low—close to its minimum value of zero. Early death "rules" as the likely cause of death when r is 32%. Death at $t=T$ is less likely to be attained.

PV_1 is a measure of expected age at death, and PV_t measures the expected time remaining until death. PV is a summary measure that includes life, as represented by a survival rate: $[1/(1+r)^t]$; the risk of early death: r; and the end of life: T. How does the concept of PV_t—specifically, PV_1, PV_2, …, PV_T—apply to a piece of music or to training modules? As addressed in chapter 8 for a piece of music, PV_1 would be its "expected life span." If the first period (say, the first measure) of the piece is "survived" without making a fatal error, then the expected life remaining is equal to PV_2 (where after $t = 1$, T now represents the periods of potential life remaining). For subsequent time periods, t, PV_t would equal the expected remaining life. If the fatal error rate, r, is high, PV_1 is low. There is a big "return" to surviving until T. $(\sum B)_1$ reflects that payoff; that is, the larger r is, the larger $(\sum B)_1$ will be, and vice versa.

Bibliography

"Afghanistan is Among Worst Places on Globe for Women's Health, say UNICEF and CDC." *reliefweb.int*, November 6, 2002. https://reliefweb.int/report/afghanistan/afghanistan-among-worst-places-globe-womens-health-say-unicef-and-cdc.

Alchian, Armen, and William R. Allen. *Exchange and Production: Competition, Coordination, and Control*, 2nd edition. Belmont, CA: Wadworth, 1977.

Aldrich, Jr., Nelson W. *George, Being George.* New York, NY: Random House, 2008.

Alexander, Gerianne M. "An Evolutionary Perspective of Sex-typed Toy Preferences: Pink, Blue, and the Brain." *Archives of Sexual Behavior* 32, no. 1 (2003): 7–14.

Alinsky, Saul D. *Rules for Radicals.* New York, NY: Vintage Books, 1989.

Allen, R. G. D. *Mathematical Analysis for Economists.* New York, NY: St. Martin's Press, 1967.

American Air Museum in Britain. *Donald James Matthew Blakeslee*, November 30, 2018. http://www.americanairmuseum.com/person/44924.

American Psychological Association (APA). "Guidelines for Psychological Practice With Lesbian, Gay, and Bisexual Clients." *American Psychologist* 67, no. 1 (January 2012): 10–42.

Anderson, James A. *An Introduction to Neural Networks.* Cambridge, MA: MIT Press, 1995.

Arbib, Michael A. *The Handbook of Brain Theory and Neural Networks.* Cambridge, MA: MIT Press, 2002.

Aristotle. *The Ethics of Aristotle: The Nicomachean Ethics.* New York, NY: Penguin Books, 1976.

———. *Great Books of the Western World: Aristotle II*, Edited by Robert Maynard Hutchins, Vol. IX. Chicago, IL: Encyclopaedia Britannica, 1982.

Aviles, Gwen. "Amazon Removes Controversial Books by 'Father of Conversion Therapy'." *nbcnews.com*, July 3, 2019. https://www.nbcnews.com/feature/nbc-out/amazon-removes-controversial-books-father-conversion-therapy-n1026446.

Axelrod, Robert. *The Evolution of Cooperation.* New York, NY: Basic Books, 1984.

"Baby Body Parts Testimony Brings Jury to Tears." *wnd.com.*, October 17, 2019. https://www.wnd.com/2019/10/baby-body-parts-testimony-brings-jury-tears/.

Barnett, Harold J., and Chandler Morse. *Scarcity and Growth.* Baltimore, MD: The Johns Hopkins Press, 1963.

Baumol, William J. *Economic Theory and Operations Analysis*, 4th edition. Englewood Cliffs, NJ: Prentice-Hall, Inc., 1977.

Beal, Matthew J. *Variational Algorithms for Approximate Bayesian Inference.* London: University of London, May 2003.

Beamon, Todd. "NYC Releases List of 31 Genders: Man, Woman, 'Something Else Entirely'." *Newsmax*, June 1, 2016. http://www.newsmax.com/Newsfront/NYC-releases-gender-list/2016/06/01/id/731809/.

Becker, Gary S. "The Economic Approach to Human Behavior." In *The Essence of Becker*, Edited by Ramon Febrero and Pedro S. Schwartz, 3–17. Stanford, CA: Hoover Institution, 1995.

Becker, Lawrence. *Reciprocity.* Chicago, IL: University of Chicago Press, 1990.

Berliner, Michael S. *Letters of Ayn Rand.* New York, NY: Dutton, 1995.

Binswanger, Harry. *The Ayn Rand Lexicon: Objectivism from A to Z.* New York, NY: Meridian, 1986.

Bissell, Roger. "A Calm Look at Abortion Arguments." *Reason* 13, no. 5 (September 1981): 27–31.

Blake, Nathaniel. "NYT Writer Says a 'Just,' 'Rational' Society Would Eliminate Pronouns 'He' and 'She'." *The Federalist*, June 15, 2019. https://thefederalist.com/2019/07/15/nyt-writer-says-just-rational-society-eliminate-pronouns/.

Bongaarts, John. "Trends in Senescent Life Expectancy." *Population Studies* 63, no. 3 (2005): 203–13.

Boorman, Georgi. "California Legislature Passes Bill to Punish Elder-Care Workers Who Don't Use Trans Pronouns." *The Federalist*, September 15, 2017. https://thefederalist.com/2017/09/15/california-legislature-passes-bill-punish-elder-care-workers-dont-use-trans-pronouns/.

Boydstun, Stephen. "Volitional Synapses: Part 2." *Objectivity* 2, no. 2 (1995): 105–29.

———. "Volitional Synapses: Part 3." *Objectivity* 2, no. 4 (1996): 183–204.

Boytim, J. F. *Solo Vocal Repertoire for Young Singers: An Annotated Bibliography*, 2nd edition. New York, NY: National Association of Teachers of Singing, 1982.

Braine, Theresa. "Not Enough Babies? Declining U.S. Birth Rate Means Population Can't Replace Itself, New Report Says." *New York Daily News*, January 10, 2019. https://www.nydailynews.com/news/national/ny-news-cdc-babies-birth-rate-pregnancy-20190110-story.html.

Branden, Nathaniel. "What Are the Respective Obligations of Parents to Children." *The Objectivist Newsletter* 1, no. 12 (December 1962): 55.

———. "Does Inherited Wealth Give Some Individuals an Unfair Advantage in a Competitive Economy?" *The Objectivist Newsletter* 2, no. 6 (1963): 22–23.

"British Medical Doctor Fired Because He Believes Gender is Fixed at Birth." *Free West Media*, July 12, 2019. http://freewestmedia.com/2019/07/12/british-medical-doctor-fired-because-he-believes-gender-is-fixed-at-birth/.

Brown, Elizabeth Nolan. "Section 230 Is the Internet's First Amendment. Now Both Republicans and Democrats Want to Take It Away." *Reason*, July 29, 2019. https://reason.com/2019/07/29/section-230-is-the-internets-first-amendment-now-both-republicans-and-democrats-want-to-take-it-away/.

Bureau of Labor Statistics. *Job-related Deaths are Less Likely for Women*, September 30, 1998. https://www.bls.gov/opub/ted/1998/Sep/wk5/art03.htm.

"California Professor Vindicated After Termination for 'Dangerous' Conservative Views." *Pacific Justice Institute*, January 9, 2019. https://www.pacificjustice.org/press/california-professor-vindicated-after-termination-for-dangerous-conservative-views.

Campbell, W. C. *Computer Analysis of Musical Performance*. Doctoral Dissertation, University of Connecticut, 1970.

Carnap, Rudolf. "The Two Concepts of Probability: The Problem of Probability." *Philosophical and Phenomenological Research* 5, no. 4 (1945): 513–32.

Carnes, Bruce A., S. Jay Olshansky, and Douglas Grahn. "Continuing the Search for a Law of Mortality." *Population and Development Review* 22, no. 2 (1996): 231–64.

Carpenter, Gail A., and Stephen Grossberg. "ART-2: Self-Organization of Stable Recognition Category Codes for Analog Input Patterns." *Applied Optics* 26, no. 23 (1987): 4919–30.

———. "A Massively Parallel Architecture for a Self-Organizing Neural Pattern Recognition Machine." *Computer Vision, Graphics, and Image Processing* 37 (1987): 54–115.

———. "ART3: Hierarchical Search Using Chemical Transmitters in Self-Organizing Pattern Recognition Architectures." *Neural Networks* 3 (1990):. 129–52.

———. "Adaptive Resonance Theory." In *The Handbook of Brain Theory and Neural Networks*, Edited by Michael A. Arbib, 1–12. Cambridge, MA: MIT Press, 2002.

Carpenter, Gail A., Stephen Grossberg, and David B. Rosen. "Neural Networks." *ART-2A: An Adaptive Resonance Algorithm for Rapid Category Learning and Recognition* 4 (1991): 493–504.

Carpenter, Gail A., Stephen Grossberg, Natalya Markuzon, John H. Reynolds, and David B. Rosen. "A Fuzzy ARTMAP: A Neural Network Architecture for Incremental Supervised Learning of Analog Multidimensional Maps." *Neural Networks* 3 (1992): 1–40.

Carpenter, Gail A., Stephen Grossberg, and John W. Reynolds. "Predictive Self-Organizing Neural Network." *United States of America Patent 5,214,715*, 1993.

Cendrillon, Raphael, and Brian C. Lovell. "Real-Time Face Recognition using Eigenfaces." *Proceedings – SPIE The International Society for Optical Engineering*, 2000, 269–76.

Central Intelligence Agency. *The World Fact Book: Country Comparisons-Maternal Mortality Rate*, 2017. https://www.cia.gov/library/publications/the-world-factbook/fields/353rank.html.

Chapman, Douglas G., and Ronald A. Schaufele. *Elementary Probability Models and Statistical Inference*. Waltham, MS: Ginn-Blaisdell, 1970.

Chiang, Alpha C. *Fundamental Methods of Mathematical Economics*, 2nd edition. New York, NY: McGraw-Hill, 1974.

Chou, Ya-Lun. *Statistical Analysis.* New York, NY: Holt, Rinehart and Winston, Inc., 1969.

Christian, Bonnie. "Teenager Who Went Viral after Arguing with His Teacher That There are Only Two Genders Barred from Returning to the School to Finish His Education." *Evening Standard*, July 3, 2019. https://www.standard.co.uk/news/uk/teenager-who-went-viral-after-arguing-with-his-teacher-that-there-are-only-two-genders-told-its-not-a4180816.html.

Chu, Singfat. "Using Soccer Goals to Motivate the Poisson Process." *INFORMS Transactions on Education* 3, no. 2 (2003): 64–70.

Clark, Michael. *Bayesian Basics*, September 11, 2015. https://14aa534a-a-ab15346e-s-sites.googlegroups.com/a/umich.edu/micl/miscfiles/IntroBayes.pdf.

Colvin, Geoff. *Talent is Overrated.* New York, NY: Penguin Group, 2008.

Connellan, J., S. Baron-Cohen, S. Wheelwright, A. Batki, and J. Ahluwalia. "Sex Differences in Human Neonatal Social Perception." *Infant Behavior and Development* 23 (2000): 113–18.

Cordell-Whitney, Dionne. "Minnesota Mom Loses Fight Against Teen's Sex Change." *Courthouse News Service*, May 24, 2017. https://www.courthousenews.com/minnesota-mom-loses-fight-teens-sex-change/.

Cox, Stepen. *The Woman and the Dynamo: Isabel Paterson and the Idea of America.* New Brunswick, NJ: Transaction Publishers, 2004.

Crovelli, Mark R. "On the Possibility of Assigning Probabilities to Singular Cases, or: Probability Is Subjective Too!" *Libertarian Papers* 1, no. 26 (2009): 1–23.

———. "A Challenge to Ludwig von Mises's Theory of Probability." *Libertarian Papers* 2, no. 23 (2010): 1–20.

———. "All Probablistic Methods Assume a Subjective Definition of Probability." *Libertarian Papers* 4, no. 1 (2012): 163–74.

Cullenberg, Stephen, Jack Amariglio, and David F. Ruccio. *Postmodernism, Economics and Knowledge.* London: Routledge, 2001.

Davidson, Jane W. "Visual Perception in Performance Manner in the Movements of Solo Musicians." *Psychology of Music* 21 (1993): 103–13.

Day, Taylor. "Where 'Section 230' Fits in the Social Media Censorship War." *American Thinker*, August 28, 2019. https://www.americanthinker.com/blog/2019/08/where_section_230_fits_in_the_social_media_censorship_war.html.

Delac, Kresimir, Mislav Grgic, and Panos Liatsis. "Appearance-based Statistical Methods for Face Recognition." *47th International Symposium ELMAR-2005*, Zadar, Croatia, 2005.

Delzell, Judith K., Debbie A. Rohwer, and Diane E. Ballard. "Effects of Melodic Pattern Difficulty and Performance Experience on Ability to Play by Ear." *Journal of Research in Music Education* 1 (1999): 53–63.

Den Uyl, Douglas J. "The Right to Welfare and the Virtue of Charity." *Social Philosophy and Policy* 10, no. 1 (1993): 192–224.

Den Uyl, Douglas J., and Douglas B. Rasmussen. "Life, Teleology, and Eudaimonia in the Ethics of Ayn Rand." In *The Philosophic Thought of Ayn Rand*, Edited by

Douglas J. Den Uyl and Douglas B. Rasmussen, 63–80. Urbana, IL and Chicago, IL: University of Illinois Press, 1986.

———. *The Philosophic Thought of Ayn Rand*. Urbana, IL and Chicago, IL: University of Illinois Press, 1986.

Desanctis, Alexandra. “The High School Fighting to Save Women’s Sports.” *National Review*, July 12, 2019. https://www.nationalreview.com/2019/07/transgender-ideology-hurts-girls-sports-undermines-feminism/.

Devlin, Hannah. “Scientist Grow Mini-brain on the Move that can Contract Muscle.” *theguardian.com*, March 18, 2019. https://www.theguardian.com/science/2019/mar/18/scientists-grow-mini-brain-on-the-move-that-can-contract-muscle.

Divers Institute of Technology. *Mark V Deep Sea Diving Suit*, 2019. https://www.diversinstitute.edu/programs/suit-up/mark-v/.

Duffey, Romney B. “The Quantification of Resilience: Learning Environments and Managing Risk.” *Proceedings of Resilience Engineering Symposium*, Nice, France, 2008.

———. “Predicting Rare Events: Risk Exposure, Uncertainty and Unknown Unknowns.” *AR2TS 19th Symposium*, Stratford, England, 2010.

———. *The Quantification of Systemic Risk and Stability: New Methods and Measures*. NBER Working Paper No. 17022. Washington, DC: National Bureau of Economic Research, 2011.

———. “Search Theory: The Probabilistic Physics and Psychology of Memory and Learning.” *Journal of Scientific Research and Studies* 4, no. 5 (2017): 107–120.

Duffey, Romney B., and John W. Saull. *Managing Risk: The Human Element*. Chichester, West Sussex: Wiley, 2008.

———. “Risk Prediction, Regulation, Perception, Acceptance and Avoidance: A General Theory.” *19th Advances in Risk and Reliability Technology Symposium (AR2TS)*, University of Nottingham, Stratford-upon-Avon, 2009.

Dutta, M. *Econometric Methods*. Cincinnati, OH: South-Western, 1975.

The Economist. “How to Deal with a Declining Population.” July 28–August 3, 2007: 11.

Ehrlich, Isaac, and Gary S. Becker. “Market Insurance, Self-Insurance, and Self-Protection.” *Journal of Political Economy* 80, no. 4 (1972): 623–48.

Ellington, Connor. “Female Athlete Alleges Retaliation by Coach Because Her Mother Complained about Transgender Policy.” *The College Fix*, July 1, 2019. https://www.thecollegefix.com/female-athlete-alleges-retaliation-by-coach-because-her-mother-complained-about-transgender-policy/.

Essentials of Fire Fighting. Stillwater, OK: Oklahoma State University, 1983.

Evans, Brian. “Police State: UK Catholic Commentator Facing Prison For Using Wrong Gender Pronoun!” *Evans News Report*, March 22, 2019. https://evansnewsreport.com/2019/03/22/police-state-catholic-commentator-in-uk-facing-prison-for-using-wrong-gender-pronoun/.

Evers, Williamson M. “The Law of Omissions and Neglect of Children.” *Journal of Libertarian Studies* 2, no. 1 (1978): 1–10.

Farnum, S. *Farnum String Scale*. Winona, MN: Hal Leonard Co., 1969.

Febrero, Ramon, and Pedro S. Schwartz. *The Essence of Becker.* Stanford, CA: Hoover Institute Press, 1995.

"The Feds Investigate Connecticut Athletics for Letting Boys Compete in Girls' Sports." *The College Fix*, August 8, 2019. https://www.thecollegefix.com/the-feds-investigate-connecticut-athletics-for-letting-boys-compete-in-girls-sports/.

Feldman, H. A. "Families of Lines: Random Effects in Linear Regression Analysis." *Journal of Applied Physiology* 64, no. 4 (1988): 1721–32.

Fiondella, Lance, and Romney D. Duffey. "Software and Human Reliability: Error Reduction and Prediction." *PSA2015 International Topical Meeting on Probabilistic Safety Assessment and Analysis*, Sun Valley, ID, 2015.

Fisher, Irving N. *The Nature of Capital and Income.* New York, NY: Sentry Press, [1906] 1965.

———. *The Theory of Interest.* New York, NY: Macmillan Co., 1930.

Fiske, H. E. "Relationship of Selected Factors in Trumpet Performance Adjudication." *Journal of Research in Music Education* 25 (1977): 256–63.

———. *The Effect of a Training Procedure in Music Performance Evaluation on Judge Reliability.* Ontario Educational Research Council Report, 1978.

Frank, Robert H. *Passions within Reason.* New York, NY: W. W. Norton & Company, 1988.

Friedman, Milton. *A Theory of the Consumption Function.* Princeton, NJ: Princeton University Press, 1957.

Friedman, Victoria. "All Adults Automatically Organ Donors Unless They Opt Out in New English Law." *breitbart.com*, March 16, 2019. https://www.breitbart.com/europe/2019/03/16/all-adults-presumed-organ-donors-new-english-law/.

———. "Teen Who Said There Are Only Two Genders Expelled from School, GoFundMe Shut Down." *breitbart.com*, July 4, 2019. https://www.breitbart.com/europe/2019/07/04/teen-who-declared-there-are-two-genders-barred-returning-school/.

Gander, Kashmira. "Scientists Create Mini-Human Brains that Produce Waves in a Lab: 'The Level of Neural Activity We Are Seeing is Unprecidented'." *Newsweek*, August 29, 2019. https://www.newsweek.com/scientists-create-mini-human-brains-lab-waves-neural-activity-1456755.

Gockowski, Anthony. "KU Dean: Diversity and Inclusion a 'Universal Value' of Libraries." *Campus Reform*, December 28, 2016. http://www.campusreform.org/?ID=8575.

Goldfarb, Stanley. "Take Two Aspirin and Call Me by My Pronouns." *wsj.com*, September 12, 2019. https://www.wsj.com/articles/take-two-aspirin-and-call-me-by-my-pronouns-11568325291.

Gordon, E. *Rating Scales and Their Uses for Evaluating Achievement in Music Performance.* Chicago, IL: GIA, 2002.

Gotthelf, Allan. "Ayn Rand's Theory of Concepts." In *Concepts and their Role in Knowledge: Reflections on Objectivist Epistemology*, Edited by Allan Gotthelf and James G. Lennox, 3–40. Pittsburgh, PA: Univeristy of Pittsburgh Press, 2013.

Gotthelf, Allan, and James H. Lennox. *Concepts and their Role in Knowledge: Reflections on Objectivist Epistemology.* Pittsburgh, PA: University of Pittsburgh Press, 2013.

Griffiths, Paul E. "Rand on Concepts, Definitions, and the Advance of Science: Comments on Gotthelf and Lennox." In *Concepts and their Role in Knowledge: Reflections on Objectivist Epistemology*, Edited by Allan Gotthelf and G. Lennox James, 139–47. Pittsburgh, PA: University of Pittsburgh Press, 2013.

Grossberg, Stephen. "Competitive Learning: From Interactive Activation to Adaptive Resonance." *Cognitive Science* 11 (1987): 23–63.

———. "The Link between Brain Learning, Attention, and Consciousness." *Consciousness and Cognition* 8 (1999): 1–44.

———. "Adaptive Resonance Theory: How a Brain Learns to Consciously Attend, Learn, and Recognize a Changing World." *Neural Networks* 37 (2013): 1–47.

———. "Grandmother Cohorts: Multiple-scale Brain Compression Dynamics during Learning of Object and Sequence Categories." *Language, Cognition, and Neuroscience* 32 (2016): 1–37.

Gutierrez, Angelina. "The Development of the Music Performance Assessment Tool (MPAT) for College Music Majors in the Piano, Strings, Voice and Guitar Departments." *Scholastica Review* 1 (2005): 1–38.

Gwartney, James D., Richard L. Stroup, Russell S. Sobel, and David A. MacPherson. *Economics: Private and Public Choice*, 11th edition. Mason, OH: Thomson, 2006.

"H.R.5—116th Congress (2019–2020)." *Congress.gov*, May 20, 2019. https://www.congress.gov/bill/116th-congress/house-bill/5/text.

Hasson, Peter. "Facebook, Amazon, Google And Twitter All Work with Left-Wing SPLC." *Daily Caller*, June 6, 2018. http://dailycaller.com/2018/06/06/splc-partner-google-facebook-amazon/.

Hastings, Hunter. "Per Bylund on Subjective Value." *Mises Institute*, May 14, 2019. https://mises.org/library/bylund-subjective-value.

Hayek, Friedrich A. *Law, Legislation and Liberty*, Vol. 1. Chicago, IL: The University of Chicago Press, 1973.

Hazlitt, Henry. *The Foundations of Morality*. Irvington-on-Hudson, NY: The Foundation for Economic Education, Inc., 1998.

Held, Virginia. "Mothering versus Contract." In *Beyond Self-Interest*, Edited by Jane J. Mansbridge, 287–347. Chicago, IL: University of Chicago, 1990.

Heldt, Brianna. "Mother Claims Son Identifies as a Girl, Father Disagrees in Texas Custody Battle." *Townhall*, November 28, 2018. https://townhall.com/tipsheet/briannaheldt/2018/11/28/mother-claims-son-identifies-as-a-girl-father-disagrees-in-texas-custody-battle-n2536661.

Helen, Nicholas. "Too Strong Trans Players in Women's Rugby are driving Referees Away." *thetimes.co.uk*, September 28, 2019. https://www.thetimes.co.uk/article/injury-fears-over-rugbys-trans-women-drive-referees-off-pitch-877hjsfz0.

Herbener, Jeffrey M. "Ludwig von Mises and the Austrian School of Economics." In *Philosophers of Capitalism: Menger, Mises, Rand, and Beyond*, Edited by Edward W. Younkins. Lanham, MD: Lexington Books, 2005.

Heron, Melonie. "Deaths: Leading Causes for 2015." *National Vital Statistics Reports*. Washington, DC: U.S. Department of Health and Human Services, Centers for Disease Control and Prevention, 2017.

Hewitson, Gillian. "Disavowal of the Sexed Body." In *Postmodernism, Economics and Knowledge*, Edited by Stephen Cullenberg, Jack Amariglio, and David F. Ruccio, 221–45. London: Routledge, 2001.

Heyes, J. D. "Apple Threatens to Ban Social Media App Parler from its Platform if it Refuses to Censor 'Offensive' (Conservative) Content." *Natural News*, June 28, 2019. https://www.naturalnews.com/2019-06-28-apple-threatens-parler-app-over-censoring-offensive-content.html.

Hinson, Maurice, and Wesley Roberts. *Guide to the Pianist's Repertoire*, 4th edition. Bloomington, IN: Indiana University Press, 2014.

Hollander, Myles, and Douglas A. Wolfe. *Nonparametric Statistical Methods*. New York, NY: John Wiley & Sons, 1973.

Hoppe, Hans-Hermann. "On Certainty and Uncertainty: How Rational Can Our Expectations Be?" *Review of Austrian Economics* 10, no. 1 (1997): 49–78.

———. "Introduction." In *The Ethics of Liberty*, Edited by Murray N. Rothbard, xi–xliii. New York, NY and London: New York University Press, 1998.

Horwitz, Steven. "Two Worlds at Once: Rand, Hayek, and the Ethics of the Micro- and Macro-cosmos." *The Journal of Ayn Rand Studies* 6, no. 2 (2005): 375–403.

Howden, David. "Single Trial Probability Applications: Can Subjectivity Evade Frequency Limitations?" *Libertarian Papers* 1, no. 42 (2009): 1–12.

Huber, Dave. "Cornell Summer Seminar Asks: Should We Still Use Concepts like 'Rationality' and 'Reason'?" *The College Fix*, June 25, 2019. https://www.thecollegefix.com/cornell-summer-seminar-asks-should-we-still-use-concepts-like-rationality-and-reason/.

Huebner, Solomon Stephen, and Kenneth Black. *Life Insurance*, 9th edition. Englewood Cliffs, NJ: Prentice-Hall, Inc., 1976.

Huron, David, and Jonathon Berec. "Characterizing Idiomatic Organization in Music: A Theory and Case Study of Musical Affordances." *Empirical Musicology Review* 4, no. 3 (2009): 103–122.

Inside Man. "97% Employees Who Die at Work are Men (2009–2014 Figures)." March 3, 2015. http://www.inside-man.co.uk/2015/03/03/97-employees-die-work-men-2009-2014-figures/.

Jacob, Madeleine. "Jury Rules against Dad Trying to Save His 7-Year-Old from Gender 'Transition'." *lifesitenews.com*, October 21, 2019. https://www.lifesitenews.com/news/breaking-jury-rules-against-dad-trying-to-save-his-7-year-old-from-gender-transition.

Jaynes, E. T. *Probability Theory: The Logic of Science*. New York, NY: Cambridge University Press, 2003.

Jetton, Merlin. "On Probability." *Objectivity* 2, no. 1 (1994): 1–29.

Johnson, Lance D. "Bank of America Just Shut Down All Bank Accounts Belonging to a Baptist Pastor Because of His Christian Beliefs." *Censorship.news*, April 23, 2019. https://www.censorship.news/2019-04-23-bank-of-america-shut-down-baptist-pastor.html.

Johnson, Manuel, and James T. Bennett. "Increasing Resource Scarcity: Further Evidence." *Quarterly Review of Economics and Business* 20, no. 1 (1980): 42–48.

Johnston, J. *Econometric Methods*, 2nd edition. New York, NY: McGraw-Hill, 1972.

"Jordan Peterson Launches Anti-Censorship Site Thinkspot." *The Guardian*, June 13, 2019. https://www.theguardian.com/technology/2019/jun/13/jordan-peterson-launches-anti-censorship-site-thinkspot.

"Judicial Watch Sues California over Gender Quota Mandate for Corporate Boards." *Judicial Watch*, August 9, 2019. https://www.judicialwatch.org/press-releases/judicial-watch-sues-california-over-gender-quota-mandate-for-corporate-boards/.

Kabbany, Jennifer. "Math Teacher Loses Job after Defending Western Civilization." *The College Fix*, July 1, 2019. https://www.thecollegefix.com/math-teacher-loses-job-after-defending-western-civilization/.

Keenan, Jeremiah. "Father Gagged, Found Guilty Of 'Family Violence' For Calling His Trans Daughter a 'She'." *The Federalist*, April 24, 2019. https://thefederalist.com/2019/04/24/father-gagged-found-guilty-family-violence-calling-trans-daughter/.

Keene, L. F., and D. B. Varnado. *Saturn Early Launch Phase: SP-79*. Instrumentation Systems Analysis Branch (K-ED2) and Tracking Branch (K-EF4), NASA Doc. No. N65-19700, John F. Kennedy Space Center, SP-79, 1964.

Kelley, David. "The Necessity of Government." *The Freeman* 24 (April 1974): 243–48.

———. *Unrugged Individualsim*. Poughkeepsie, NY: Institute for Objectivist Studies, 1996.

———. "Ruled – Or Principled?" *IOS Journal* 6, no. 6 (February 1997): 1, 5–7.

———. "Happiness or Life, or Both: Reply to Ole Martin Moen." *Reason Papers* 37, no. 1 (2015): 65–79.

Khan, Shazma. "Scientists Put Human Gene into Monkeys to Make them Smarter, Human-like." *Business Recorder*, April 11, 2019. https://www.brecorder.com/2019/04/11/488194/scientists-put-human-gene-into-monkeys-to-make-them-smarter-human-like/.

King, J. Charles. "Life and the Theory of Value: The Randian Argument Reconsidered." In *The Philosophic Thought of Ayn Rand*, Edited by Douglas J. Den Uyl and Douglas B. Rassmussen, 102–21. Urbana, IL and Chicago, IL: The University of Illinois Press, 1986.

Kirkup, James. "The NHS Has Quietly Changed its Trans Guidance to Reflect Reality." *The Spectator*, June 4, 2020. https://www.spectator.co.uk/article/the-nhs-has-quietly-changed-its-trans-guidance-to-reflect-reality.

Klein, Andreas. *The Chopin "Etudes": An Indispensable Pedagogical Tool for Developing Piano Technique*. Dissertation, Rice University, 1989.

Knight, Randall D. *Physics for Scientists and Engineers: A Strategic Approach*. San Francisco, CA: Pearson, 2004.

Knox, Taryn, Lynley C. Anderson, and Alison Heather. "Transwomen in Elite Sport: Scientific and Ethical Considerations." *Journal of Medical Ethics* 45, no. 6 (2019): 395–403.

Kruschke, John K. *Doing Bayesian Data Analysis: A Tutorial with R and BUGS*. Oxford: Elsevier, 2011.

Kuhn, Thomas. *The Structure of Scientific Revolutions*, 2nd edition, Vol. 2. Chicago, IL: The University of Chicago Press, 1970.

Kurtz, E. B. *Life Expectancy of Physical Property: Based on Mortality Laws*. New York, NY: The Ronald Press Company, 1930.

Latimer, Jr., Marvin E., Martin J. Bergee, and Mary L. Cohen. "Reliability and Perceived Pedagogical Utility of a Weighted Music Performance Assessment Rubric." *Journal of Research in Music Education* 58, no. 2 (2010): 168–83.

Lefler, Dion, and Jonathan Shorman. "Kansas to Allow Transgender People to Change Their Gender on Birth Certificates." *kansascity.com*, June 24, 2019. https://www.kansascity.com/news/politics-government/article231903843.html.

Lehmann, Andreas C., and K. Anders Ericsson. "Sight-reading Ability of Expert Pianists in the Context of Piano Accompanying." *Psychomusicology* 12 (1993): 182–95.

Lennox, James G. "Concepts, Context, and the Advance of Science." In *Concepts and their Role in Knowledge: Reflections on Objectivist Epistemology*, Edited by Allan Gotthelf and James G. Lennox, 112–33. Pittsburgh, PA: University of Pittsburgh Press, 2013.

Leoni, Bruno. *Freedom and the Law*. Princeton, NJ: Van Nostrand, 1961.

Leskovec, Jure, Anand Rajaraman, and Jeffrey D. Ullman. *Mining of Massive Data Sets*, 2014. infolab.stanford.edu/~ullman/mmds/book.pdf.

Machan, Tibor R. *Human Rights and Human Liberties*. Chicago, IL: Nelson-Hall Company, 1975.

———. *Classical Individualism: The Supreme Importance of Each Human Being*. London and New York, NY: Routledge, 1998.

———. *Generosity: Virtue in Civil Society*. Washington, DC: Cato Institute, 1998.

Mack, Eric. "The Fundamental Moral Elements of Rand's Theory of Rights." In *The Philosophic Thought of Ayn Rand*, Edited by Douglas J. Den Uyl and Douglas B. Rasmussen, 122–61. Urbana, IL and Chicago, IL: University of Illinois Press, 1986.

"Male Prisoners Self-Identifying as Trans for 'Perks'." *The Christian Institute*, July 26, 2019. https://www.christian.org.uk/news/male-prisoners-self-identifying-as-trans-for-perks/.

Malthus, Thomas. *Principle of Population*. Homewood, IL: Irwin, [1803] 1963.

Mansbridge, Jane J. *Beyond Self-Interest*. Chicago, IL: University of Chicago, 1990.

McPherson, Gary E., and William F. Thompson. "Assessing Music Performance: Issues and Influences." *Research Studies in Music Education* 10, no. 1 (1998): 12–24.

Meadows, Donella H., Dennis L. Meadows, Jorgen Randers, and William W. Behrens III. *The Limits to Growth*, Vol. 2nd revised. New York, NY: Signet, 1975.

"Men Dominate in Workplace Deaths." *Los Angeles Times*, August 4, 1995. http://articles.latimes.com/1995-08-04/business/fi-31566_1_workplace-deaths.

Merrill, Ronald E. *The Ideas of Ayn Rand*. LaSalle, IL: Open Court, 1991.

———. "Objectivist Ethics: A Biological Critique." *Objectivity* 2, no. 5 (1997): 67–93.

Mesarovic, Mihajlo, and Eduard Pestel. *Mankind at the Turning Point*. New York, NY: Signet, 1976.

Miller, Heidi. "Difference Between Male And Female Structures (Mental And Physical)." *Steady Health*, June 14, 2017. https://www.steadyhealth.com/articles/difference-between-male-and-female-structures-mental-and-physical.

Mills, Janet. "Assessing Musical Performance Musically." *Educational Studies* 17 (1991): 173–81.

Mises, Ludwig von. *Human Action*, 4th edition. San Francisco, CA: Fox & Wilkes, [1949] 1996.

Mises, Richard von. *Positivism.* New York, NY: Dover, [1951] 1968.

———. *Probability, Statistics and Truth*, 2nd edition. New York, NY: Macmillian, 1957.

Morton, Victor. "Transgender Weightlifter Wins Two Gold Medals in Women's Competition." *The Washington Times*, July 15, 2019. https://www.washingtontimes.com/news/2019/jul/15/laurel-hubbard-transgender-weightlifter-wins-two-g/?utm_campaign=shareaholic&utm_medium=twitter&utm_source=socialnetwork.

Mueller, John D. *Redeeming Economics: Rediscovering the Missing Element.* Wilmington, DE: ISI Books, 2010.

Murphy, Robert P. *What Universities Won't Teach College Students About the Economics of Climate Change*, June 10, 2019. https://mises.org/wire/what-universities-wont-teach-college-students-about-economics-climate-change.

Narveson, Jan. "Ayn Rand as Moral & Political Philosopher." *Reason Papers* 23, Fall (1998): 96–100.

Navarrete, Pablo, and Javier Ruiz-del-Solar. "Comparative Study between Different Eigenspace-Based Approaches for Face Recognition." In *Advances in Soft Computing—AFSS 2002. Lecture Notes in Computer Science*, Edited by N. R. Pal and M. Sugeno, Vol. 2275. Berlin, Heidelberg: Springer, 2002.

Norton, David L. *Personal Destinies: A Philosophy of Ethical Individualism.* Princeton, NJ: Princeton University Press, 1976.

NYCCHR. "Gender Identity Expression." *New York City Commission on Human Rights*, June 2016. http://freebeacon.com/wp-content/uploads/2016/06/GenderID_Card2015.pdf.

Ollen, Joy. "A Criterion-related Validity Test of Selected Indicators of Musical Sophistication Using Expert Ratings." *9th International Conference on Music Perception and Cognition*, Bologna, Italy, 2006.

O'Neil, Tyler. "Retaliation? Google Whistleblower Claims FBI, SWAT, Bomb Squad Appeared at His Home." *PJ Media*, August 15, 2019. https://pjmedia.com/trending/retaliation-google-whistleblower-claims-fbi-swat-bomb-squad-appeared-at-his-home/.

O'Neill, William F. *With Charity toward None: An Analysis of Ayn Rand's Philosophy.* Totowa, NJ: Littlefield, Adams & Co., 1972.

Oyeshile, O. A. "A Critique of the Maximin Principle in Rawls' Theory of Justice." *Humanity & Social Sciences Journal* 3, no. 1 (2008): 65–69.

Pal, N. R., and M. Sugeno. *Advances in Soft Computing—AFSS 2002. Lecture Notes in Computer Science.* Berlin, Heidelberg: Springer, 2002.

Parke, Caleb. "Conservative Students Threatened with Doxxing at Texas College." *Fox News*, June 25, 2019. https://www.foxnews.com/us/texas-college-campus-conservative-threatened.

Pateman, C. *The Sexual Contract.* Cambridge: Polity, 1988.

Paterson, Isabel. *The God of the Machine.* Caldwell, ID: The Caxton Printers, [1943] 1968.

Peikoff, Leonard. "The Philosophy of Objectivism. Lecture Series (1976), Lecture 8." In *The Ayn Rand Lexicon: Objectivism from A to Z*, Edited by Harry Binswinger, 479. New York, NY: Meridian, 1986.

———. *The Ominous Parallels.* New York, NY: Mentor, 1982.

———. "The Analytic-Synthetic Dichotomy." In *Introduction to Objectivist Epistemology*, Edited by Ayn Rand. New York, NY: Meridian, 1990.

———. *Objectivism: The Philosophy of Ayn Rand.* New York, NY: Dutton, 1991.

Pitacco, Ermanno. "Survival Models in Actuarial Mathematics: From Halley to Longevity Risk." *Invited talk at 7th International Congress Insurance: Mathematics & Economics, ISFA*, Lyon, France, 2003, 1–42.

Plimpton, George. "C-Span: Truman Capote." *c-span.org*, December 4, 1997. https://www.c-span.org/video/?97126-1/truman-capote/.

———. *A Conversation with George Plimpton*, March 16, 2000. https://www.youtube.com/watch?v=SkatvkE8Zpw.

Preinreich, Gabriel A. D. "Annual Survey of Economic Theory: The Theory of Depreciation." *Econometrica* 6, no. 3 (1938): 219–41.

"President Trump Ended Ghoulish Contract to Create 'Humanized Mice' Using Aborted Babies." *lifenews.com*, December 6, 2019. https://www.lifenews.com/2019/12/06/president-trump-ended-ghoulish-contract-to-create-humanized-mice-using-aborted-babies/.

Pulman, Bertrand. "Malinowski and Ignorance of Physiological Paternity." *Revue Française de Sociologie: Supplement: An Annual English Selection* 45 (2004): 125–46.

Radocy, R. E. "On Quantifying the Uncountable in Musical Behavior." *Bulletin of the Council of Research in Music Education* 88 (1986): 22–31.

———. "Evaluating Student Achievement." *Music Educators Journal* 76, no. 4 (1989): 30–33.

Ralston, Janette. "The Development of an Instrument to Grade the Difficulty of Vocal Solo Repertoire." *Journal of Research in Music Education* 47, no. 2 (1999): 163–73.

Rand, Ayn. *The Fountainhead.* Chicago, IL: Sears Readers Club, 1943.

———. *Atlas Shrugged.* New York, NY: Random House, 1957.

———. "Atlas Shrugged." In *For the New Intellectual*, Edited by Ayn Rand, 87–192. New York, NY: Signet, 1961.

———. *For the New Intellectual.* New York, NY: Signet, 1961.

———. "The Fountainhead." In *For the New Intellectual*, Edited by Ayn Rand, 68–86. New York, NY: Signet, 1961.

———. *Alvin Toffler's 'Playboy' Interview with Ayn Rand.* The Objectivist, Reprint, 1964.

———. "The Ethics of Emergencies." In *The Virtue of Selfishness*, Edited by Ayn Rand. New York, NY: Signet, 1964.

———. "Government Financing in a Free Society." In *The Virtue of Selfishness*, Edited by Ayn Rand, 116–20. New York, NY: Signet, 1964.

———. "Man's Rights." In *The Virtue of Selfishness*, Edited by Ayn Rand. New York, NY: Signet, 1964.

———. "The Nature of Government." In *The Virtue of Selfishness*, Edited by Ayn Rand, 107–15. New York, NY: Signet, 1964.

———. "The Objectivist Ethics." In *The Virtue of Selfishness*, Edited by Ayn Rand, 13–35. New York, NY: Signet, 1964.

———. *The Virtue of Selfishness.* New York, NY: Signet, 1964.

———. *Capitalism: The Unknown Ideal.* New York, NY: Signet, 1967.

———. "Conservatism: An Obituary." In *Capitalism: The Unknown Ideal*, Edited by Ayn Rand, 192–201. New York, NY: Signet, 1967.

———. "The Property Status of Airwaves." In *Capitalism: The Unknown Ideal*, Edited by Ayn Rand, 122–29. New York, NY: Signet, 1967.

———. "What is Capitalism?" In *Capitalism: The Unknown Ideal*, Edited by Ayn Rand, 11–34. New York, NY: Signet, 1967.

———. "The Wreckage of the Consensus." In *Capitalism: The Unknown Ideal*, Edited by Ayn Rand, 221–35. New York, NY: Signet, 1967.

———. "Of Living Death (2)." *The Objectivist* 7, no. 10 (October 1968): 1–6.

———. "The Comprachicos." In *The New Left: The Anti-Industrial Revolution*, 187–239. New York, NY: Signet, 1975.

———. *The New Left: The Anti-Industrial Revolution.* New York, NY: Signet, 1975.

———. "The Psycho-Epistemology of Art." In *The Romantic Manifesto*, 15–24. New York, NY: Signet, 1975.

———. *The Romantic Manifesto.* New York, NY: Signet, 1975.

———. "Causality Versus Duty." In *Philosophy: Who Needs It*, Edited by Ayn Rand, 95–101. New York, NY: Signet, 1982.

———. "Egalitarianism and Inflation." In *Philosophy: Who Needs It*, Edited by Ayn Rand, 120–36. New York, NY: Signet, 1982.

———. "Faith and Force: The Destroyers of the Modern World." In *Philosophy: Who Needs It*, Edited by Ayn Rand, 58–76. New York, NY: Signet, 1982.

———. "The Metaphysical Versus the Man-Made." In *Philosophy: Who Needs It*, Edited by Ayn Rand, 23–34. New York, NY: Signet, 1982.

———. "Philosophical Detection." In *Philosophy: Who Needs It*, 12–22. New York, NY: Signet, 1982.

———. "Philosophy: Who Needs It." In *Philosophy: Who Needs It*, Edited by Ayn Rand, 1–11. New York, NY: Signet, 1982.

———. *Philosophy: Who Needs It.* New York, NY: Signet, 1982.

———. "The Sanction of the Victims. The Objectivist Forum (Apr): 6, April 1982: 6." In *The Ayn Rand Lexicon: Objectivism from A to Z*, Edited by Harry Binswinger, 434. New York, NY: Meridian, 1986.

———. *Introduction to Objectivist Epistemology.* New York, NY: Signet, 1990.

Rasmussen, Douglas B., and Douglas J. Den Uyl. *Liberty and Nature: An Aristotelian Defense of Liberal Order.* La Salle, IL: Open Court, 1991.

Rasmussen, Mary. "A System of Numerical Symbols for Indicating Rhythmic Difficulty." *Music Educators Journal* 48, no. 3 (1962): 78.

Raul. "Who is More Powerful – Countries or Companies?" *howmuch.net*, July 11, 2019. https://howmuch.net/articles/putting-companies-power-into-perspective.

Repp, Bruno H. "The Aesthetic Quality of a Quantitatively Average Music Performance: Two Preliminary Experiments." *Music Perception: An Interdisciplinary Journal* 14, no. 4 (1997): 419–44.

Richardson, Bradford. "California First-Grader Sent to Principal's Office for Misgendering Classmate." *The Washington Times*, August 23, 2017. https://www.washingtontimes.com/news/2017/aug/23/california-parents-feel-betrayed-transgender-revea/.

Rothbard, Murray N. "Free Law in a Free Society: Review of 'Freedom and the Law' by Bruno Leoni." *National Review*, July 21, 1972: 803, 805.

———. *The Ethics of Liberty*. New York, NY: New York University Press, 1998.

Russell, James A., Leon G. Epstein, David M. Greer, Matthew Kirschen, Michael A. Rubin, and Lewis Ariane. "Brain Death, the Determination of Brain Death, and Member Guidance for Brain Death Accommodation Requests." *Neurology* 92 (January 29, 2019): 1–5.

Sachko, Anna Maria. *An Analysis of the Demand for Life Insurance*. Ph.D. Dissertation, Dept. of Economics, Columbia University, 1975.

Sacks, Jonathan. "Judaism Has No Kings." *the algemeiner*, July 22, 2019. https://www.algemeiner.com/2019/07/22/judaism-has-no-kings/.

Salerno, Joseph T. "Ludwig von Mises as Social Rationalist." *The Review of Austrian Economics* 4 (1990): 26–54.

Salvatore, Dominick. *Managerial Economics*, 3rd edition. New York, NY: McGraw-Hill, 1996.

Salzberg, Rita S., and Cecilia Chu Wang. "A Comparison of Prompts to Aid Rhythmic Sight-Reading of String Students." *Psychology of Music* 17 (1989): 123–31.

Sciabarra, Chris Matthew. *Ayn Rand: The Russian Radical*. University Park, PA: Pennsylvania State University Press, 1995.

Sébastien, Véronique, Henri Ralambondrainy, Olivier Sébastien, and Noël Conruyt. "Score Analyzer: Automatically Determining Scores Difficulty Level for Instrumental E-Learning." *13th International Society for Music Information Retrieval Conference*, Porto, Portugal, 2012, 571–76.

Shao, Stephen P. *Statistics for Business and Economics*, 3rd edition. Columbus, OH: Charles E. Merrill Publishing Co., 1976.

Shelton, Ray. "Epicurus and Rand." *Objectivity* 2, no. 3 (1995): 1–47.

Shlens, Jon. *A Tutorial on Principal Component Analysis: Version 1*, March 25, 2003. https://www.cs.princeton.edu/picasso/mats/PCA-Tutorial-Intuition_jp.pdf.

Showalter, Brandon. "Drugs Used as Puberty Blockers in Youth Linked to Thousands of Adult Deaths, FDA Shows." *The Christian Post*, October 4, 2019. https://www.christianpost.com/news/drugs-used-as-puberty-blockers-in-youth-linked-to-thousands-of-adult-deaths-fda-shows.html?fbclid=IwAR1mBayInXJKcrfl7hO9ysfSKfnKIiNQt8QdbL0uakKupWL8JTX7mpj_NQo.

Simon, Herbert A. "Theories of Decision-Making in Economics and Behavioral Science." *American Economic Review* 49, no. 3 (1959): 253–83.

Simpson, Thomas Marshall, Zareh M. Pirenian, and Bolling H. Crenshaw. *Mathematics of Finance*, 3rd edition. Englewood Cliffs, NJ: Prentice-Hall, 1951.

Smith, Adam. *The Wealth of Nations*. New York, NY: The Modern Library, [1776] 1937.

Smith, Allan. "After Years of Big Spending, Tech's Political Machine Turns to High Gear." *NBC News*, July 3, 2019. https://www.nbcnews.com/politics/congress/after-years-big-spending-tech-s-political-machine-turns-high-n1025096.

Smith, Lindsay I. *A Tutorial on Principal Components Analysis*. Ithaca, NY: Cornell University, February 2002. http://studylib.net/doc/10658014/a-tutorial-on-principal-components-analysis-lindsay-i-smi.

Spencer, Herbert. *Social Statics*. New York, NY: Robert Schalkenbach Foundation, [1892] 1954.

Spencer, Robert. "Amazon Bans Tommy Robinson's Book, 'Mohammed's Koran'." *PJ Media*, March 5, 2019. https://pjmedia.com/homeland-security/amazon-bans-tommy-robinsons-book-mohammeds-koran/.

SPSS® Base 10.0 Application Guide. Chicago, IL: SPSS, 1999.

Sugden, Robert. *The Economics of Rights, Cooperation and Welfare*. Oxford: Basil Blackwell, 1986.

Thompson, Sam, and Aaron Williamon. "Evaluating Evaluation: Musical Performance Assessment as a Research Tool." *Music Perception* 21, no. 1 (2003): 21–41.

Thompson, W. F., C. T. P. Diamond, and L. Balkwill. "The Adjudication of Six Performances of a Chopin Etude: A Study of Expert Knowledge." *Psychology of Music* 26 (1998): 154–74.

Touchstone, K. "Interdependent Decision-Making, Game Theory and Conformity." *Reason Papers* 20 (1995): 68–108.

———. *Then Athena Said: Unilateral Transfers and the Transformation of Objectivist Ethics*. Lanham, MD: University Press of America, 2006.

———. "Economic Decision-Making and Ethical Choice." *The Journal of Ayn Rand Studies* 10, no. 1 (2008): 171–91.

———. "Ethical Principles, Charity, and a Criterion for Giving." *Reason Papers* 30, Fall (2008): 37–58.

———. "Rand, Rothbard, and Rights Reconsidered." *Libertarian Papers* 2, no. 18 (2010): 1–40.

———. "Reproductivity, Capital Theory, and Objectivist Ethics." *Humanomics* 26, no. 3 (2010): 224–40.

———. "Rand and the Austrians: The Ultimate Value and the Non-interference Principle." *Libertarian Papers* 7, no. 2 (2015): 169–204.

———. "Charity, Childcare, and Crime: From Objectivist Ethics to the Austrian School." *Libertarian Papers* 8, no. 1 (2016): 23–57.

———. "When 'A is not A': Reflections on a Conversation." *Journal of Ayn Rand Studies* 17, no. 2 (2017): 238–74.

———. "On Life and Value within Objectivist Ethics." *Journal of Ayn Rand Studies* 18, no. 1 (2018): 55–83.

Turk, Matthew, and Alex Pentland. "Eigenfaces for Recognition." *Journal of Cognitive Neuroscience* 3 (1991): 71–86.

———. "Face Recognition Using Eigenfaces." *Proceedings of the 1991 IEEE Computer Science Conference on Computer Vision and Pattern Recognition*, 1991, 586–91.

U. S. Navy Diving Manual, Vol. I. Washington, DC: Naval Sea Systems Command, 1978.

United States Undersea Museum. *MK V Diving Rig*, September 19, 2016. http://www.navalunderseamuseum.org/mk-v/.

"Univ. of Louisville to Faculty: Express Your Views at Your Own Risk." *Alliance Defending Freedom*, March 28, 2019. http://centerforacademicfreedom.org/newsroom/univ-louisville-faculty-express-views-risk/.

Using Pronouns. Eugene, OR: University of Oregon. https://studentlife.uoregon.edu/pronouns (accessed August 31, 2019).

Valentine, Lloyd M., and Dennis F. Ellis. *Business Cycles and Forecasting*, 8th edition. Cincinnati, OH: South-Western Publishing Company, 1991.

Vibes, John. "Scientists Say They've Created the World's First Human-Monkey Hybrid." *themindunleashed.com*, September 3, 2019. https://themindunleashed.com/2019/09/human-monkey-hybrid.html.

Volokh, Eugene. "At the University of Oregon, No More Free Speech for Professors on Subjects such as Race, Religion, Sexual Orientation." *Reason*, December 26, 2016. https://reason.com/2016/12/26/at-the-university-of-oregon-no/.

Walden, Celia. "How Dare the BBC Teach Children that there are '100 genders'?" *The Telegraph*, September 9, 2019. https://www.telegraph.co.uk/women/life/dare-bbc-teach-children-100-genders/.

Walker, Jeff. *The Ayn Rand Cult.* LaSalle, IL: Open Court, 1999.

Ward, Emily. "Virginia Governor Describes How Post-Birth Abortion Would Proceed." *cnsnews.com*, January 30, 2019. https://www.cnsnews.com/news/article/emily-ward/virginia-governor-describes-how-post-birth-abortion-would-proceed.

Watkins, J., and S. Farnum. *The Watkins-Farnum Performance Scale: A Standardized Achievement Test for All Band Instruments.* Winona, MN: Hal Leonard Music, 1954.

———. *The Watkins-Farnum Performance Scale: A Standardized Achievement Test for All Band Instruments.* Winona, MN: Hal Leonard Music, 1962.

Weatherbe, Steve. "Fire Me, Fine Me, Jail Me. I Won't Back Down to Speech Police, Says U of T Prof." *LifeSiteNews*, October 28, 2016. https://www.lifesitenews.com/news/watch-fire-me-fine-me-jail-me.-i-wont-back-down-to-speech-police-says-u-of.

Weatherford, Roy. *Philosophical Foundations of Probability Theory.* London: Routledge & Kegan Paul Ltd., 1982.

Wetzstein, Cheryl. "Planned Parenthood Kept Aborted Babies Alive to Harvest Organs, Ex-technician Says." *The Washington Times*, August 19, 2015. https://www.washingtontimes.com/news/2015/aug/19/planned-parenthood-kept-aborted-babies-alive-to-ha/.

Williamon, A. "The Value of Performing from Memory." *Psychology of Music* 27 (1999): 87–95.

Winston, Wayne L., and S. Christian Albright. *Practical Management Science.* Belmont, CA: Duxbury Press, 1997.

World Chess Federation. *World Top Chess Players: Top 100 Women February 2015*, 2019. https://ratings.fide.com/toparc.phtml?cod=342.

Yaari, Menahem E. "On the Consumer's Lifetime Allocation Process." *The International Economic* 3, no. 5 (1964): 304–17.

Yeager, Leland B. *Ethics as Social Science.* Cheltenham, UK: Edward Elgar, 2001.

Younkins, Edward W. "Menger, Mises, Rand, and Beyond." *The Journal of Ayn Rand Studies* 6, no. 2 (Spring 2005): 337–74.

———. *Philosophers of Capitalism: Menger, Mises, Rand, and Beyond.* Lanham, MD: Lexington Books, 2005.

Zdzinski, Stephen F. "Measurement of Solo Instrumental Music Performance: A Review of Literature." *Bulletin of the Council for Research in Music Education* 109 (1991): 47–58.

Zikmund, William G. *Business Research Methods*, 5th edition. Fort Worth, TX: Dryden, 1997.

Zúñiga, Gloria L. "Truth in Economic Subjectivism." In *Philosophers of Capitalism: Menger, Mises, Rand, and Beyond*, Edited by Edward W. Younkins. Lanham, MD: Lexington Books, 2005.

Index

About the Author

Kathleen Touchstone is a retired educator and the author of *Then Athena Said: Unilateral Transfers and the Transformation of Objectivist Ethics* (2006) as well as several articles.

www.ingramcontent.com/pod-product-compliance
Lightning Source LLC
LaVergne TN
LVHW100348290926
849146LV00002B/27
* 9 7 8 1 4 9 8 5 9 6 9 9 2 *